Microsoft® Office
FrontPage® 2003
ILLUSTRATED

INTRODUCTORY

Microsoft® Office
FrontPage® 2003
ILLUSTRATED

INTRODUCTORY

Jessica Evans

THOMSON
COURSE TECHNOLOGY™

Australia • Canada • Mexico • Singapore • Spain • United Kingdom • United States

THOMSON

COURSE TECHNOLOGY

Microsoft® Office FrontPage® 2003 - Illustrated Introductory

Jessica Evans

Executive Editor:
Nicole Jones Pinard

Developmental Editor:
M. T. Cozzola

Associate Product Manager:
Emilie Perreault

Production Editors:
Daphne Barbas, Christine Gatliffe

Text Designer:
Joseph Lee, Black Fish Design

Editorial Assistant:
Abbey Reider

QA Manuscript Reviewers:
Christian Kunciw, Sean Franey

In-house Product Manager:
Christina Kling Garrett

Composition House:
GEX Publishing Services

Product Manager:
M. T. Cozzola

The Illustrated Series Vision

Teaching and writing about computer applications can be extremely rewarding and challenging. How do we engage students and keep their interest? How do we teach them skills that they can easily apply on the job? In developing the Illustrated series, our goals were to provide you with a textbook that:

- works for a beginning student

- provides varied, flexible, and meaningful exercises and projects to reinforce the skills

- serves as a reference tool

- makes your job as an educator easier, by providing resources above and beyond the textbook to help you teach your course

Our popular, streamlined format is based on advice from instructional designers and customers. This flexible design presents each lesson on a two-page spread, with step-by-step instructions on the left, and screen illustrations on the right. This signature style, coupled with high-caliber content, provides a comprehensive yet manageable introduction to Microsoft Office FrontPage 2003—it is a teaching package for the instructor and a learning experience for the student.

Acknowledgments

Once again, I have had the pleasure of working with a talented group of people during this book's development. I'd like to thank Christina Kling Garrett, my in-house Product Manager, who coordinated all of the book's details and ensured its timely publication. My Quality Assurance testers, Christian Kunciw and Sean Franey, went through the manuscript and the final pages of this book multiple times to ensure quality and accuracy in the final product. Their sharp eyes caught things that I missed and I truly appreciate their efforts. I'd also like to thank my Production Editors, Christine Gatliffe and Daphne Barbas, for their careful proofreading and willingness to push the book through production to make sure it was published as error-free and as early as possible. And finally, my appreciation goes to Mary-Terese Cozzola, Developmental Editor and Product Manager, who always met our deadlines, even when I was returning stuff to her "last minute." MT's suggestions have greatly improved this book, and it's been a pleasure working with her.

Finally, I'm fortunate to have many good friends, neighbors, and family members whose lives and businesses have served as the creative inspiration for many of the cases you'll find in this book. I would like to thank my wonderful husband, Richard, and our beautiful daughter, Hannah, for their love and support. I am also grateful to my Dad, whose encouragement and support have been constants in my life. I also appreciate his eagerness to take Hannah fishing or to the movies when I need a few extra hours to finish up a unit.

Jessica Evans

Preface

Welcome to *Microsoft® Office FrontPage® 2003— Illustrated Introductory*. Each lesson in this book contains elements pictured to the right.

How is the book organized?

The book is organized into eight units on FrontPage; covering planning and creating a FrontPage Web site; customizing the appearance of a Web site; creating and maintaining hyperlinks; working with pictures; creating tables, Web pages with frames, and forms; and publishing a Web site.

What kinds of assignments are included in the book? At what level of difficulty?

The lesson assignments develop a fictional Web site for the Vail Valley Marathon. Data files and case studies, with many international examples, provide a great variety of interesting and relevant business applications. Assignments include:

- **Concepts Reviews** include multiple choice, matching, and screen identification questions.

- **Skills Reviews** provide additional hands-on, step-by-step reinforcement.

- **Independent Challenges** are case projects requiring critical thinking and application of the unit skills. The Independent Challenges increase in difficulty, with the first one in each unit being the easiest (most are step-by-step with detailed instructions). Independent Challenges 2 and 3 build from unit to unit, with students learning how to enhance Web sites as they learn new skills throughout the book.

- **E-Quest Independent Challenges** are case projects with a Web focus. E-Quests require the use of the World Wide Web to conduct research to complete the project.

- **Visual Workshops** show a completed file and require that the file be created without any step-by-step guidance, involving problem solving and an independent application of the unit skills.

Each 2-page spread focuses on a single skill.

Concise text introduces the basic principles in the lesson and integrates a real-world case study.

UNIT F
FrontPage 2003

Deleting a Frame from a Frames Page

In some cases, you might need to delete a frame from a frames page. When you delete a frame from a frames page, you are only deleting the HTML tag that *creates* the frame. You are not deleting the Web page that appears in the frame. If you need to delete the page itself, you must do so in Folders view. After viewing the frames page in a browser, Jason decides the Vail Valley Marathon logo is too small to be effective. He asks you to delete the frame that holds the logo and its file.

STEPS

TROUBLE
Don't worry if you selected the picture. Selecting an object or text in a frame also selects the frame.

1. Close your browser
2. If necessary, click in the frame in the upper-left corner to select it
3. Click Frames on the menu bar
   The Frames menu, as shown in Figure F-15, contains options for working with frames. Table F-2 provides a description of the Frames menu commands.
4. Click Delete Frame
   The frame is deleted from the frames page. The banner frame, which is the frame that you split to create the deleted frame, returns to its original size automatically.
5. Click the Save button ⊞ on the Standard toolbar
   FrontPage saves the revisions to the frames page, which once again contains three frames.
6. Click the Web Site tab at the top of the Contents pane
   The Vail Valley Marathon Logo page still exists in the marathon Web site, even though you deleted the frame that contained this page from the frames page.
7. Right-click vvm.htm in the Contents pane, click Delete on the shortcut menu, then click Yes
   The Vail Valley Marathon Logo Web page is deleted from the marathon Web site.

TABLE F-2: Frames menu commands

command	description
Split Frame	Opens a dialog box in which you can split a selected frame into rows or columns, instead of using the mouse
Delete Frame	Deletes the currently selected frame from the frames page, but does not delete the page displayed in that frame from the Web site
Open Page in New Window	Opens the Web page in the selected frame as a regular Web page, without the frames page
Save Page	Saves the Web page in the currently selected frame, without saving any changes that you may have made to the frames page itself
Save Page As	Saves the Web page in the currently selected frame using a different filename
Frame Properties	Opens the Frame Properties dialog box, which contains options for setting the frame's size, initial page, and other options

FRONTPAGE F-14 CREATING A FRAMES PAGE

Hints and troubleshooting advice, right where you need it–next to the step itself.

Tables provide quickly accessible summaries of key terms, toolbar buttons, or other key information connected with the lesson material. Students can refer easily to this information when working on their own projects at a later time.

Every lesson features large, full-color representations of what the screen should look like as students complete the numbered steps.

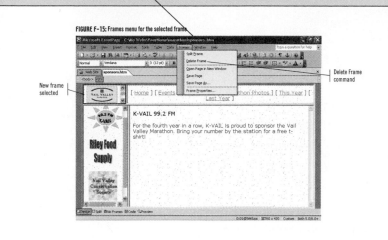

FIGURE F-15: Frames menu for the selected frame

New frame selected

Delete Frame command

Clues to Use

Printing a frames page in a browser

As you browse the Internet, you'll visit many Web sites that use frames pages to organize the way that you view Web pages. Printing a frames page is different from printing a Web page that does not use frames. Each browser handles printing a frames page differently. In Internet Explorer, you have the option of printing the page as it appears in the browser, printing only the page displayed in the selected frame, or printing the page in each frame on a separate sheet of paper. To print a frames page in these different ways, click the Print command on the File menu, which opens a Print dialog box similar to the one shown in Figure F-16. (Your dialog box might look different.)

There are two other options in the Internet Explorer Print dialog box that you might find useful when printing Web pages. If you add a check mark to the Print all linked documents check box, you will print the page that appears in the browser window and all pages that are linked to that page. For example, you might print the home page and all pages that open using links on the home page. Use this option carefully, however, as some pages contain many links. If you

add a check mark to the Print table of links check box, you will print the page that appears in the browser window and a separate sheet that lists all of the documents that are linked to that page.

FIGURE F-16: Print dialog box in Internet Explorer

CREATING A FRAMES PAGE FRONTPAGE F-15

Clues to Use boxes provide concise information that either expands on the major lesson skill or describes an independent task that in some way relates to the major lesson skill.

The pages are numbered by unit. As shown here, F indicates the unit and 15 indicates the page.

Instructor Resources

The Instructor Resources CD is Course Technology's way of putting the resources and information needed to teach and learn effectively into your hands. With an integrated array of teaching and learning tools that offers you and your students a broad range of technology-based instructional options, we believe this CD represents the highest quality and most cutting edge resources available to instructors today. Many of these resources are available at www.course.com.

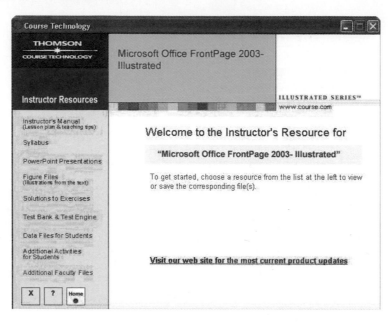

The resources available with this book are:

- **Solutions to Exercises**—Solutions to Exercises contains every file students are asked to create or modify in the lessons and End-of-Unit material. A Help file on the Instructor Resources CD includes information for using the Solution Files. There is also a document outlining the solutions for the End-of-Unit Concepts Review, Skills Review, and Independent Challenges.

- **PowerPoint Presentations**—Each unit has a corresponding PowerPoint presentation that you can use in lecture, distribute to your students, or customize to suit your course.

- **Instructor's Manual**—Available as an electronic file, the Instructor's Manual is quality-assurance tested and includes unit overviews and detailed lecture topics with teaching tips for each unit.

- **Sample Syllabus**—Prepare and customize your course easily using this sample course outline.

- **Figure Files**—The figures in the text are provided on the Instructor Resources CD to help you illustrate key topics or concepts. You can create traditional overhead transparencies by printing the figure files. Or you can create electronic slide shows by using the figures in a presentation program such as PowerPoint.

- **ExamView**—ExamView is a powerful testing software package that allows you to create and administer printed, computer (LAN-based), and Internet exams. ExamView includes hundreds of questions that correspond to the topics covered in this text, enabling students to generate detailed study guides that include page references for further review. The computer-based and Internet testing components allow students to take exams at their computers, and also saves you time by grading each exam automatically.

- **Data Files for Students**—To complete most of the units in this book, your students will need **Data Files**. Put them on a file server for students to copy. The Data Files are available on the Instructor Resources CD-ROM, the Review Pack, and can also be downloaded from www.course.com.

Instruct students to use the **Data Files List** located on the Review Pack and the Instructor Resources CD. This list gives instructions on copying and organizing files.

Brief Contents

Preface   vi

UNIT A   **Getting Started with FrontPage 2003**   **A-1**

UNIT B   **Creating a Web Site**   **B-1**

UNIT C   **Working on the Web Site's Hyperlinks and Appearance**   **C-1**

UNIT D   **Working with Pictures**   **D-1**

UNIT E   **Creating a Table**   **E-1**

UNIT F   **Creating a Frames Page**   **F-1**

UNIT G   **Creating a Form**   **G-1**

UNIT H   **Working in a Published Web Site**   **H-1**

Glossary   1

Index   4

Contents

Preface vi

| UNIT A | **Getting Started with FrontPage 2003** | **A-1** |

Understanding FrontPage A-2
    Creating disk-based and server-based Web sites

Planning a Web Site A-4
    Creating a subsite

Starting FrontPage 2003 ....A-6

Opening an Existing Web Site A-8
    Using the Getting Started task pane

Changing the Web Site View A-10
    Working in Remote Web Site view

Changing the Page View A-12

Using Tasks View A-14
    Completing and managing tasks

Getting Help A-16
    Using the Office Assistant

Closing a Web Site and FrontPage A-18
    Changing the option to open the previously used Web site

Concepts Review A-20

Skills Review A-21

Independent Challenges A-22

Visual Workshop A-24

| UNIT B | **Creating a Web Site** | **B-1** |

Creating a New Web Site B-2
  Filenaming conventions for Web pages

Setting the Web Site's Page Options B-4

Entering and Inserting Text in a Web Page B-6
  Creating a new page in a Web site

Formatting Text B-8

Applying Paragraph Styles B-10
  Formatting text with the Format Painter

Importing Pages into a Web Site B-12
  Importing pages from the Internet

Checking the Spelling in a Web Site B-14

Previewing and Printing a Web Page B-16
  Using a browser to view an HTML document

Concepts Review B-18

Skills Review B-20

Independent Challenges B-21

Visual Workshop B-24

| UNIT C | **Working on the Web Site's Hyperlinks and Appearance** | **C-1** |

Understanding Navigation View C-2

Adding Existing Pages to the Navigation Structure C-4

Adding Blank Pages to the Navigation Structure C-6

Turning on Shared Borders C-8
  Some things to consider when using shared borders

Changing Link Bar Properties C-10
  Using FrontPage link bars to navigate a Web site

Changing the Content of a Shared Border C-12
  Turning off shared borders for a single Web page

Applying a Theme to a Web Site C-14
    Changing the theme for individual pages

Customizing a Theme C-16
    Deleting a theme

Concepts Review C-18

Skills Review C-19

Independent Challenges C-21

Visual Workshop C-24

| UNIT D | **Working with Pictures** | **D-1** |

Inserting a Picture D-2
    Inserting a background picture

Changing a Picture's Properties D-4
    Estimating download times for Web pages

Adding Text over a Picture D-6

Creating an Image Map D-8
    Highlighting and working with hotspots

Creating WordArt D-10
    Inserting drawings and shapes

Creating a Thumbnail Picture D-12
    Enhancing a thumbnail picture

Creating a Photo Gallery D-14

Changing a Photo Gallery's Properties D-16

Concepts Review D-18

Skills Review D-19

Independent Challenges D-21

Visual Workshop D-24

UNIT E	**Creating a Table**	**E-1**

Adding a Table to a Web Page E-2

Changing Table Properties E-4
     Changing the border colors of tables and cells

Entering Table Data and Resizing Cells E-6
     Removing table borders

Inserting and Deleting Cells E-8
     Converting existing text to a table

Merging and Splitting Cells E-10

Inserting a Picture in a Cell E-12
     Using a background picture for a table

Aligning and Formatting Cells E-14

Applying an AutoFormat to a Table E-16

Concepts Review E-18

Skills Review E-19

Independent Challenges E-20

Visual Workshop E-24

UNIT F	**Creating a Frames Page**	**F-1**

Understanding Frames F-2
     Creating "No Frames" pages for browsers that can't display frames

Creating a Frames Page Using a Template F-4

Setting Pages to Open in a Frames Page F-6

Creating a New Page in a Frames Page F-8
     Saving multiple pages in a frames page

Setting Multiple Pages to Open in a Frame F-10

Creating a New Frame in a Frames Page F-12

Deleting a Frame from a Frames Page F-14
    Printing a frames page in a browser

Setting Frame Properties F-16

Concepts Review F-18

Skills Review F-19

Independent Challenges F-20

Visual Workshop F-24

UNIT G   **Creating a Form**   **G-1**

Understanding Forms G-2

Opening a Web Page That Contains a Form G-4

Adding a Text Box and a Text Area G-6

Adding a Drop-Down Box G-8

Adding an Option Button Group G-10

Adding a Check Box G-12
    Options for storing a form's results

Setting Form Properties G-14

Creating a Search Form G-16
    Creating a "Search the Web" component

Concepts Review G-18

Skills Review G-19

Independent Challenges G-21

Visual Workshop G-24

Publishing a Web Site H-2
  Publishing a Web site to an Internet Web server
Opening a Web Site from a Server H-4
  Selecting an ISP to host your Web site
Recalculating and Verifying Hyperlinks H-6
Testing a Page That Contains a Form Component H-8
  Viewing a results file
Testing a Page That Contains a Search Component H-10
  Starting the Indexing Service for IIS
Setting Permissions in a Web Site H-12
Creating a Hit Counter H-14
Maintaining a Published Web Site H-16
  Submitting your Web site to search engines
Concepts Review H-18
Skills Review H-20
Independent Challenges H-21
Visual Workshop H-24

Glossary   1

Index   4

Read This Before You Begin

In this book, you will create disk-based Web sites in a location of your choice; the default used in the units is C:\My Webs\[YourName]\[Web folder name], which is referenced throughout the book as "the location where your Web sites are stored," so you will know where to create new Web sites. To identify your Web sites in a lab situation, you should create all of your disk-based Web sites in a folder with your name as part of the path (as directed in the lessons). In Unit H, you will publish a Web site on a server. The default server name is *localhost*.

Before beginning your work, make sure that you have the Data Files provided by Course Technology. Check with your instructor or go to **www.course.com** to download the files. You can store your Data Files on a Zip drive, hard drive, network drive, or other file location. Throughout the book, the Data Files are referenced as "the drive and folder where your Data Files are stored," because file locations will vary.

Installation

The Setup program provides different options for installing FrontPage, allowing you to choose exactly how to install it. You can do a typical, custom, or complete installation. As part of a custom installation, you also have three other installation options. You can:

- Set a feature to be installed immediately or the first time it is used. If you do not install a feature and need to use it later, FrontPage will prompt you to insert your CD in the correct drive when you need to install the feature.
- Install a feature to run directly from the CD or over a network, conserving hard drive space.
- Choose not to install a feature. If you attempt to use an uninstalled feature, FrontPage will prompt you to insert the CD so it can install the feature for you.

If you chose a typical installation, some features of FrontPage 2003 covered in this book might not be installed on your computer. If you need to install a feature, FrontPage will prompt you to do so. However, to avoid needing the CD to install features on first use, select the complete installation option when installing FrontPage 2003.

Toolbars and Menus

By default, FrontPage 2003 uses personalized toolbars and menus. For the purposes of completing the exercises in this book, these features have been disabled. To disable personalized toolbars and menus, click Tools on the menu bar, click Customize, click the Options tab, click the Show Standard and Formatting toolbars on two rows and Always show full menus check boxes to add check marks to them, then click Close.

Installing Internet Information Services (IIS)

The steps in Unit H are written to publish a Web site using IIS 5.1 or higher with the FrontPage 2002 Server Extensions installed on it. (*Note*: There are no FrontPage 2003 Server Extensions.) You can also publish Web sites to any compatible server running the FrontPage 2002 Server Extensions or SharePoint Services, which runs on Windows 2003 Server. If you need to install IIS, open the Windows Control Panel, double-click Add or Remove Programs, then click Add/Remove Windows Components. In the Windows Components Wizard dialog box, click Internet Information Services (IIS) in the Components list to select it, then click Details. In the Subcomponents of Internet Information Services (IIS) list box, make sure that every item contains a check mark *except* for FrontPage 2000 Server Extensions. Click OK, make sure that Indexing Service in the Components list box contains a check mark, then click Next. Setup will install IIS. Go to **www.office.microsoft.com** for more information about the Server Extensions and SharePoint Services.

If your instructor asks you to publish and create server-based Web sites on a network server, follow your instructor's directions for logging on to the server. The steps in this book for creating and publishing Web sites will work correctly as long as the server has the FrontPage 2002 Server Extensions or SharePoint Services installed on it.

Browsers

We recommend using Microsoft Internet Explorer 6.0 or higher or Netscape Navigator 7.0 or higher for browser output.

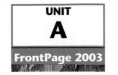

Getting Started with FrontPage 2003

OBJECTIVES

Understand FrontPage
Plan a Web site
Start FrontPage 2003
Open an existing Web site
Change the Web site view
Change the Page view
Use Tasks view
Get Help
Close a Web site and FrontPage

Microsoft Office FrontPage 2003 is a program that lets you create, manage, publish, and maintain a Web site. A **Web site** is a collection of Web pages that are organized around a specific organization or topic and connected to each other using hyperlinks. A **hyperlink** is text or a picture that, when clicked, opens a location in the same Web page, a different Web page in the same Web site, or a different Web site. After using FrontPage to create a Web site and its Web pages, you publish the site to a Web server, which makes the site accessible to Internet users. You have recently been hired as a Web design intern by the Vail Valley Marathon. This marathon is in its seventh year and attracts a wide following of enthusiastic runners who are willing to face the challenging terrain offered by the Colorado Rocky Mountains. Jason Tanaka, manager of the Vail Valley Marathon, asks you to use FrontPage to create a Web site so he can publish information about the event on the Internet.

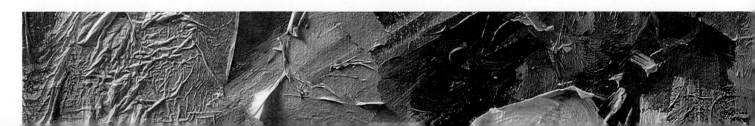

Understanding FrontPage

FrontPage 2003 is a program that lets you create, manage, publish, and maintain a Web site. In most cases, a Web site is stored on a Web server or on a network. A **Web server** is a computer that is connected to the Internet and that uses server software to store and deliver Web pages. A **network** consists of two or more computers that are connected to each other in order to share information and resources. The **Internet** is a worldwide collection of computer networks that are connected to each other using cables, phone lines, and other resources. A Web site published to a Web server is accessible to Internet users. FrontPage is an effective tool for creating Web sites and publishing them. ▓▓▓▓ Before planning the Vail Valley Marathon Web site, Jason asks you to explore FrontPage to learn more about creating Web sites and Web pages.

DETAILS

- ### Create a Web site

  In FrontPage, the term **Web site** refers to the collection of files and folders that run the Web site and provide its content. A FrontPage Web site also contains files that operate the Web site on a Web server.

- ### Create Web pages

  A **Web page** is a document that is written in a language called **HTML (Hypertext Markup Language)**. You can create a Web page using any text editor by typing the content and necessary HTML tags to create the page. FrontPage, however, simplifies the process of creating a Web page by automatically generating the HTML document when you use its commands and tools to create the Web page content. A Web site can contain one or more Web pages. Usually, the Web site's main page, around which all other Web pages in a Web site are organized, is called the **home page**.

- ### Organize the Web site's pages

  FrontPage includes tools to manage the files and folders that make up the content and functionality of a Web site. For example, when you create a Web site, FrontPage automatically creates a folder named images, in which you can store all of the Web site's graphic and multimedia files. In addition, FrontPage includes tools that you can use to examine the hierarchy of how pages are related to the site's home page and to each other.

- ### Publish a Web site

  FrontPage includes tools that make it easy to transfer a Web site from your computer to a Web server. Publishing a Web site to a Web server connected to the Internet makes your Web site accessible to Internet users. When you **publish** a Web site, you transfer all of the site's files and folders to the Web server you selected to host the Web site. A Web server also accepts requests from other computers that are connected to it and shares some or all of its resources, such as files and programs, with those computers. In this type of configuration, the computers that are connected to the server are called **clients**. When multiple clients are connected to a server, the configuration is called a **client/server network**. See Figure A-1. The software that lets a client interact with a Web server is called a **Web browser**. Two popular browsers are Microsoft Internet Explorer and Netscape Navigator.

- ### Interact with the Internet

  Each Web server connected to the Internet has a unique address called a **domain name** or **URL (Uniform Resource Locator)**. To connect to a Web server using a URL, a Web browser uses **HTTP (Hypertext Transfer Protocol)**, which is the set of rules that a browser uses to retrieve and display the pages that you request.

- ### Manage and update a Web site

  After you publish a Web site, you will need to update its content by adding new pages, deleting old pages, and correcting any problems identified by users. FrontPage includes a variety of reports to help you perform site maintenance. In addition, you can use the different reports to identify your site's visitors, its most popular pages, and other information to help you improve the site.

Fiber-optic
cable

Web clients
running Web
browser
software

Web server running Web server
software and hosting Web sites

Telephone line

Clues to Use

Creating disk-based and server-based Web sites

There are two ways to create a Web site in FrontPage. You can create a **disk-based Web site**, which stores the site and its files on your computer's hard drive, a network, or an external drive such as a Zip drive. Alternatively, you can create a **server-based Web site**, which creates the Web site and its files directly on a Web server. When you choose to create a Web site on a Web server, you can access and use all of the pages using HTTP. In this book, you will create a disk-based Web site and then publish it to a server.

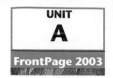

Planning a Web Site

Before you create a Web site, it's important to have a clear vision of what you want the Web site to accomplish and how the elements of the site will function to achieve this vision. Careful planning is critical to the development of any Web site. Before developing a Web site, you should ask questions, such as: Who will be the primary visitors to the site? How will I attract and keep visitors' attention? How will users navigate the site to find the information they need? Will my site allow visitors to interact with it by completing forms and sending information? ▰▰▰ You begin planning the Vail Valley Marathon Web site by meeting with Jason to learn more about his vision for the site. You learn that he wants to use the Web site to post information about the race. He also wants to use the site to provide a registration form for entering the race. You review basic planning guidelines with Jason as you work to create the initial design for the site.

DETAILS

- **Define the site's goal and purpose**

  Jason wants to use the site as a marketing tool for increasing the number of runners in this year's marathon. Having detailed information about the marathon on the Internet will make it easier for people to learn about and enter the marathon, which ultimately contributes to the success of the race. A well-designed, informative site will reduce the number of calls that staff members receive from interested applicants, asking about the race and requesting registration forms. The long-term savings related to fewer staff members and decreased phone and postage costs will offset the initial investment of preparing and maintaining the site.

- **Determine how visitors will use the site and the information they require**

  Jason tells you that visitors to the Web site will use it to get logistical information about the race, including its time, location, and route. Runners will want to be able to register for the race using the site. Finally, race sponsors will appreciate acknowledgments for their support.

- **Plan the site's pages and their relationships to each other**

  Based on the site's goal and purpose, as well as its projected audience, you decide to create several Web pages. First, the site's home page will include general information about the race and links to the site's other pages. Additional pages will contain a map of the race route, a registration form, and detailed information about the race. You also plan to include a page with information about the race's sponsors. An effective way of planning the content of a Web site is to sketch the pages you intend to include and their relationships to each other. Your initial design of the Web site appears in Figure A-2.

- **Prepare the site's content**

  Different team members will be responsible for the different pages in the site. For example, the marketing department will contact the sponsors of the race and ask permission to use their company logos in the page that features information about the marathon's sponsors.

- **Plan the site's navigation options**

  You know that users want to be able to move quickly through a site to find the information they need. Each page in the site must contain links to other pages in the site, so that visitors can navigate to any page without first returning to the home page.

- **Plan the appearance of pages in the site**

  Jason tells you that most runners who participate in this challenging race are serious marathoners, but they also enjoy many other outdoor activities. The marathoners often stay in the Vail Valley after the marathon to hike up a mountain pass and enjoy the area's natural beauty. You decide that a casual, fun Web site that uses vibrant colors will fit very well with the marathon's overall personality.

- **Test the site**

  After thoroughly testing the disk-based Web site, you will be ready to publish the site to a Web server. After publishing the site, you plan to test the site again thoroughly to ensure that the site's hyperlinks and features work correctly using multiple versions of current browsers.

FIGURE A-2: Initial design of the Web site

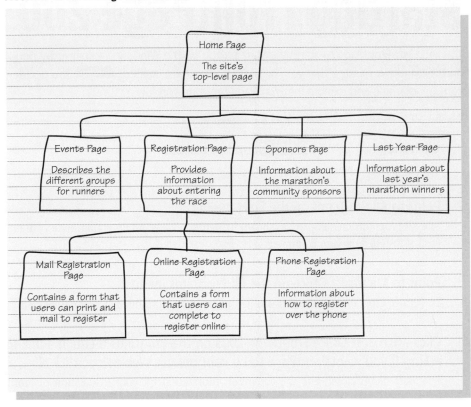

Clues to Use

Creating a subsite

A **subsite** (or **subweb**) is a Web site within a Web site. The main Web site is usually called the **root Web**, and a root Web can have multiple subsites within it. When a root Web contains a subsite, the subsite has a different URL and is functionally separate from the root Web. It has its own pages and can have a different design and overall appearance from the root Web. You create a subsite when you want to limit access to the subsite's pages, which contain information associated with the root Web. For example, you might create a subsite named "runners" within the vailrace root Web. You could use this subsite to store information about the runners, such as contact information, previous races run and their times, medical information, and so on. You could restrict usage of this subsite so that only designated staff members could add, update, and delete information. By creating a subsite, the two different sites—one that has pre-race information available to the general public and another that has information about runners with restricted access—are separate. In general, anything that you can do in a root Web is also permitted in a subsite.

Starting FrontPage 2003

You can start FrontPage by using the Start button on the Windows taskbar or by double-clicking a shortcut on the Windows desktop that you, or another user, have created. You decide to start FrontPage so you can examine and explore the FrontPage program window.

STEPS

TROUBLE
If a double arrow appears at the bottom of the All Programs menu, click it to display all of the program groups installed on your computer.

TROUBLE
If a dialog box opens and asks you to enter your name and initials, do so, then click OK.

TROUBLE
If a Web site name appears on the title bar, click File on the menu bar, then click Close Site.

1. **Click the Start button** 🏁 start **on the taskbar**
   The Start menu opens.

2. **Point to All Programs on the Start menu**
   The All Programs menu opens, as shown in Figure A-3. The All Programs menu contains a list of the program groups installed on your computer.

3. **Point to Microsoft Office on the All Programs menu**
   The Office programs installed on your computer appear on the Microsoft Office menu.

4. **Click Microsoft Office FrontPage 2003 on the Programs menu; if a dialog box opens asking if you want FrontPage to be your default Web editor, click No**
   The Start menu closes, and the copyright information for your installation of FrontPage appears on the screen. After a few seconds, the FrontPage program window opens, as shown in Figure A-4.

5. **If necessary, click the Maximize button on the FrontPage title bar to maximize the program window**

6. **If necessary, click the Show Design View button** Design **to change to Design view**

FIGURE A-3: All Programs menu

All Programs menu (your All Programs menu options might differ)

Start menu (your Start menu options might differ)

Start button

Microsoft Office FrontPage 2003 command

Taskbar

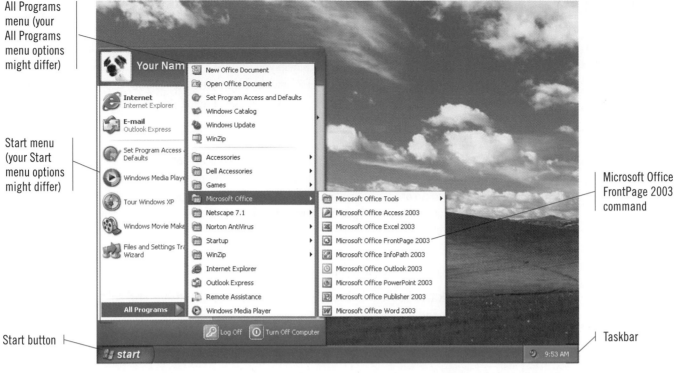

FIGURE A-4: Microsoft FrontPage 2003 program window

FrontPage title bar

Menu bar

Standard toolbar

Formatting toolbar (your toolbar might not appear on its own row)

Getting Started task pane (your options might differ)

Show Design View button is selected

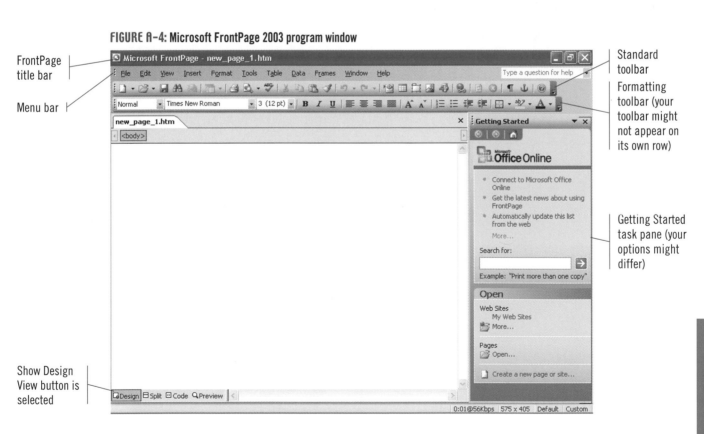

FrontPage 2003

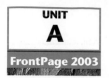

UNIT A — FrontPage 2003

Opening an Existing Web Site

When you open an existing Web site in FrontPage, you can access all of its files, pages, and folders. After opening a Web site, you can use different views to help you understand the organization and content of the site. Jason created a prototype of the Vail Valley Marathon Web site for you. You decide to open this Web site to learn more about FrontPage and the Web site you will create.

STEPS

QUICK TIP

The appearance of the Open button changes depending on whether you last opened a file or a Web site. Your Open button might look like.

1. **Click the Open button list arrow on the Standard toolbar**

   The Open button menu appears, as shown in Figure A-5. There are two Open options in FrontPage. You use the first option, Open, to open a single Web page. You use the second option, Open Site, to open a Web site. Most of the time, you will use the Open Site option to open a Web site, which gives you access to all of the Web pages in the Web site.

2. **Click Open Site**

   The Open Site dialog box opens, as shown in Figure A-6.

3. **If necessary, click the Look in list arrow, then browse to the drive and folder where your Data Files are stored**

4. **Double-click the UnitA folder to open it**

   The UnitA folder contains two Web sites: vailrace and irma. FrontPage places a blue dot in folders that contain Web sites. A folder that does not contain a Web site appears without the blue dot.

TROUBLE

Depending on your FrontPage configuration, the Web site might open in a different view than the one shown in Figure A-7. If necessary, click the Folders View button to change to Folders view.

5. **Click vailrace to select it, then click Open**

   The vailrace Web site opens in FrontPage, as shown in Figure A-7. When you open a Web site, you are really opening all the folders and files that make up the Web site. The Getting Started task pane closes automatically. You can tell that a Web site is open because its path and name appear on the FrontPage title bar.

6. **If necessary, click the Toggle Pane button on the Standard toolbar to close the Folder List**

   The **Folder List** displays the folders and files in a Web site. You can open or close the Folder List, so your Folder List might already be closed.

Clues to Use

Using the Getting Started task pane

As you have seen, the Getting Started task pane automatically opens on the right side of the FrontPage program window when you first start FrontPage. It contains options for opening existing Web pages and Web sites. These options are also available on the File menu or by clicking the Open button list arrow on the Standard toolbar. Depending on your current action, the Getting Started task pane might open and close automatically. To display or hide the task pane, click View on the menu bar, then click Task Pane.

Open button list arrow

Keyboard shortcut for the Open command

Open button menu

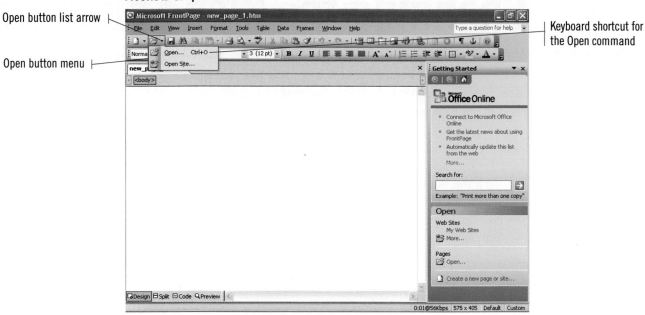

Current location (yours might differ)

Use the list arrow to navigate to the drive or folder where your Data Files are stored

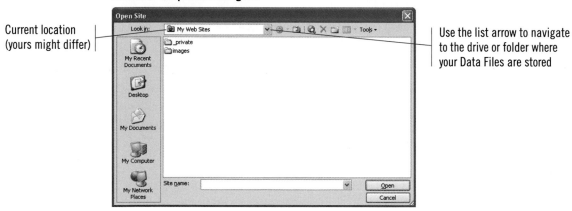

Toggle Pane button

Folder List (your Folder List might be closed)

Title bar indicates the Web site's path and name (your path might differ)

Contents pane

Folders View button is selected

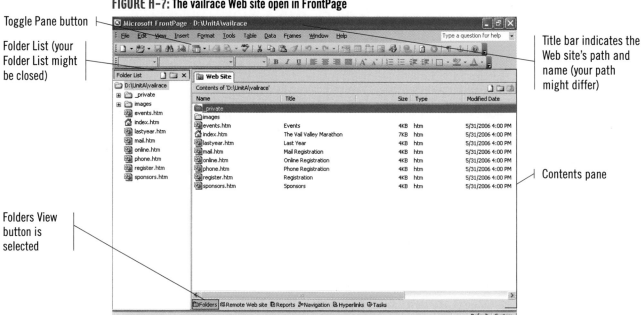

FrontPage 2003

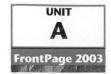

Changing the Web Site View

After you open a Web site in FrontPage, you can choose from seven different views for working with its local and published pages, file and folder structure, navigation options, site reports, hyperlinks, and tasks. Changing the view does not change the site itself; it simply lets you see the site's content in the most appropriate way for your current task. ▓▓▓▓ You examine some of the different views of the vail-race Web site to familiarize yourself with the purpose of each view.

STEPS

1. **Click the Reports View button** 🗎 Reports **at the bottom of the Contents pane**

   You use **Reports view** to analyze, summarize, and produce various types of reports about a Web site. Each individual report is listed in the Name column; the collection of reports shown in Figure A-8 is called a **Site Summary report**. You can use Reports view as you develop a Web site to determine the overall size of your site, pages that are slow to download, usage reports, and other important information.

TROUBLE
You might need to use the horizontal scroll bar in the Contents pane to view all of the information for each file.

2. **Click the Folders View button** 🗁 Folders **at the bottom of the Contents pane**

   You use **Folders view** to examine, create, delete, copy, and move files and folders in the open Web site. Notice that the vailrace Web site shown in Figure A-9 contains two folders, _private and images. FrontPage creates these folders when you create a Web site. The underscore in the _private folder name indicates that this folder is hidden. A **hidden folder** is not accessible to site visitors after you publish a Web site. You use a hidden folder to store files that contain sensitive data. The Contents pane shows that the Web site contains eight files and two folders. Each file is listed using its name, title, size, type, last modified date, the person who last modified the file, and optional comments.

3. **Click the Navigation View button** 🔠 Navigation **at the bottom of the Contents pane**

   You use **Navigation view** to create or display a Web site's navigation structure, which identifies the relationships between pages in the Web site. The top-level page in a Web site is usually the site's home page.

QUICK TIP
The Toggle Pane button "toggles" the display of the Folder List off and on. If the Folder List is on, clicking 🖻 turns it off; if it is off, clicking 🖻 turns it on.

4. **Click the Hyperlinks View button** 🗟 Hyperlinks **at the bottom of the Contents pane, click the Toggle Pane button** 🖻 **on the Standard toolbar to turn on the Folder List, then click index.htm in the Folder List**

   Hyperlinks view for the home page appears, as shown in Figure A-10. You use **Hyperlinks view** to view the hyperlinks leading to and from the page selected in the Folder List. In Hyperlinks view, you can click a plus box for any page to expand the diagram, showing the hyperlinks leading to and from the selected page. You can click the minus box for any page to collapse the view of hyperlinks associated with that page.

5. **Double-click index.htm in the Contents pane, then click** 🖻 **to turn off the Folder List**

   The home page opens in Page view. You use **Page view** to create, edit, and format the content of a Web page. Page view has different viewing options that let you see the Web page, the HTML document that creates the Web page, and a preview of the Web page as it will appear in a browser. Because this Web site is a prototype, it contains incomplete pages, which you will create during the Web site's development.

6. **Click the Web Site tab at the top of the Contents pane, then click the Tasks View button** 🗐 Tasks **at the bottom of the Contents pane**

   You use **Tasks view** to maintain a list of the tasks required to complete a Web site. This Web site does not yet include any tasks. For each task, you can identify its status, name, the person to whom the task is assigned, a priority level, the page with which the task is associated, the date the page was last modified, and a task description.

7. **Click the index.htm tab at the top of the Contents pane**

   The home page is displayed again in Page view.

FIGURE A-8: Reports view of the vailrace Web site

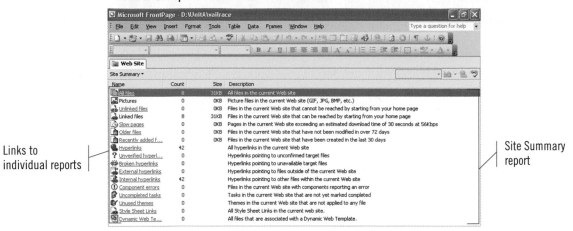

Links to individual reports

Site Summary report

FIGURE A-9: Folders view of the vailrace Web site

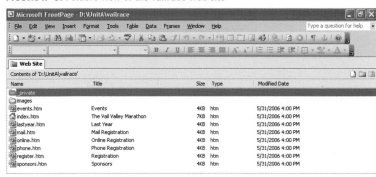

FIGURE A-10: Hyperlinks view of the home page

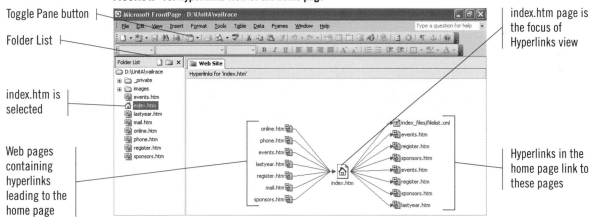

Toggle Pane button

Folder List

index.htm is selected

Web pages containing hyperlinks leading to the home page

index.htm page is the focus of Hyperlinks view

Hyperlinks in the home page link to these pages

Clues to Use

Working in Remote Web Site view

After you finish a Web site, you are ready to move its files and folders to the Internet service provider you selected to host your Web site. **Remote Web Site view** lets you transfer files between a local computer or network and a Web server using different methods, including Web Distributed Authoring and Versioning (WebDAV), File Transfer Protocol (FTP), and HTTP. The method you choose to transfer your files depends on the type of transfers supported by the Web server to which you are publishing files. After publishing a Web site, you can use Remote Web Site view to synchronize copies of the Web site stored in different locations to ensure consistency between copies of the Web site, and to create a backup of the Web site in case there is a problem with the site stored on the server.

FrontPage 2003

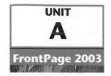
Changing the Page View

Page view has four options for examining a Web page. The default Page view, which shows the formatted Web page and is where you'll do most of your work, is called **Design view**. Clicking the Show Code View button at the bottom of the Contents pane displays the HTML document that creates your Web page in **Code view**. If you know HTML, you can use Code view to make changes to your Web page. The third view, called **Split view**, splits the Page view window into two panes, with the HTML document (Code view) on top and the Web page (Design view) on the bottom. This view lets you see the HTML document and the Web page at the same time; as you make changes in one pane, the other pane is updated automatically. Finally, **Preview view** lets you see your Web page as it will appear in a browser, without needing to start a browser program. You decide to examine the Sponsors page using the different view options in the Page view window so you are familiar with the different ways to view a Web page.

STEPS

1. **Point to the** Sponsors link **in the home page, press and hold** [Ctrl]**, click the** Sponsors link**, then release** [Ctrl]

   The Sponsors page opens in Design view. Notice that a new page tab for this file, sponsors.htm, appears at the top of the Contents pane.

2. **Click the** Show Code View button ⊡Code **at the bottom of the Contents pane, then press** [Ctrl][Home]

   As shown in Figure A-11, Code view displays the HTML document that creates the Sponsors page. Notice that FrontPage automatically inserted the required HTML tags for all Web pages. The <html> and </html> tags enclose the entire HTML document, the <head> and </head> tags enclose the head section of the HTML document, and the <body> and </body> tags enclose the body section of the Web page. Finally, FrontPage added <meta> tags that identify the default language, character set, and other information about the Web page. The content of the Web page appears in the body section.

3. **Click** Tools **on the menu bar, then click** Optimize HTML

   The Optimize HTML dialog box opens, as shown in Figure A-12. You can set FrontPage to create some additional HTML tags when it creates a Web page, such as the tag that identifies the HTML document as being created by FrontPage. You use the Optimize HTML dialog box to remove these optional tags if you don't want to use them in your Web page. These tags usually won't cause any problems, but they are not standard HTML tags.

4. **Compare your Optimize HTML dialog box with Figure A-12 and check and clear the check boxes so your screen matches the one shown, then click** OK

   FrontPage removes the nonstandard HTML tags from the home page.

5. **Click the** Show Split View button ⊟Split **at the bottom of the Contents pane**

   Split view splits the window into two panes, with Code view on top and Design view on the bottom.

QUICK TIP
When you select text in one view, it is also selected in the other view.

6. **Use the pointer to select the word** all **in Design view, then click the** Bold button **B** **on the Formatting toolbar**

   As shown in Figure A-13, the text you selected in Design view is bold, and the HTML tags that format bold text, <b> and </b>, appear around the same text in Code view.

7. **Click the** Show Preview View button 🔍Preview **at the bottom of the Contents pane**

   The Web page, with the new bold text, appears as it will be shown in a browser.

8. **Click the** Show Design View button ▣Design **at the bottom of the Contents pane, then click the** Save button 🖫 **on the Standard toolbar**

   The Web page reappears in Design view, and you saved your changes. The text you selected in Split view is still selected.

FIGURE A-11: Code view for the Sponsors page

Head section

Body section

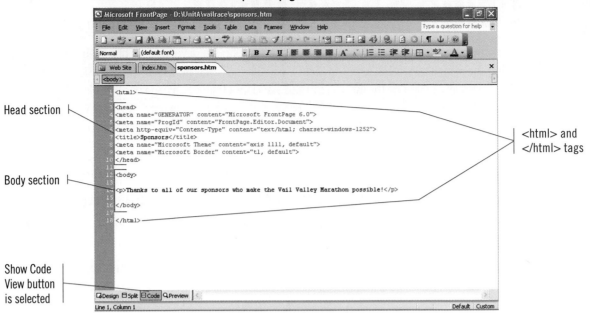

<html> and
</html> tags

Show Code
View button
is selected

FIGURE A-12: Optimize HTML dialog box

Select the options
shown here
(Step 4)

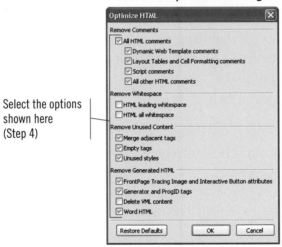

FIGURE A-13: Split view for the Sponsors page

HTML tags for
formatting bold
text (the </b>
might also be
selected on
your screen)

Selected bold
text in the
Web page

Show Preview
View button

Show Split
View button
is selected

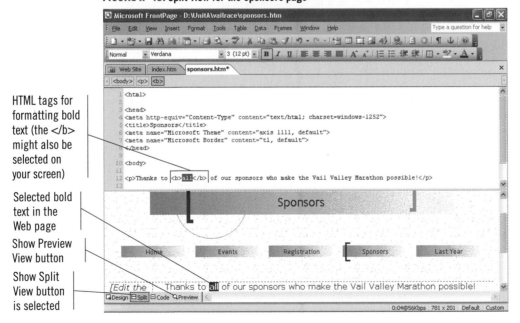

FrontPage 2003

Using Tasks View

Tasks view is a very useful tool when a team is coordinating the development of a Web site. Each task for completing the Web site can be added to Tasks view, then as tasks are completed, reassigned, and re-evaluated, team members can update the list. You can also associate a task with a page or other file in the site to clarify connections between tasks and files. 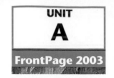 Because different staff members for the Vail Valley Marathon will contribute to the Web site's content, you decide to use Tasks view to organize its many tasks. You start by adding some of the tasks you need to complete to Tasks view.

STEPS

TROUBLE

Clicking 🗋 will create a new Web page. If this occurs, click File on the menu bar, click Close, then repeat Step 2.

1. **Click the** Web Site tab **at the top of the Page view window, then make sure that the** Tasks View button ⊘ Tasks **is selected at the bottom of the Contents pane**

   Because you have not added any tasks, Tasks view is empty.

2. **Click the** Create a new normal page button list arrow 🗋 ▾ **on the Standard toolbar**

   The Create a new normal page menu opens. You use this menu to create a new page, Web site, folder, or task.

TROUBLE

The Assigned to list box might display the current logon name for your computer. This is not a problem.

3. **Click** Task **in the list**

   The New Task dialog box opens. The insertion point appears in the Task name text box. The dialog box automatically includes your name and the current date and time.

4. **Type** Create Map page; **if your name doesn't appear automatically in the Assigned to list box, press [Tab], then type your first and last names**

   You created the task and assigned it to yourself.

5. **Click the** High option button **in the Priority section**

   You use the option buttons to select the priority for a task. The default priority for a new task is Medium.

6. **Click in the** Description text box, **then type** The route will circle U.S. Hwy 6 and U.S. Hwy 24, which will be closed to traffic.

   As shown in Figure A-14, the specifications for the new task are complete.

QUICK TIP

When an ellipsis (...) appears in the entry for a column, point to the right edge of the column header so the pointer changes to ✛, then double-click to expand the column to best fit the data it contains.

7. **Click** OK

   You recorded the task in Tasks view. See Figure A-15. When this task has been completed, you can right-click it and click Mark Complete on the shortcut menu to change the status from Not Started to Completed. If you need to update a task, double-click it in Tasks view to open the Task Details dialog box, where you can make the necessary changes.

8. **Click the** Folders View button 📁 Folders **at the bottom of the Contents pane, click** phone.htm **in the Contents pane, click** 🗋 ▾ **(remember to click the list arrow), then click** Task

   The New Task dialog box opens. The Associated With section shows that this new task will be associated with the page named phone.htm. When you want to associate a task with a specific page, you select that page in Folders view before opening the New Task dialog box.

9. **Type** Set up toll-free number **in the Task name text box, make sure the task is assigned to you, click the** High option button **in the Priority section, then click in the** Description text box **and type** Must include new toll-free number in this page.

10. **Click** OK **in the New Task dialog box, then click** ⊘ Tasks **at the bottom of the Contents pane**

    As shown in Figure A-16, the new task appears in Tasks view. The Associated With column displays the title of the page with which the task is associated. You don't need to save a task in a Web site—once you create it, it is saved in the Web site automatically.

Create a new normal
page button list arrow

Web Site tab

This task does not
have a Web page
associated with it

Tasks View button
is selected

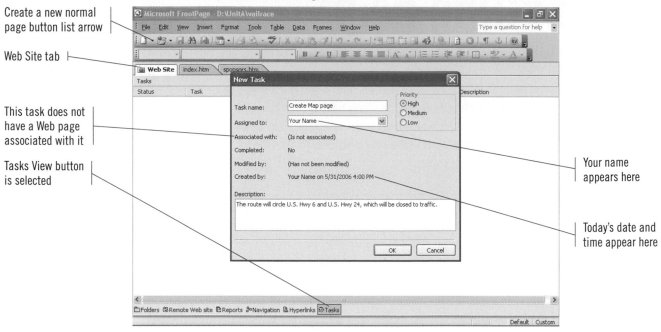

Your name
appears here

Today's date and
time appear here

FIGURE A-15: New task added to Tasks view

Task status indicates
that this task has not
been started

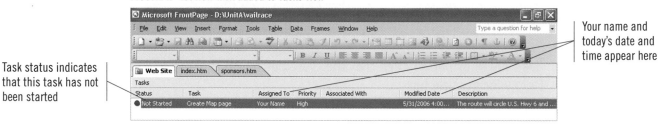

Your name and
today's date and
time appear here

FIGURE A-16: Task associated with phone.htm page added to Tasks view

Title of page associated
with this task

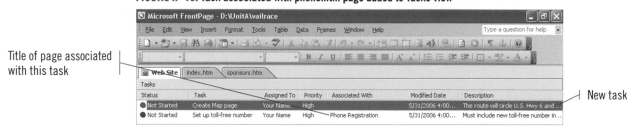

New task

Clues to Use

Completing and managing tasks

After completing a task, you can mark it as complete by right-clicking it in Tasks view, and then clicking Mark Complete on the shortcut menu. Completed tasks are hidden automatically, unless you right-click the Tasks pane and click Show History on the shortcut menu. To delete a task, right-click it in the Tasks pane, then click Delete Task. The task will be deleted from the Web site permanently when you click Yes.

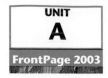

Getting Help

To take advantage of the many features available in FrontPage, you can rely on its extensive Help system for examples, tips, and instructions. There are several methods for getting Help, so you can use the one that you like the best. The fastest way of getting Help is to type a question or keyword(s) in the Type a question for help text box, which appears on the menu bar. You can also click the Microsoft Office FrontPage Help button on the Standard toolbar, which opens the FrontPage Help task pane. ▰▰▰ You are anxious to learn more about using FrontPage to create a new Web site. You decide to use the Type a question for help text box to search for Help on this topic.

STEPS

1. **Click in the** Type a question for help text box **on the menu bar**

   The text in the Type a question for help text box is deleted, and the insertion point appears in the text box.

2. **In the Type a question for help text box, type** How do I create a new Web site?

   As you type, the text scrolls to the left.

3. **Press** [Enter]

   The Search Results task pane opens and displays some topics that might answer your question, as shown in Figure A-17. You can scroll down the results to see all of the topics related to your search. The "Can't find it?" link and "Other places to look" section at the bottom of the results list offer tips and links to other resources for answering your question. The Search panel at the bottom of the Search Results task pane offers the option of searching other Help resources.

QUICK TIP

You can maximize the Microsoft Office FrontPage Help window or resize it as desired so it best suits your needs.

4. **In the Search Results task pane, click** Create a Web site

   The Microsoft Office FrontPage Help window opens and displays information about the topic you selected, "Create a Web site." See Figure A-18.

5. **Read the information, then click the** Close button **on the Microsoft Office FrontPage Help window title bar**

6. **Click the** Other Task Panes list arrow **on the Search Results task pane, click** Help, **then click the** Table of Contents link

   The Table of Contents pane opens. This pane lets you search for Help by viewing related topics and their subtopics, as shown in Figure A-19. To expand a topic, click it; to collapse a topic, click it again. Expanding a topic displays subtopic titles, which might contain pages or additional subtopics. Clicking a topic opens its link in the Microsoft Office FrontPage Help window. Use this method for getting Help when you want to learn about a general category, such as "Working with Graphics."

7. **Click the** Close button **on the Microsoft Office FrontPage Help task pane**

Clues to Use

Using the Office Assistant

The **Office Assistant** is an animated character that offers tips, answers questions, and provides access to the FrontPage Help system. To get Help using the Office Assistant, click Help on the menu bar, then click Show the Office Assistant. Then you type a question or keyword(s) in the Office Assistant's text box and click Search. The Office Assistant displays topics related to your question or keyword(s); you then click a hyperlink to open the Microsoft Office FrontPage Help window, where you can search for additional Help or read the Help page that appears.

FIGURE A-17: Using the Type a question for help text box

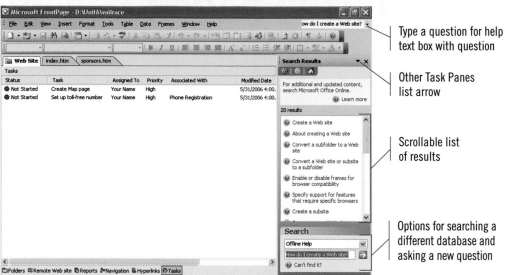

Type a question for help text box with question

Other Task Panes list arrow

Scrollable list of results

Options for searching a different database and asking a new question

FIGURE A-18: Microsoft Office FrontPage Help window

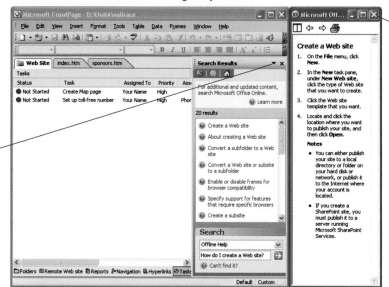

Close button for the Microsoft Office FrontPage Help window

Other Task Panes list arrow

FIGURE A-19: Table of Contents pane

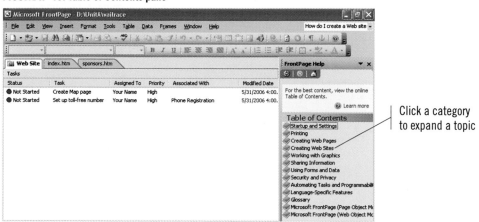

Click a category to expand a topic

FrontPage 2003

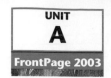

Closing a Web Site and FrontPage

FrontPage has an option that you can set so the Web site that you were working in when you (or another user) last closed FrontPage opens automatically when you start FrontPage again. Because of this option, it's a good idea to close the current Web site before closing FrontPage. If you close your Web site before closing FrontPage, other users won't have access to your site and will receive disk errors when FrontPage attempts to open a Web site stored in an inaccessible location. ▩▩▩▩ You are finished viewing the prototype of the vailrace Web site, so you close the Web site and FrontPage.

STEPS

1. **Click File on the menu bar**

   The File menu opens, as shown in Figure A-20. There are two Close options. You use the first option, Close, when you want to close the active Web page or report. The Close option is dimmed because you are in Tasks view, so no Web page or report is active. You use the second option, Close Site, when you want to close the current Web site and any open Web pages. In either case, if any pages contain unsaved changes, FrontPage will prompt you to save them.

2. **Click Close Site on the File menu**

   The vailrace Web site closes. The title bar now displays the text "Microsoft FrontPage 2003," indicating that there is no open Web site.

3. **Click File on the menu bar, then click Exit**

   FrontPage closes, and you return to the Windows desktop.

FIGURE A-20: File menu

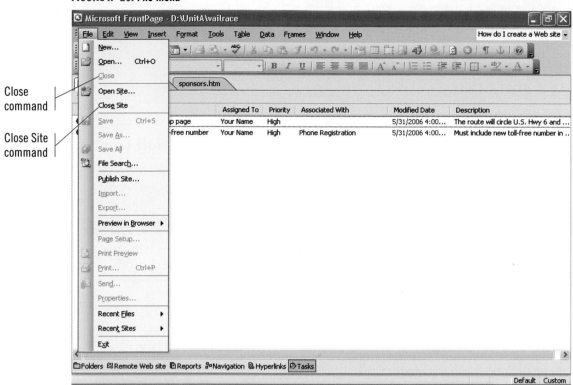

Close command

Close Site command

Clues to Use

Changing the option to open the previously used Web site

By default, FrontPage is set to open the previously used Web site when you start the program again. This feature is convenient when you are the only user on a computer and you are working in the same Web site all the time. If you want to disable this feature, however, you can do so by clicking Tools on the menu bar, clicking Options, and then clicking the Open last Web site automatically when FrontPage starts check box to clear it (see Figure A-21). After clicking OK, the next time you start FrontPage it will not open a Web site automatically. You can quickly open recently used files and Web sites by clicking File on the menu bar, and then pointing to Recent Files (to view a list of specific Web pages) or Recent Sites (to view a list of specific Web sites).

FIGURE A-21: Options dialog box

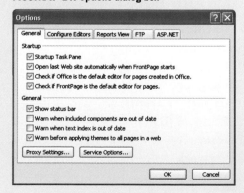

FrontPage 2003

Practice

▼ CONCEPTS REVIEW

Refer to Figure A-22 to answer the following questions about the Microsoft FrontPage program window.

FIGURE A-22

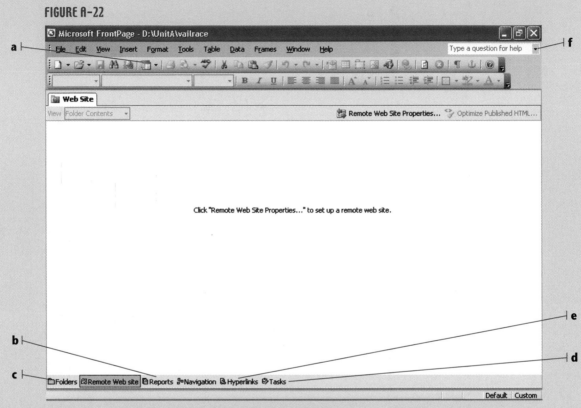

1. Which element do you click to view the Web site's files and folders?
2. Which element do you click to analyze, summarize, and produce various types of reports about a Web site?
3. Which element do you click to view a graphical representation of the hyperlinks in a Web site?
4. Which element do you click to view the tasks for completing a Web site?
5. Which element do you click to turn on the Folder List?
6. Which element do you use to get Help while working in a Web site?

Match each of the following terms with the statement that describes its function or purpose.

7. **Client/server network**
8. **Domain name**
9. **Hypertext Markup Language (HTML)**
10. **Hypertext Transfer Protocol (HTTP)**
11. **Internet**
12. **Network**
13. **Web page**
14. **Web site**

a. A collection of client computers and server computers connected to each other
b. A collection of Web pages that are organized around a specific organization or topic and connected to each other using hyperlinks
c. A document written in HTML
d. A worldwide collection of computer networks
e. The language used to create Web pages
f. The set of rules a browser uses to connect to and display a Web page
g. The unique address that identifies every Web site on the Internet
h. Two or more computers that are connected to each other to share information and resources

Select the best answer from the following list of choices.

15. **The software that lets your computer interact with a network is called a:**
    a. Web client.
    c. Web site.
    b. Web browser.
    d. Web page.

16. **The language that you use to create a Web page is called:**
    a. HTTP.
    c. HTML.
    b. URL.
    d. None of the above

17. **The purpose of testing a Web site after you publish it to a Web server is to:**
    a. Ensure that the site's hyperlinks work correctly.
    b. Ensure that the site performs as expected using multiple browsers.
    c. Determine if the expected number of people are visiting the site.
    d. Both A and B are correct

18. **Which of the following locations can be opened using a hyperlink?**
    a. A location in a Web page
    c. A different Web site
    b. A different Web page in the same Web site
    d. All of the above

19. **Which of the following Page views shows the HTML document that creates a Web page?**
    a. Design view
    c. Code view
    b. Preview view
    d. HTML view

▼ SKILLS REVIEW

1. **Plan a Web site.**
   a. Irma Mooney creates and paints small figurines and other objects for different holidays. She displays her work in a local bakery. The bakery manages her accounts and receives a 25% commission for all objects sold, and Irma keeps the rest. Many people anxiously await Irma's creations for each holiday because they can combine the bakery's delicious baked items with a porcelain object to create a gift basket. The bakery receives orders from outside its local area, so the management has decided to create a Web site to reach a larger audience.
   b. Plan a Web site that includes a home page and a page for each of the following holidays: Valentine's Day, St. Patrick's Day, Easter, Mother's Day, Father's Day, Independence Day (U.S.), Rosh Hashanah, Halloween, Thanksgiving Day, Hanukkah, and Christmas. Using Figure A-2 as a guide, sketch the pages in the site and their relationships to each other. (You do not need to provide a description of each page.)

2. **Start FrontPage 2003.**
   a. Start FrontPage.
   b. If necessary, maximize the FrontPage program window.
   c. If a Web site opens automatically, close it.
   d. If the Folder List opens, close it.

3. **Open an existing Web site.**
   a. Open the Open Site dialog box.
   b. Browse to the drive and folder where your Data Files are stored, double-click the UnitA folder, then open the irma Web site.

4. **Change the Web site view.**
   a. Change to Navigation view. What is the Web site's top-level page? How many pages appear below the home page?
   b. Change to Folders view. How many files and folders are in the Web site?
   c. Change to Hyperlinks view, then turn on the Folder List and select the home page (index.htm). How many hyperlinks lead to and away from the home page?
   d. Change to Reports view. How many pictures are in the Web site? How many linked files are in the Web site?
   e. Close the Folder List, then change to Folders view.

5. **Change the Page view.**
   a. Open the home page (index.htm) in Design view.
   b. Change to Code view and examine the HTML document for the home page.

   c. Open the Optimize HTML dialog box. If necessary, change the settings in the Optimize HTML dialog box to match those shown in Figure A-12, then click OK.

   d. Change to Split view, then change the text **Irma Mooney's** in the first line of the home page to bold and watch the update in the HTML document.

   e. Change to Preview view and examine the Web page.

   f. Change to Design view.

   g. Save the home page.

6. Use Tasks view.

   a. Change to Tasks view.

   b. Add a new task to the Web site named **Passover Page**. Assign the task to yourself, assign it a high priority, and then enter the following description: **Create the Passover page in the Web site.**

7. Get Help.

   a. Use the Type a question for help text box on the menu bar to ask the question, **What is a hyperlink?**

   b. Click the About hyperlinks link in the Search Results task pane. (You might need to scroll the search results to find this link.) If desired, maximize the Microsoft Office FrontPage Help window.

   c. Read the information provided in the **Ways to use hyperlinks**, **How URLs work**, and **How hyperlinks are displayed** pages.

   d. Close the Microsoft Office FrontPage Help window, then close the Search Results task pane.

8. Close a Web site and FrontPage.

   a. Close the Web site.

   b. Exit FrontPage.

▼ INDEPENDENT CHALLENGE 1

Sarah Gravis just accepted an internship position for her hometown state representative, Dean Keeton. Representative Keeton wants Sarah to use FrontPage to create a Web site to communicate important information with his constituents via the Internet. Sarah took an HTML course in college but has never used FrontPage. As she views the FrontPage program window for the first time, she is curious about the tools FrontPage provides for working with HTML and another markup language used on the Web, Extensible Markup Language (XML), which is used to create structured documents with customized formats. She uses the Help system to learn more about the tools FrontPage provides for working with HTML and XML.

   a. Start FrontPage, then use the Other Task Panes list arrow to display the FrontPage Help task pane.

   b. Click the Table of Contents link.

   c. Click the Creating Web Pages topic to expand it. A list of pages appears below the expanded Creating Web Pages topic. Below the list of pages are subtopics that you can click to expand, revealing the pages with information relevant to each subtopic.

   d. Click the Authoring HTML subtopic to expand it, click the General subtopic to expand it, then read some of the pages that might interest Sarah, such as **About working with HTML** and **About working with XML**. Then expand the **Quick Tag Tools** subtopic and read some of the topics about working with HTML that might interest Sarah.

   e. After reading several pages of information that you think are relevant, answer the following questions on a piece of paper with your name on it:

      1. What information is supplied to a browser in an HTML tag? (*Hint:* Clicking blue text in the Microsoft Office FrontPage Help window displays additional information about the term. Clicking the blue text again hides the additional information.)

      2. Can you show HTML tags when working in Design view? If so, how?

      3. Does XML replace HTML? Why or why not?

      4. What are the two Quick Tag tools? Describe each one and its function.

   f. Use the Type a question for help text box to learn more about **IntelliSense**. What is IntelliSense?

   g. Close FrontPage.

▼ INDEPENDENT CHALLENGE 2

The Villages at Kensington is a neighbourhood association of approximately 350 single-family homes located in Vancouver, British Columbia. At a recent meeting, a resident made a motion for the association to commission the development of a Web site. The motion passed unanimously. It was agreed that the Web site's design needs to provide easy access to information about association events, such as picnics, pool parties, tennis leagues and tournaments, neighbourhood meetings, and other special events. The site also needs to provide information about area crime and alerts concerning local construction and road changes. Jim Wheeler is the president of the Board of Directors. He asks you to help him plan the Web site. In the following units of this book, you will develop the entire Web site for Jim.

a. On a piece of paper with your name on it, use the information provided in this unit to prepare a Web site plan for Jim that answers the following questions. Use the information provided in this Independent Challenge and your own knowledge to answer the questions.
1.   What is the site's goal and purpose?
2.   How will visitors use the site?
3.   What information will site visitors require?
4.   What content should the site's pages include? Briefly describe some of the pages that you might include in the site.
5.   What kind of design should the site have? Would you design the site using a casual or a formal style? Why?

b. On a piece of paper with your name on it, prepare a sketch of your proposed Web site that shows the relationships between the pages. Your sketch should look similar to Figure A-2. Supply as much information as you can.

▼ INDEPENDENT CHALLENGE 3

Tryon, North Carolina is a small town located outside of Asheville on the Saluda River and on the edge of the Blue Ridge Mountains. This beautiful city is home to many retired individuals and full-time and seasonal residents. In recent years, the city's numerous horse shows, bed-and-breakfast inns, and shopping opportunities for folk art and antiques have made Tryon a great destination for tourists. In an effort to increase tourism in the area, the city manager, Nick Dye, has commissioned you to develop a Web site. The Web site will include a home page for the city of Tryon as well as links to local attractions and areas of interest, such as restaurants, scenic drives, river activities, antique malls, theaters, and golf resorts. Much of the content for the Web site will come from the local vendors, restaurants, and shops that will benefit from the Web site's creation. Nick asks you to start planning the Web site's content and structure. In the following units of this book, you will develop the entire Web site for Nick.

a. On a piece of paper with your name on it, use the information provided in this unit to prepare a Web site plan for Nick that answers the following questions. Use the information provided in this Independent Challenge and your own knowledge to answer the questions. In doing this research, you might use a search engine, such as AltaVista, Yahoo!, or Google, to find and visit Web sites for small cities and towns that may have similar features to those found in Tryon.
1.   What is the site's goal and purpose?
2.   How will visitors use the site?
3.   What information will site visitors require?
4.   What content should the site's pages include? Briefly describe some of the pages that you might include in the site.
5.   What kind of design should the site have? Would you design the site using a casual or a formal style? Why?

b. On a piece of paper with your name on it, prepare a sketch of your proposed Web site that shows the relationships between the pages. Your sketch should look similar to Figure A-2. Supply as much information as you can.

▼ INDEPENDENT CHALLENGE 4

You are leading the Web development team at The Aquarium, a tropical fish store specializing in saltwater fish and saltwater aquariums. Your FrontPage Web site is complete, and now you need to publish it to the ISP you selected to host it. You haven't published a Web site to a Web server, so you decide to use the Internet to learn more about publishing.

▼ INDEPENDENT CHALLENGE 4 (CONTINUED)

a. Start FrontPage, then use the Type a question for help text box to ask **How do I publish a Web site?** In the Search Results task pane, locate and click the About publishing files and folders link.

b. In the Microsoft Office FrontPage Help window, click the Show All link to expand all of the Help topics, and then read the topics. After reading the information, answer the following questions on a piece of paper with your name on it.

1. What happens to the files and folders in a Web site when you publish it?
2. What are three reasons for publishing a Web site?
3. What is a local Web site? What is a remote Web site?
4. What is an extended Web server?
5. What information do you need to know in order to publish a Web site to a Web server using Remote Web Site view?
6. What is a component?
7. What does it mean to synchronize files between sites?
8. What are the FrontPage Server Extensions?

c. Close the Microsoft Office FrontPage Help window, and then close FrontPage.

▼ VISUAL WORKSHOP

Start FrontPage and open the irma Web site from the UnitA folder in the drive and folder where your Data Files are stored. Create the tasks shown in Figure A-23. (*Hint*: You can resize the columns by double-clicking ✛ on the right side of the column heading.) Be sure to assign the tasks to yourself. After creating the tasks, compare your screen to Figure A-24. (*Note*: Your screen will show your name in the Assigned To column and the current date and time in the Modified Date column.) Press [Print Screen] and paste the image into a word-processing program to print the page, then close the word processor and the Web site and exit FrontPage.

FIGURE A-23

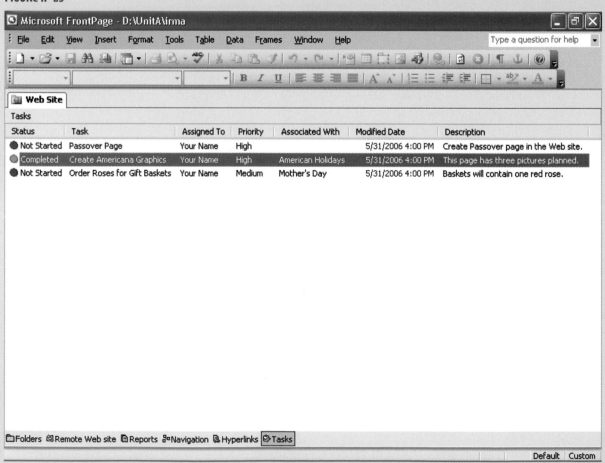

Creating a Web Site

OBJECTIVES

Create a new Web site
Set the Web site's page options
Enter and insert text in a Web page
Format text
Apply paragraph styles
Import pages into a Web site
Check the spelling in a Web site
Preview and print a Web page

When you create a new Web site in FrontPage, you use a template to create the initial content and folder structure of the Web site. A **Web site template** contains one or more sample pages and other structural information for creating a Web site so you don't have to create everything from scratch. Depending on the content that you need, you might be able to use a template that not only creates the Web site, but also fills it with pages and sample content about your topic. Or you might choose to use a template that creates the Web site structure and a home page, but nothing else. In either case, after you create the Web site's structure, you can begin to edit any existing pages created by the template and add new pages to make the Web site consistent with your needs. After finalizing your initial plan for the content, organization, and structure of the Web site for the Vail Valley Marathon, you are ready to use FrontPage to create the new site and some of its pages.

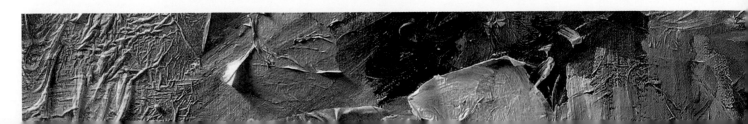

Creating a New Web Site

FrontPage includes 10 templates that you can use to create a new Web site (see Table B-1). Some of these templates are wizards that create the Web site's structure and sample pages, which you can edit and replace with your own content. When you create a new Web site, you have the option of storing the Web site's folders and files on a disk (a disk-based Web site) or on a server (a server-based Web site). Regardless of where you store the Web site, FrontPage creates a Web folder with the files that support the site in the location you specify. ▰▰▰▰ You decide to use the Web Site Templates dialog box to choose a template for the marathon Web site and specify the location of the new site's folders and files.

1. **Start Microsoft FrontPage; if necessary, click File on the menu bar, then click Close Site to close any open Web site**

   Microsoft FrontPage starts, and the Getting Started task pane opens.

2. **Click the Other Task Panes list arrow on the Getting Started task pane, then click New**

   The New task pane contains options for creating a new Web page or a new Web site. When you begin your work, you must create a Web site in which to store your Web pages. If you create Web pages without first creating a Web site in which to store them, you will just have a collection of files.

3. **Click More Web site templates in the New Web site section of the New task pane**

   The Web Site Templates dialog box opens, as shown in Figure B-1. Table B-1 describes the types of Web sites you can create using templates in this dialog box.

4. **Click the Personal Web Site icon, then read the description**

   When you click an icon, a brief description of the selected template appears in the Description section of the dialog box.

5. **Click the One Page Web Site icon**

   As shown in the Description section, you use the One Page Web Site template to create a new Web site with a single blank page. This is the template you want to use to create the marathon Web site.

6. **Click in the Specify the location of the new Web site list box**

   The existing text in the list box is selected.

7. **Type C:\My Webs\[YourName] (replace the [YourName] part of the location—including the square brackets—with your first and last names, without any spaces)**

   Your entry replaces the existing text. To distinguish your Web site from others in the My Webs folder on the drive or server on which you are creating it, you created a subfolder using your first and last names. This book assumes that you are creating Web sites in the location C:\My Webs\[YourName]. If you are unsure of where to create your Web sites, ask your instructor or a technical support person for help.

8. **Type \marathon**

   As the last item in the Web site's location, "marathon" indicates the name of the Web site. The Web site's location is complete.

9. **Click OK**

   FrontPage creates the marathon Web site in the location you specified and opens it in Folders view. The FrontPage title bar indicates the drive, path, and Web site name. The New task pane closes automatically.

TABLE B-1: Web site templates and their descriptions

template	description
One Page Web Site	Creates a Web site that contains one blank page, index.htm, which becomes the site's home page
Corporate Presence Wizard	Creates a Web site with sample pages that a corporation can customize
Customer Support Web Site	Creates a Web site with sample pages for companies providing customer support, such as software companies
Database Interface Wizard	Creates a Web site that you can connect to a database so that you can add, view, update, and delete records
Discussion Web Site Wizard	Creates a Web site that contains a table of contents, full-text searching capability, and threads organized around a specific discussion topic
Empty Web Site	Creates a Web site structure of folders containing no pages
Import Web Site Wizard	Creates a Web site that contains pages you import from another location, such as another Web site or a file location
Personal Web Site	Creates a Web site with sample pages that an individual can personalize to promote his or her interests and favorite Web sites
Project Web Site	Creates a Web site with sample pages for a list of members, a schedule, a status, and a discussion archive related to a specific project
SharePoint Team Site	Creates a Web site with tools that group members can use to collaborate on a project, including a calendar, a library for storing shared documents, a tasks list, and a contacts list

FIGURE B-1: Web Site Templates dialog box

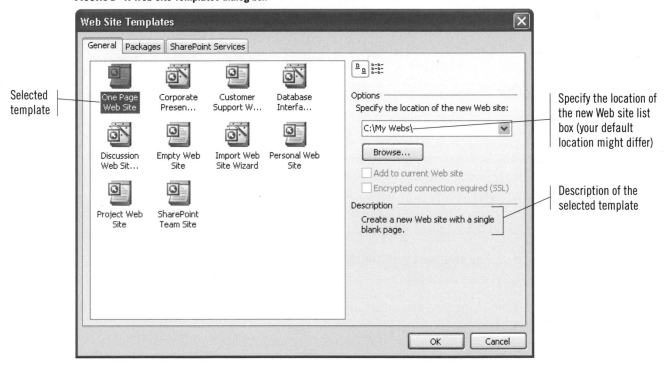

Selected template

Specify the location of the new Web site list box (your default location might differ)

Description of the selected template

FrontPage 2003

Design Matters

Filenaming conventions for Web pages

Although long filenames (such as registration.htm), mixed-case filenames (such as Registration.htm), and filenames containing spaces (such as Registration Form.htm) are valid filenames in a disk-based FrontPage Web site, some Web servers will not accept these types of filenames. Some Internet Service Providers (ISPs) limit the number of characters in filenames to eight, permit only lowercase letters, and restrict the use of spaces and other special characters. Because filenaming conventions can vary, it is important to understand what restrictions exist on the Web server on which you will ultimately store your Web site. In this book, you will practice good Web design by creating filenames that are legal for most Web servers.

Setting the Web Site's Page Options

Part of the planning phase for a Web site includes conducting sufficient research to determine who will visit it and how it will be used. You should design your Web site for this target audience. Table B-2 describes some Internet technologies that you can enable or disable in a FrontPage Web site. Web programmers with advanced skills can write code to support these technologies in various browsers and then add that code to the pages in a Web site. You can also enable a Web site to support specific browsers. FrontPage also includes a feature that lets you set a default page size for all pages you create in a Web site. Because Web site visitors might display the Web pages at different screen resolutions and using different monitors, the size of your Web pages might differ among its users. ▓▓▓▓▓ Jason Tanaka's research indicates that the Vail Valley Marathon audience uses the latest browsers, which support current Internet technologies. He asks you to configure the marathon Web site to optimize the features supported by FrontPage and the latest versions of Internet Explorer and Navigator and to set the default page size.

STEPS

QUICK TIP

You can quickly see your Web site's authoring settings using the status bar. Double-click the current authoring setting (such as "Default" or "Custom") on the status bar to open the Authoring tab of the Page Options dialog box.

1. **Click Tools on the menu bar, click Page Options, then click the Authoring tab**

   The Authoring tab options are shown in Figure B-2. The settings on this tab are collectively called the Web site's "authoring settings." Your initial authoring settings might differ from those shown in Figure B-2.

2. **In the FrontPage and SharePoint technologies section, clear and select the check boxes as necessary so your screen matches Figure B-2**

   You enable the Web site features that you will use as you complete the Web site.

3. **Click the Browsers list arrow, then click Both Internet Explorer and Navigator**

   This setting enables all Web features commonly supported by both Microsoft Internet Explorer and Netscape Navigator.

QUICK TIP

When you change a Web site's settings, all future Web sites created in FrontPage will use those same settings unless you change them again.

4. **Click the Browser versions list arrow, then click 5.0/6.0 browsers and later**

   This setting enables support for all features of Internet Explorer and Navigator, versions 5.0/6.0 and later. Notice that the ActiveX controls and JavaScript/JScript check boxes are dimmed and that the VBScript check box is deselected. The selected browsers and browser versions do not support VBScript and have limited support for ActiveX controls and JavaScript/JScript.

5. **Make sure all your settings match those shown in Figure B-2, then click OK**

   The Page Options dialog box closes, and you return to Folders view.

6. **Open the home page (index.htm) in Design view**

   You must be in Page view to change the default page size.

7. **Point to the Page Size pane on the status bar (see Figure B-3), then click the Page Size pane**

8. **In the Page Size menu, click 760 x 420 (800 x 600, Maximized)**

   The default page size displayed by most monitors is 800 x 600 pixels.

FIGURE B-2: Authoring tab of the Page Options dialog box

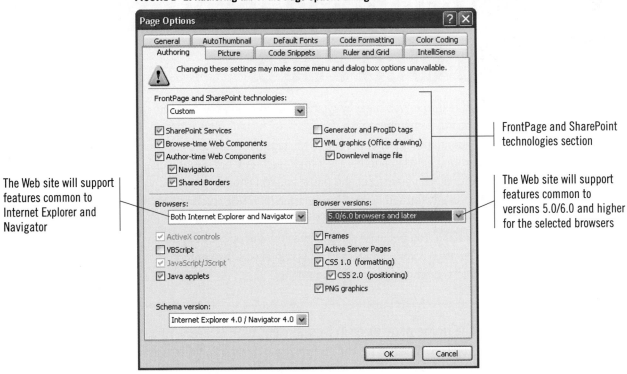

The Web site will support features common to Internet Explorer and Navigator

FrontPage and SharePoint technologies section

The Web site will support features common to versions 5.0/6.0 and higher for the selected browsers

FIGURE B-3: Setting the default page size

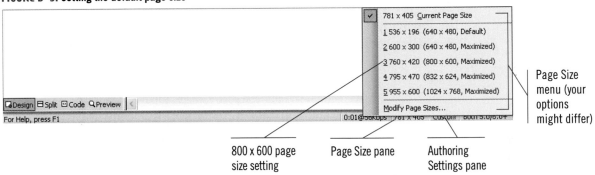

800 x 600 page size setting

Page Size pane

Authoring Settings pane

Page Size menu (your options might differ)

TABLE B-2: Popular Internet technologies that you can enable or disable in a FrontPage Web site

Internet technology	description
ActiveX controls	Applications that create animation, interactive objects, and other multimedia effects in a Web page
VBScript	A scripting language used to embed interactive elements in Web pages
JavaScript/JScript	A scripting language used to create dynamic content in Web pages
Java applets	Programs written in the Java programming language and run by a browser that add multimedia effects, interactivity, and other effects to Web pages
Frames	Web pages that display multiple Web pages simultaneously in separate, scrollable windows
Active Server Pages	Dynamic Web pages containing scripts that process active content in a Web page
CSS 1.0 (formatting)	An HTML specification that lets you apply text attributes, such as color and font size, to text in one or more Web pages
CSS 2.0 (positioning)	An HTML specification that lets you precisely position objects in a Web page
PNG graphics	Graphic files saved in the PNG file format (some browsers cannot display .png files)

Entering and Inserting Text in a Web Page

You can add text to a Web page by typing it, by inserting the contents of a file, or by pasting the contents of the Clipboard. Remember that a Web page is created using HTML. When you enter text in a Web page, FrontPage automatically generates the HTML tags necessary to create and format the text. When you need to insert text that exists in another file format, such as Word, FrontPage automatically converts the inserted text to HTML. When you use cut and paste, you can choose to insert only the text, without any formatting, or the text and any formatting that is supported by HTML (such as bold and alignment). When you insert a file, all of the content appears exactly as it does in the original file, with the exception of styles not supported by HTML. ▓▓▓▓ You begin working on the Web site by entering the site's name and sponsor in the home page. As you are working, you receive a file containing the content for the home page from Jason, so you decide to insert it rather than retype its contents.

STEPS

TROUBLE

If you make a typing mistake, press [Backspace] to erase characters to the left of the insertion point or press [Delete] to erase characters to the right of the insertion point, then type the correct text.

1. **With the home page open in Design view, type** The Vail Valley Marathon, **then press** [Enter]

   When you press [Enter] at the end of a line in a Web page, FrontPage creates a new paragraph. Creating a new paragraph in FrontPage is different from creating a new paragraph in a word-processing program, such as Word, because FrontPage automatically inserts a blank space below the previous paragraph. If you need to start text on a new line but do not want a blank space to appear below the previous line, press [Shift][Enter].

2. **Type** Sponsored by The Colorado Chronicle, **then press** [Enter]

3. **Use the pointer to select both lines in the page, then click the** Center button ▤ **on the Formatting toolbar**

   As shown in Figure B-4, both lines are centered; you will change the format of these lines in another unit. Notice that the page tab, which contains the filename index.htm, now has an asterisk (*) to the right of the filename. This asterisk reminds you that the page contains unsaved changes.

TROUBLE

Depending on your FrontPage configuration, you might see a double arrow at the bottom of menus. Click the double arrow to open the full menu.

4. **Click the** Save button 🖫 **on the Standard toolbar**

   FrontPage saves the home page, and the asterisk no longer appears on the page tab. You created this page and gave it a filename when you used the One Page Web Site template to create the Web site, so FrontPage saves it with the same filename.

5. **Click below the second line of text in the home page, click** Insert **on the menu bar, then click** File

   The Select File dialog box opens.

TROUBLE

If you do not see the filename extensions, Windows might be configured to hide them. This is not a problem.

6. **Click the** Look in list arrow, **navigate to the drive and folder where your Data Files are stored, then double-click the** UnitB **folder to open it**

7. **Click the** Files of type list arrow, **then click** Word 97-2003 (*.doc)

   The file Jason gave you, welcome.doc, appears in the list, as shown in Figure B-5. Filename extensions help you identify a file's type. For example, a file with the ".doc" filename extension is a Word document, and a file with the ".htm" filename extension is a Web page.

TROUBLE

If a warning message about installing a converter appears, insert your FrontPage 2003 CD in the correct drive, then click Yes.

8. **Click** welcome.doc **to select it, then click** Open

   A Transferring RTF file to HTML message box opens and closes, and the contents of the welcome.doc file are inserted in the home page. See Figure B-6. The dashed line above the word "Sponsors" is the bottom of a page that appears in a browser window set to 800 x 600 pixels. FrontPage added this dashed line when you set the page size to use this setting.

FIGURE B-4: Text entered in the home page

Asterisk on page tab indicates that this page contains unsaved changes

Center button

Centered lines

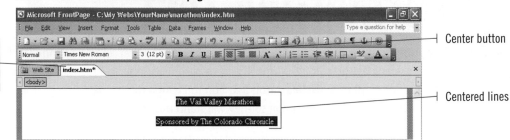

FIGURE B-5: Select File dialog box

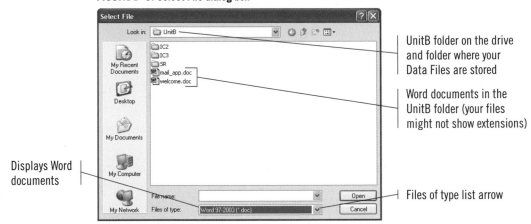

UnitB folder on the drive and folder where your Data Files are stored

Word documents in the UnitB folder (your files might not show extensions)

Displays Word documents

Files of type list arrow

FIGURE B-6: File inserted in the home page

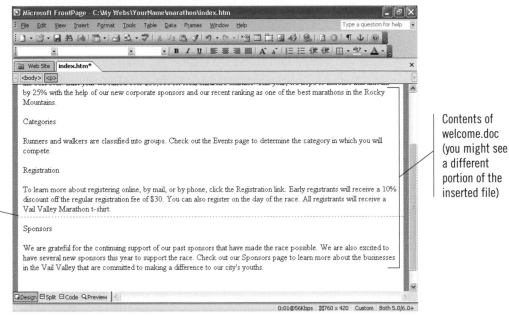

Bottom of this Web page when viewed using a browser set to 800 x 600 pixels

Contents of welcome.doc (you might see a different portion of the inserted file)

Clues to Use

Creating a new page in a Web site

When you create a new page in a Web site, you have the option of creating a new blank page or a page based on a template. A **Web page template** is similar to a Web site template in that it already contains content related to a specific topic. (You will learn more about page templates in another unit.) To create a new blank page, click the Blank page option in the New page section of the New task pane. To save the new page, click the Save button on the Standard toolbar. The Save As dialog box opens. Use the Save in list arrow to select the location in which to save the file, type a filename in the File name text box, then click Change title. In the Set Page Title dialog box, type the page title that you want to appear on the browser's title bar when the page opens. Click OK, then click Save. FrontPage saves the Web page in the location you specified.

FrontPage 2003

Formatting Text

The Formatting toolbar in FrontPage contains many tools that let you change the font, font size, font style (bold, underlined, or italic), alignment, and color of text. Table B-3 identifies the Formatting toolbar buttons and their descriptions. ▰▰▰▰▰ Jason asks you to change the format of the name "Vail Valley Marathon" in the paragraphs in the home page so they will stand out. You will format the page's heading later.

STEPS

1. **Press [Ctrl][Home]**

2. **Select the text** Vail Valley Marathon **in the second sentence of the first paragraph**

3. **Click the** Bold button **B** **on the Formatting toolbar**
   The text changes to bold.

4. **Click the** Font Color button list arrow **A·** **on the Formatting toolbar**
   A color palette opens with 16 standard colors, such as white, yellow, and green. You can select a color in the Standard Colors section by clicking it.

5. **Click** More Colors
   The More Colors dialog box opens. This palette lets you choose from all 216 Web safe colors. A **Web safe color** is one that is displayed consistently and correctly on computers running different operating systems.

6. **Click the** dark orange color **(last row, third color from the left)**
   The New box in the More Colors dialog box shows the color you selected, as shown in Figure B-7.

7. **Click** OK**, then click anywhere in the** Vail Valley Marathon **text to deselect it**
   The Vail Valley Marathon text is now bold and dark orange.

8. **Scroll down the Web page if necessary to see the last line of the Registration paragraph, select the** Vail Valley Marathon **text, click** **B**, **then click the Font Color button** **A**
   The page is complete, as shown in Figure B-8. Because you clicked the Font Color button instead of the list arrow, the text is formatted in the previously applied color, dark orange.

9. **Click the** Save button **🖫** **on the Standard toolbar**

TABLE B-3: Formatting toolbar buttons and their descriptions

button name	button	use to
Style list box	Normal ▼	Apply a style to selected text; click the list arrow to select the desired style
Font list box	Times New Roman ▼	Apply a font to selected text; click the list arrow to select the desired font
Font Size list box	3 (12 pt) ▼	Apply different font sizes to selected text; click the list arrow to select sizes compatible with HTML, where 1 is the smallest and 7 is the largest
Bold	B	Change selected text to bold
Italic	I	Change selected text to italic
Underline	U	Change selected text to underlined
Align Left	▤	Change the alignment of the selected paragraph or object to left
Center	▤	Change the alignment of the selected paragraph or object to centered
Align Right	▤	Change the alignment of the selected paragraph or object to right
Justify	▤	Change the alignment of the selected paragraph to justified

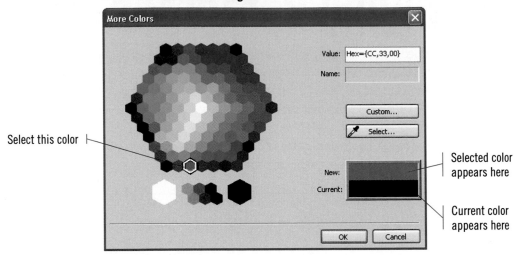

FIGURE B-7: More Colors dialog box

Select this color

Selected color appears here

Current color appears here

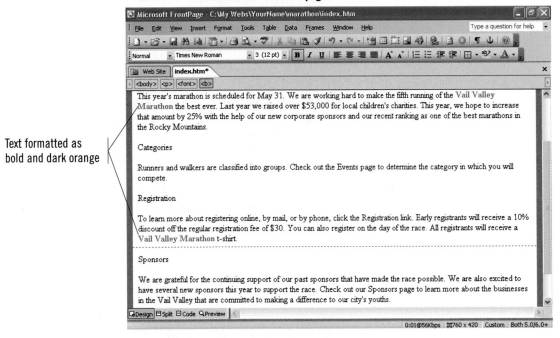

FIGURE B-8: Formatted text in the home page

Text formatted as bold and dark orange

TABLE B-3: Formatting toolbar buttons and their descriptions (continued)

button name	button	use to
Increase Font Size	A▴	Increase the font size of the selected text to the next higher HTML level
Decrease Font Size	A▾	Decrease the font size of the selected text to the next lower HTML level
Numbering	▦	Change selected paragraphs to a numbered list
Bullets	▦	Change selected paragraphs to a bulleted list
Decrease Indent	▦	Move the indentation of a selected paragraph left by one tab stop (0.5 inch)
Increase Indent	▦	Move the indentation of a selected paragraph right by one tab stop (0.5 inch)
Borders	▦ ▾	Add a border to the selected text; use the list arrow to select a different border option from the one displayed on the button
Highlight	ab▾	Highlight the selected text; click the list arrow to choose a different highlight color from the one displayed on the button or choose None to remove highlighting from the selected text
Font Color	A ▾	Change the color of the selected text; click the list arrow to choose a different color from the one displayed on the button

Applying Paragraph Styles

You have learned how to format text by selecting the text and changing one or more attributes, such as font style and font color. You can also apply formatting to an entire paragraph by applying a **paragraph style** to it. The styles and formatting that you can apply to text in a Web page must be ones supported by HTML. For example, HTML supports seven font sizes, with size 1 being the smallest and size 7 being the largest. These font sizes correspond to point sizes from 8 to 36. Similarly, you can apply six levels of headings to text in a Web page. The heading with size 1 is the largest, and the heading with size 6 is the smallest. ▰▰▰▰ You are ready to format the headings in the home page.

STEPS

1. **Click the Show All button ¶ on the Standard toolbar**

   The ¶ symbol appears to indicate the end of each paragraph in the Web page. Showing and hiding the **nonprinting characters**, such as ¶, in a Web page is a matter of personal preference. When working with more advanced FrontPage features, such as tables and absolute positioning, showing the nonprinting characters can make it easier for you to do your work.

QUICK TIP

In a Web page, a "paragraph" can be a single line containing one word or a paragraph consisting of multiple lines and words.

2. **Press [Ctrl][Home], then click anywhere in the text Welcome near the top of the home page**

   When you apply a heading style, the style is applied to the paragraph and the text it contains automatically.

3. **Click the Style list arrow on the Formatting toolbar**

   The Style list opens, as shown in Figure B-9. The listed styles are ones supported by HTML.

4. **Click Heading 2 in the Style list**

   The "Welcome" paragraph, which in this case is a single word, is formatted with the default Heading 2 style, which is an 18-point, bold, Times New Roman font. See Figure B-10.

5. **Double-click the Format Painter button ▱ on the Standard toolbar, then move the pointer into the Web page**

   The pointer changes to ▰▯. The **Format Painter** lets you apply the formatting and style of existing text to other text in a Web page, which can save time. If you want to copy the formatting once, you click the Format Painter button one time. If you plan to copy the formatting to multiple text instances, you double-click the Format Painter button so that the Format Painter feature remains active. Clicking the active Format Painter button again turns it off.

QUICK TIP

When you select text, the style and format settings of the selected text appear on the Formatting toolbar.

6. **Click in the text Categories**

   The "Categories" paragraph is formatted with the Heading 2 style. The Format Painter copies the style from the text at the location of the insertion point or the currently selected text to the text you click next. You could have repeated Steps 3 and 4 to make this formatting change, but using the Format Painter saves time and effort.

7. **Click in the text Registration, use the vertical scroll bar to scroll down the home page, click in the text Sponsors, then click ▱ on the Standard toolbar**

   Four headings are formatted with the Heading 2 style, and the Format Painter is turned off.

8. **Click ¶ on the Standard toolbar, then click the Save button ▱ on the Standard toolbar**

   The Show All feature is turned off, and the home page is saved in the Web site.

FIGURE B-9: Changing the text style

Style list arrow

Available text styles

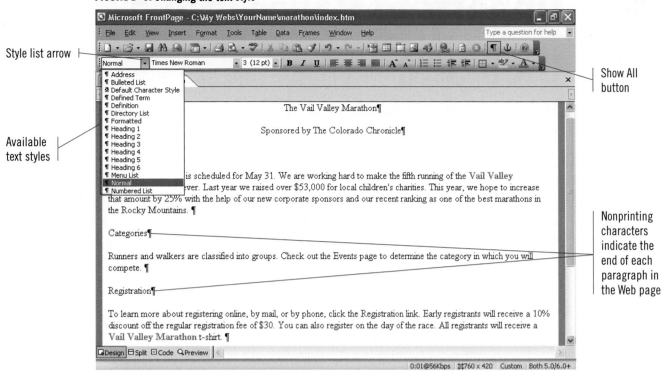

Show All button

Nonprinting characters indicate the end of each paragraph in the Web page

FIGURE B-10: Heading created in the home page

Heading 2 style applied to the current paragraph ("Welcome")

Paragraph formatted with the Heading 2 style

Format these paragraphs with the Heading 2 style in Steps 6 and 7

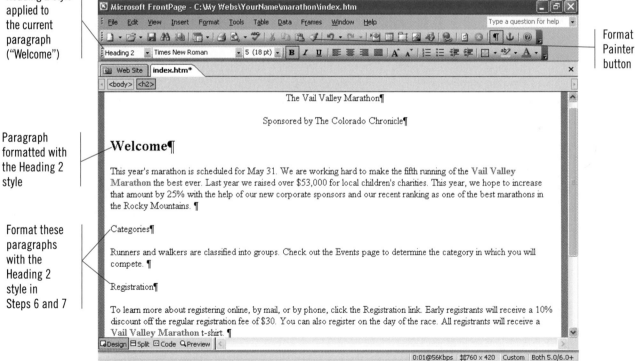

Format Painter button

Clues to Use

Formatting text with the Format Painter

When the Format Painter feature is turned on, you have several options for pasting the selected format to other text in a Web page. If you click 🖌 in any single word, you'll copy the format to the entire word. You can also drag the I-beam in the 🖌 pointer to select more than one word or several characters in a single word. To apply a format to an entire line of text, click 🖌 to the left of the line.

Importing Pages into a Web Site

You already know that you can use FrontPage to create a Web page. You can also use other programs, such as Word and Excel, to create Web pages by saving files as Web pages with the .htm filename extension. Sometimes you might need to use Web pages created by authors using other Web development tools in your FrontPage Web site, especially when you collaborate on a Web site's development with other team members who are responsible for creating pages related to their specialties. Often, these pages are saved in HTML and other file formats that you can import into a FrontPage Web site. You can insert the content of a file into a Web page—just as you did for the home page. In addition to importing the content of a file into an existing Web page, you can import entire files into a Web site. In this case, each imported file becomes a new file in the Web site. ▰▰▰ Jason gives you some files he collected from other members of the Web site development team and asks you to import them into the marathon Web site.

STEPS

1. **Click the Close button on the Contents pane**

   The home page closes, and the Web site is displayed in Folders view. You can import pages into the Web site in Page, Folders, or Navigation view.

2. **Click the Toggle Pane button 🔳 on the Standard toolbar to open the Folder List**

   Before importing pages into a Web site, you need to select the folder in which to store them. In most cases, you will import files into the root folder of the Web site.

3. **Make sure that the marathon Web site's root folder (see Figure B-11) is selected, click File on the menu bar, then click Import**

   The Import dialog box opens, as shown in Figure B-11. You can import one or more files from a file location or from the Internet; or you can import a folder and all of the files it contains.

4. **Click Add File**

   The Add File to Import List dialog box opens.

5. **If necessary, click the Look in list arrow and open the UnitB folder from the drive and folder where your Data Files are stored**

6. **Click events.htm, press and hold [Ctrl], click lastyear.htm, mail.htm, mail_app.doc, online.htm, phone.htm, register.htm, and sponsors.htm, then release [Ctrl]**

   Eight files are selected, as shown in Figure B-12. You press and hold [Ctrl] when you need to select two or more files in the list.

7. **Click Open**

   The Import dialog box shows the eight files that you selected.

8. **Click OK**

   The eight files are imported into the marathon Web site.

9. **Click 🔳**

   The imported files appear as individual files in the Web site, as shown in Figure B-13, and the Folder List closes.

FIGURE B-11: Import dialog box

Root folder

Imports file(s)

Imports all the files in a specified folder as a new folder in the Web site

Imports file(s) using a URL

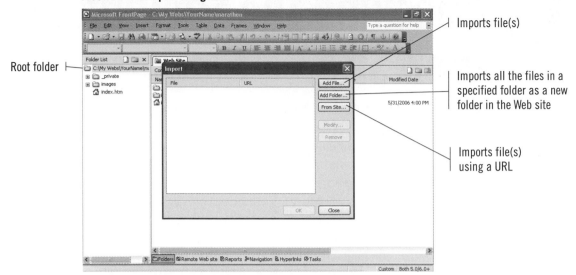

FIGURE B-12: Files selected to import

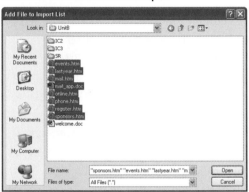

FIGURE B-13: Files imported into the marathon Web site

Your column widths might differ or be hidden

Imported files (your files might be sorted in a different order)

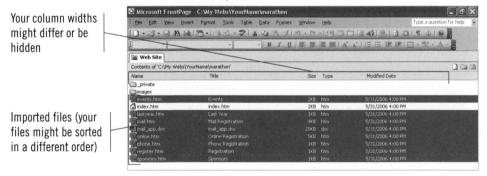

Clues to Use

Importing pages from the Internet

Sometimes you might need to import files into your Web site from an Internet URL. To do so, follow these steps. After clicking Import on the File menu, click From Site. The Import Web Site Wizard - Welcome dialog box will open and prompt you to specify how to transfer the files into your Web site. You can transfer them using the FrontPage Server Extensions or SharePoint Services, WebDAV (Distributed Authoring and Versioning, an extension of File Transfer Protocol), FTP (File Transfer Protocol), File System (files from a hard drive or a network drive), or HTTP (files from a Web site). After selecting the transfer type, type the location of the files to import in the Web Site Location text box, then click Next. FrontPage will ask you to specify the new location of the imported files; you can choose the current Web site or create a new Web site. Click Next, select the options as necessary to limit the download with regard to text and image files and the maximum amount of material to download, click Next, then click Finish. FrontPage will download the requested files and store them in the specified location. You can create a new Web site and import files into it at the same time by using the Import Web Site Wizard in the Web Site Templates dialog box.

Checking the Spelling in a Web Site

As you are working in a Web site, it is a good idea to check the spelling in your pages. In FrontPage, you can check the spelling in a single Web page by selecting it in Folders view or opening it in Page view and then clicking the Spelling button on the Standard toolbar. You can also check the spelling of every Web page in the Web site at the same time by initiating the spell check from Folders view. FrontPage searches Web pages in the Web site for spelling errors and highlights words that it doesn't recognize. You then have the option of changing a highlighted word to a suggested spelling, changing it using your own spelling, ignoring the word, or adding the word to the FrontPage dictionary. FrontPage does not search files in the Web site that do not have valid filename extensions for Web pages (such as .htm). You check the spelling of every Web page in the marathon Web site.

STEPS

1. **Click below the selected files in the Contents pane to deselect them, then click the Spelling button 🗹 on the Standard toolbar**

   The Spelling dialog box opens, as shown in Figure B-14. To check the spelling in one or more pages, press and hold [Ctrl] to select the page(s) in Folders view before opening the Spelling dialog box, then click the Selected page(s) option button. To check the spelling in every Web page, without needing to select pages in Folders view, click the Entire Web site option button.

> **QUICK TIP**
> To resize the spelling dialog box, position ⬉ over the lower-right corner and drag. To resize a column, double-click ↔ on the right border of the column heading.

2. **Click the Entire Web site option button (if necessary), then click Start**

   FrontPage checks the spelling in every page in the Web site. Figure B-15 shows that eight pages were searched and that four misspelled words appear in two of the eight Web pages.

3. **Double-click the Events (events.htm) page in the Spelling dialog box**

   The events.htm page opens, and the word "waklers" is selected in the first sentence. The Change To text box displays the word "walkers" as a suggestion for correcting this misspelled word.

4. **Click walkers in the Suggestions list box, then click Change**

   FrontPage corrects the misspelled word, "walkers." The word "Lionshead," which is the name of a resort area, is selected. Although FrontPage does not recognize this word, it is spelled correctly.

5. **Click Ignore**

   The Continue with next page? dialog box opens.

6. **Make sure that the Save and close this page check box contains a check mark, then click Next Page**

   The lastyear.htm page opens in Page view, and FrontPage selects the first word that it does not recognize. The selected word, "Keraro," is the last name of last year's male marathon winner. It is spelled correctly, so you can ignore it.

> **QUICK TIP**
> To ignore all instances of a word that FrontPage does not recognize but that is spelled correctly, click Ignore All.

7. **Click Ignore**

   FrontPage selects the next misspelled word, "Tatyana," which is the first name of last year's female marathon winner. This word is also spelled correctly.

8. **Click Ignore**

   FrontPage is finished checking the pages and opens the Finished checking pages dialog box. See Figure B-16.

9. **Click Back To List**

   The lastyear.htm page closes. Notice that in the Spelling dialog box the Status column now shows that the Events and Last Year pages have been edited. See Figure B-17.

10. **Click Cancel**

    The Spelling dialog box closes.

FIGURE B-14: Spelling dialog box

Checks the spelling of selected page(s) in Folders view

Checks the spelling of all pages in the Web site

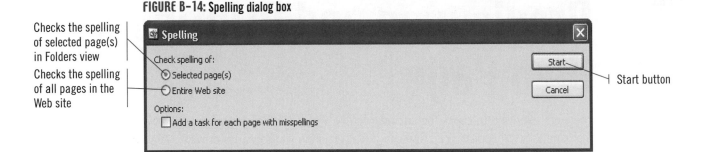

Start button

FIGURE B-15: Spelling dialog box after searching all pages

These pages contain spelling errors

Information about the spell check

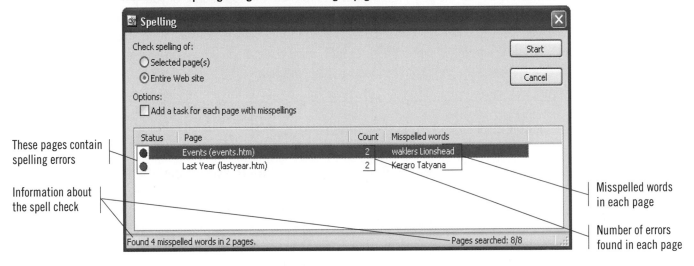

Misspelled words in each page

Number of errors found in each page

FIGURE B-16: Finished checking pages dialog box

Option to close the current page

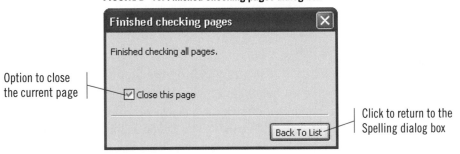

Click to return to the Spelling dialog box

FIGURE B-17: Completed Spelling dialog box

"Edited" status indicates that you have reviewed errors in these pages

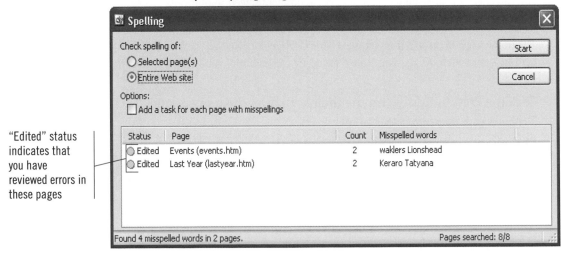

Previewing and Printing a Web Page

There are two ways to check the appearance of a Web page. You already used Preview view, which shows the page as it will appear in a browser without requiring you to start a browser. The second way is to view the Web page in a browser either by clicking the Preview button on the Standard toolbar to open the page in your default browser, or by clicking the Preview button list arrow to select a browser or multiple browsers with which to display the page. It is a good idea to check the appearance of your pages in a browser periodically to ensure that text and other objects are being displayed correctly. For any Web page open in Page view, you can also check the status bar to obtain the approximate download time for the Web page. The default download time is expressed in seconds, using a specified connection speed. ▄▀▄▀ You want to check the appearance and download time of the home page.

STEPS

1. **Double-click** index.htm **in the Contents pane**

    The home page opens in Design view.

2. **Point to the** Estimated Time to Download pane **on the status bar, then click it**

    The Estimated Time to Download menu opens, as shown in Figure B-18. The first two options, 28.8 and 56, are connection speeds for dial-up modems. Digital Subscriber Lines (DSLs) transfer data at a rate of approximately 256Kbps to 512Kbps. Cable modems transfer data at a rate of 1,000Kbps, and T1 connections are considered the fastest connections with transfers of up to 1,500Kbps.

3. **Click** 56 **in the list (even if it has a check mark next to it)**

    The download time for the home page is 0:01, or one second, at 56Kbps.

4. **Click the** Print button 🖨 **on the Standard toolbar**

    The home page prints; your name appears in the URL at the top of the page. You can print a Web page from Design view or Code view.

5. **Click the** Preview button list arrow 🔍▾ **on the Standard toolbar**

    When you click the Preview button list arrow on the Standard toolbar, you can choose which Web browser (from a list of installed browsers on your computer) to use to open the page. See Figure B-19. Once you select a browser from the list, you can click the Preview button on the Standard toolbar to preview pages using the Web browser you selected because it becomes your default Web browser. If more than one browser is installed on your computer, clicking the Preview in Multiple Browsers option starts all browsers on your computer and opens the Web page in each of them. Notice that you can also open pages in specific browser window sizes so you can check the appearance of your pages at different screen resolutions.

6. **Click the default browser for your computer**

    The home page opens in a browser. See Figure B-20. As expected, the page looks the same in the browser as it does in Design view. As you continue developing the Web site, you will use one or more browsers to test the Web site.

TROUBLE

If you are using Netscape Navigator, click 🖨 to print the home page.

7. **Click the** Print button 🖨 **on the toolbar to print the home page**

    The home page prints from your browser.

8. **Click the** Close button **on the browser title bar**

9. **In FrontPage, click** File **on the menu bar, click** Close Site, **click** File **on the menu bar, then click** Exit

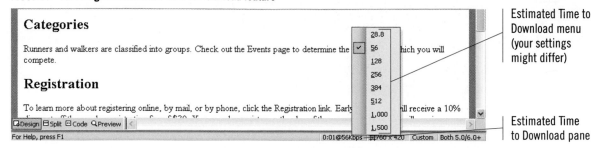

FIGURE B-18: Using the Estimated Time to Download feature

Estimated Time to Download menu (your settings might differ)

Estimated Time to Download pane

FIGURE B-19: Preview button list

Preview button list arrow

Options to open the Web page in more than one browser (if you have only one browser installed, you won't see these options)

Installed browsers (your list might differ)

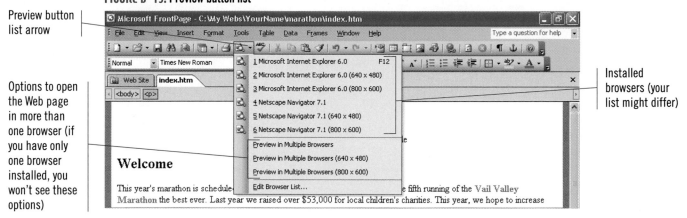

FIGURE B-20: Home page in a browser

Print button

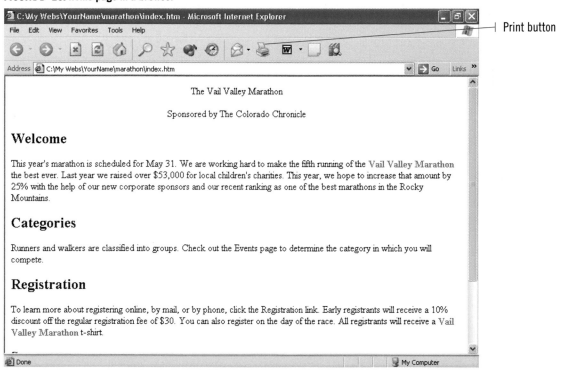

Clues to Use

Using a browser to view an HTML document

For most Web pages that you open using a browser, you can see the HTML document that created them by accessing the browser's menu commands. If you are using Internet Explorer, click View on the menu bar, then click Source. A Notepad program window opens and displays the HTML document for the Web page you are currently viewing. If you are using Navigator, click View on the menu bar, then click Page Source. The HTML document opens in a new window.

Practice

▼ CONCEPTS REVIEW

Label each element in the Microsoft FrontPage window shown in Figure B-21.

FIGURE B-21

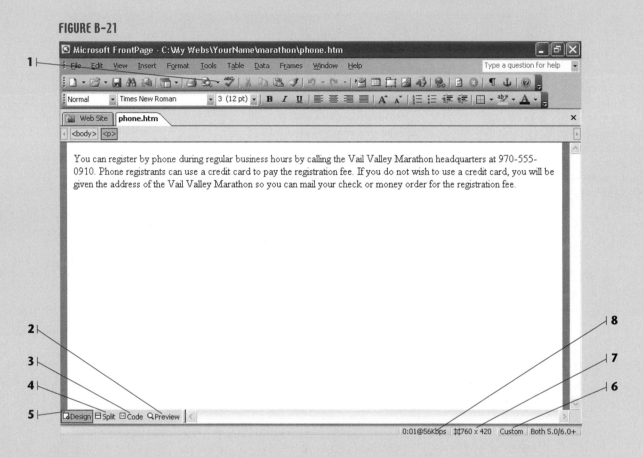

Match each of the following terms with the statement that describes its function.

9. **Empty Web Site**
10. **Font size 1**
11. **Font size 7**
12. **Heading 1 style**
13. **Heading 6 style**
14. **index.htm**
15. **SharePoint Team Site**

a. A Web site template that creates a Web site with no pages in it
b. A Web site template that creates a Web site with tools used for collaboration
c. The default name of a home page in a FrontPage Web site
d. The equivalent of 36 points
e. The equivalent of 8 points
f. The largest HTML heading style
g. The smallest HTML heading style

Select the best answer from the following list of choices.

16. To create a new Web site in FrontPage, click _____ in the New task pane.
    a. More page templates
    b. Blank page
    c. More Web site templates
    d. Go

17. Acceptable locations for creating a new Web site are:
    a. On a hard drive.
    b. On an external drive.
    c. On a server.
    d. All of the above

18. The Web site template that lets you create a Web site with pages in it that you retrieve from a disk location or another Web site is the:
    a. One Page Web Site.
    b. Project Web Site.
    c. Import Web Site Wizard.
    d. Personal Web Site.

19. The FrontPage and SharePoint technologies, the selected browser and version, and the selected Internet technologies that are enabled for a Web site are collectively called the Web site's:
    a. General settings.
    b. Schema settings.
    c. Authoring settings.
    d. None of the above

20. When you press [Enter] in a Web page in Design view, what happens?
    a. The insertion point moves to the next line, with no space below the previous paragraph.
    b. The insertion point moves to the next line, with space below the previous paragraph.
    c. You create a new heading.
    d. None of the above

21. Which of the following buttons lets you copy and paste text formats in a Web page?
    a.
    b.
    c.
    d.

22. What is affected when you apply a paragraph style?
    a. The selected text
    b. The paragraph that contains the insertion point
    c. The word that contains the insertion point
    d. All of the above

▼ SKILLS REVIEW

1. Create a new Web site.

   a. Start FrontPage.

   b. Display the New task pane, then open the Web Site Templates dialog box.

   c. Use the Personal Web Site template to create a new Web site named **hobbies** in the location where your Web sites are stored.

   d. In Folders view, double-click the first page listed in the Contents pane to open it in Design view, then examine its content.

   e. Change to Folders view, then repeat this process to open the remaining pages created by the template. The pages contain sample content and features that are created by the template.

   f. Switch to the aboutme.htm page in Design view.

2. Set the Web site's page options.

   a. Open the Page Options dialog box, then switch to the Authoring tab.

   b. In the FrontPage and SharePoint technologies section, make sure a check mark appears in every check box *except* Generator and ProgID tags.

   c. Select Internet Explorer and Navigator as the target browsers, and select versions 5.0/6.0 and later as the target browser versions.

   d. Close the Page Options dialog box.

   e. If necessary, set the default page size to 600 x 300 (640 x 480, Maximized).

3. Enter and insert text in a Web page.

   a. Select the first paragraph in the aboutme.htm page (that begins **This is a page that can be used to describe**), then delete it and the blank paragraph that follows it.

   b. Select the text **[Your Name Here]** in the first sentence, then type your first and last names.

   c. Select the text **[Location Name]**... in the first sentence, type the name of the city and state or province in which you live, then type a period.

   d. Start Word or WordPad, then type one paragraph that describes your favorite hobby or class. When you are finished, save the document as **aboutme.doc** in the hobbies Web folder in the location where your Web sites are stored. Close your word-processing program.

   e. In FrontPage, select the four paragraphs that contain the text **[Place your text here]**.

   f. Insert the aboutme.doc word-processing file that you saved in the hobbies Web site. This text should now be part of the paragraph containing your name.

   g. Save the page.

4. Format text.

   a. Format your name with italics and change the font color to blue.

   b. Format your location with italics and change the font color to blue.

   c. Save the page.

5. Apply paragraph styles.

   a. Apply the Heading 5 style to the paragraph that begins **Hello my name is...**

   b. Change the style of the **Welcome to my Web site!** paragraph to Heading 2.

   c. Save the page.

6. Import pages into a Web site.

   a. Change to Folders view.

   b. If necessary, turn on the Folder List, then select the Web site's root folder.

   c. Open the Import dialog box.

   d. Select the option to add a file.

e. Open the UnitB\SR folder from the drive and folder where your Data Files are stored, select the files favorite.htm, interest.htm, and photo.htm, then import these three files into the root folder of the hobbies Web site.

f. Click Yes to All in the Confirm Save dialog box to overwrite the existing files.

g. Close the Folder List.

7. **Check the spelling in a Web site.**

a. Check the spelling of all pages in the hobbies Web site.

b. Double-click the first page listed in the Spelling dialog box to open it, then correct any problems that you find. (*Hint*: You do not need to change the spelling of URLs or other content that is correct.)

c. Click Next Page to move to the next page, and correct any errors.

d. Click Next Page to move to the next page, and correct any errors.

e. Click Back To List, then close the Spelling dialog box.

8. **Preview and print a Web page.**

a. Display the aboutme.htm page in Design view.

b. Change the Estimated Time to Download setting to 28.8 and note the page's download time. Then set the Estimated Time to Download setting to 512 and note its download time.

c. Change to Preview view and examine the page.

d. Change to Design view, then print the page.

e. Preview the aboutme.htm page in your default browser, then print the page using the browser.

f. Close the browser and the hobbies Web site, then exit FrontPage.

▼ INDEPENDENT CHALLENGE 1

Television station WHME-11 in Birmingham, Alabama, sponsors a yearly fan drive to collect electric fans for distribution to elderly people on fixed incomes. The general manager asks you to create the Web page shown in Figure B-22. She will post this page to the WHME Web site to provide more information about the fan drive to potential donors and volunteers.

a. Start FrontPage and use the One Page Web Site template to create a new Web site named **fans** in the location where your Web sites are stored.

b. Open the home page (index.htm) in Design view.

c. Set the Web site's authoring settings by making sure a check mark appears in every check box in the FrontPage and SharePoint technologies section *except* Generator and ProgID tags, and for Internet Explorer and Navigator versions 5.0/6.0 and later.

d. If necessary, change the default page size to 800 x 600 maximized.

e. Change the estimated time to download speed to 56Kbps.

f. Use the skills that you learned in this unit to create the page shown in Figure B-22. (*Note:* This page contains bold text, italic text, and text formatted with the Heading 1 style.)

g. Save the page, then preview it using your browser.

h. Print the page using your browser, then close your browser.

i. Close the fans Web site, then exit FrontPage.

FIGURE B-22

FrontPage 2003

▼ INDEPENDENT CHALLENGE 2

After meeting with the Web site development team, you are ready to begin work on the Web site for the Villages at Kensington Neighbourhood Association using the Web site plan that you developed earlier. (If you did not work on this Web site in Unit A, contact your instructor for assistance.)

a. Start FrontPage and use the One Page Web Site template to create a new Web site named **village** in the location where your Web sites are stored.

b. Open the home page in Design view. If necessary, set the Web site's default page size to 800 x 600 maximized.

c. Enable all features *except* Generator and ProgID tags in the FrontPage and SharePoint technologies section of the Authoring tab; enable both Internet Explorer and Navigator versions 5.0/6.0 and higher.

d. On the first line of the home page, type **The Villages at Kensington**. Start a new line by pressing [Shift][Enter], then type **Neighbourhood Association**.

e. Format the lines that you typed with center alignment and the Heading 1 style.

f. Position the insertion point below the second line, then insert the file named village.doc from the UnitB\IC2 folder on the drive and folder where your Data Files are stored.

g. Format all three instances of the text **Villages at Kensington** in the text that you inserted to bold and teal. (*Note:* Do not format this text in the heading.)

h. Press [Ctrl][End], type your first and last names, then right-align the paragraph. Save the home page.

i. Import all the files *except* village.doc (a total of eight files) in the UnitB\IC2 folder into the root folder of the village Web site.

j. Open each page that you imported and view its content. In addition, format any text that serves as a column or section heading with the Heading 2 style. (*Hint:* The Format Painter also works to format content in multiple documents.) Save and close each page when you are finished with it. (*Note:* Some pages contain minimal text or are blank; you will develop each page as you complete the units in this book.)

k. Check the spelling of all pages in the Web site and make any necessary corrections. (*Hint:* **Neighbourhood** is the correct spelling of this word in Canada; click Ignore All to skip checking it in every page. People's names are spelled correctly.)

l. Preview the home page using your default browser, use your browser to print the page, then close the browser.

m. Close the village Web site, then exit FrontPage.

▼ INDEPENDENT CHALLENGE 3

Now that you have planned the Web site for the city of Tryon, North Carolina, you are ready to use FrontPage to create it. (If you did not work on this Web site in Unit A, contact your instructor for assistance.)

a. Start FrontPage and use the One Page Web Site template to create a new Web site named **tryon** in the location where your Web sites are stored.

b. Open the home page in Design view. If necessary, set the Web site's default page size to 800 x 600 maximized.

c. Enable all features *except* Generator and ProgID tags in the FrontPage and SharePoint technologies section of the Authoring tab; enable both Internet Explorer and Navigator versions 5.0/6.0 and higher.

d. Change to Split view for the home page, then in the lower pane type **Thank you for visiting the Tryon Web site!**

e. Format the paragraph that you typed with center alignment and apply the Heading 1 style.

f. Click below the heading to position the insertion point, then insert the file named tryon.doc from the UnitB\IC3 folder on the drive and folder where your Data Files are stored.

▼ INDEPENDENT CHALLENGE 3 (CONTINUED)

g. Format all three instances of the word **Tryon** in the text that you inserted in bold and purple. (*Note:* Do not format this word in the heading.)

h. Press [Ctrl][End], type your first and last names, and then right-align the paragraph. Save the home page, then switch to Design view.

i. Import all files *except* tryon.doc (a total of seven files) in the UnitB\IC3 folder into the root folder of the tryon Web site.

j. Open each page that you imported and view its content. (*Note:* Some pages contain only minimal text; you will develop each page as you complete the units in this book.) In the hotspots.htm page, format the text used as section headings using the Heading 2 style, then save the page.

k. Check the spelling of all pages in the Web site and make any necessary corrections. (*Hint:* The word **showring** should be two words.)

l. Preview the home page using your default browser, use your browser to print the page, then close the browser.

m. Close the tryon Web site, then exit FrontPage.

▼ INDEPENDENT CHALLENGE 4

As the Webmaster for your company, a not-for-profit organization that provides advice to first-time parents, you are in charge of managing its Web site. The Web site development team wants to create a new site that has similar characteristics to existing Web sites for new parents. This will make your new site easier to navigate. You decide to visit some of these sites to determine the effectiveness of their elements and features.

a. Use your favorite search engine and enter a search query such as **Where can new parents find advice?** or **Advice for new parents**. You might use AltaVista, Yahoo!, Excite, Infoseek, or another search engine of your choice. (Check with your instructor if you prefer to analyze a group of Web sites focused on a different topic.)

b. Visit at least three sites. Print the home page and one other page that is linked to the home page.

c. Write a brief report in which you comment on each site's visual appearance. Based on your research, what kinds of features make the Web sites easy to read and use? Which Web site was the most attractive? What would you change in the Web sites that you visited to make them more visually appealing and easier to use? Did you experience any problems while navigating the sites? If so, what kinds of problems did you experience? Make sure your name appears at the top of the report.

d. Attach your completed report to the pages you printed.

e. Close your browser.

Start FrontPage and use the One Page Web Site template to create a new Web site named **picnic** in the location where your Web sites are stored. Create the home page shown in Figure B-23. When you are finished, save the page, preview and print it using your browser, close the browser and the picnic Web site, then exit FrontPage.

FIGURE B-23

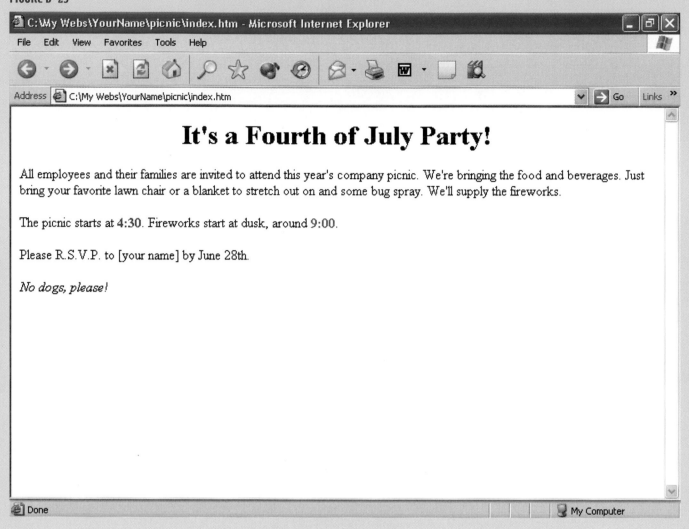

Working on the Web Site's Hyperlinks and Appearance

OBJECTIVES

Understand Navigation view
Add existing pages to the navigation structure
Add blank pages to the navigation structure
Turn on shared borders
Change link bar properties
Change the content of a shared border
Apply a theme to a Web site
Customize a theme

When viewing a Web site, clicking a hyperlink might open a location in the same Web page (an **internal link**) or a location in another Web page or Web site (an **external link**). One of the easiest and most efficient ways of creating the hyperlinks that connect the pages in a Web site is to use shared borders. A **shared border** is an area that appears in every page in a Web site that uses it. Another way to enhance your Web site's appearance is to apply a theme to it. A **theme** is a collection of coordinated graphics, colors, and fonts applied to individual pages or all pages in a Web site. The marathon Web site contains several pages now, and Jason Tanaka, manager of the Vail Valley Marathon, asks you to work on the site's hyperlinks and appearance. You decide to create hyperlinks in the Web site's shared borders to connect the pages, and to apply a theme to the Web site to enhance its appearance.

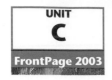

Understanding Navigation View

As you have learned, Navigation view shows a Web site's navigation structure, which identifies the relationships between pages in the Web site. When you first create a Web site, FrontPage automatically adds the home page to the navigation structure. If you used a template to create the Web site, FrontPage might add other pages created by the template to the navigation structure, as well. When you add new pages to a Web site, you must manually add them to the site's navigation structure in Navigation view. ▨▨▨▨ You used the One Page Web Site template when you created the marathon Web site, and then you imported pages into it. You will use Navigation view to add these pages to the navigation structure and define the hierarchical relationships between the Web site's pages.

DETAILS

- **Identify the relationships between pages in Navigation view**

  Much like an organization chart, the navigation structure in Navigation view illustrates the relationships between Web pages in a site. The home page is usually the top-level page in the site and includes links to all of the child pages below it. Therefore, when you add new pages to the Web site, you usually add them on the level below the home page. The home page becomes a **parent page**, and the pages below it become **child pages**. You might create additional levels of child pages to show subtopics of the child pages. The navigation structure shown in Figure C-1 shows how a bookstore might organize Web pages for cookbooks. FrontPage uses the navigation structure you create to identify the page relationships.

  After you add pages to the navigation structure in Navigation view, you can move, rename, delete, and open pages. Moving a page changes its relationship to other pages in the Web site. Renaming a page changes its title, which appears on the page icon. When you delete a page from the navigation structure, you can delete the page from the navigation structure or delete it from the Web site. Double-clicking a page icon in the navigation structure opens the page in Design view.

  Some Web sites will include pages that you won't need to add to the navigation structure because they don't need to appear in components dependent on the navigation structure (such as link bars that provide hyperlinks to other pages in the Web site and site maps that identify Web pages according to their category). Adding a page to the navigation structure is necessary only when you need the page to use these types of components. In addition, you cannot add files that are not Web pages, such as Word documents and Excel workbooks, to the navigation structure.

- **Position pages in the navigation structure to impact the appearance of some FrontPage components in a Web site**

  Some FrontPage components, such as link bars, shared borders, and page banners, are based on the Web site's navigation structure. If you try to insert these components in a Web page without first adding the page to the navigation structure, FrontPage will display the message shown in Figure C-2 as a reminder to do so. After you add the page to the navigation structure, the link bar, shared borders, and page banner components appear with actual content, as shown in Figure C-3. If you don't add the page to the navigation structure, then FrontPage won't have the necessary information to create components, such as shared borders and link bars, based on the relationships between the current page and the other pages in the Web site.

  By using components, such as link bars, shared borders, and page banners, you ensure that every page in the site has a similar appearance. If you add a link bar and a page banner at the top of all the pages, then they will all contain familiar and easily located features that help your site's users navigate the site.

FIGURE C-1: Sample navigation structure for a bookstore Web site

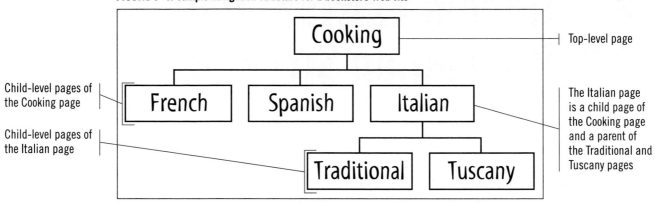

Top-level page

Child-level pages of the Cooking page

Child-level pages of the Italian page

The Italian page is a child page of the Cooking page and a parent of the Traditional and Tuscany pages

FIGURE C-2: Placeholders for components appear in a page that hasn't been added to the navigation structure

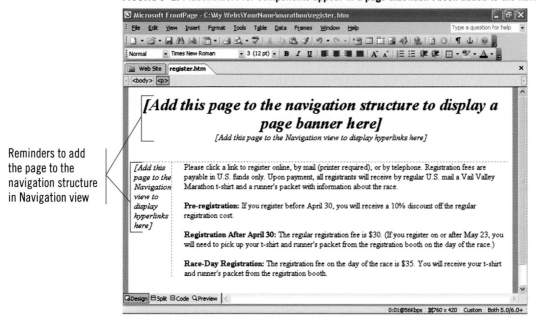

Reminders to add the page to the navigation structure in Navigation view

FIGURE C-3: Web page shown in Figure C-2 after being added to the navigation structure

Page banner in top shared border uses page title shown in the navigation structure

Link bars with links based on this page's position in the navigation structure

Left shared border contains links to child pages of the current page

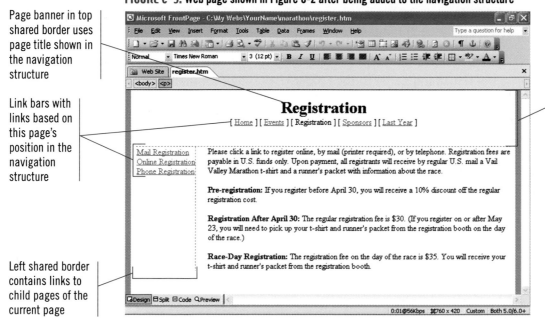

Top shared border contains links to the home page and to pages at the same level as the current page

Adding Existing Pages to the Navigation Structure

You can use Navigation view to add an existing page in a Web site to the navigation structure by dragging its filename from the Folder List and dropping it in the correct position in the navigation structure. Once the page is positioned in the navigation structure, you can insert components that are dependent on the navigation structure in the page. In addition, you can rearrange the pages in the navigation structure at any time to redefine the relationships between the site's pages. ▬▬▬▬ You plan to use components that require you to identify the relationships between pages, so you add the existing pages in the marathon Web site to the navigation structure. The home page is the top-level page. Below the home page, you want to add the following child pages: Events, Registration, Sponsors, and Last Year. In addition, the Registration page has three child pages: Mail Registration, Online Registration, and Phone Registration.

STEPS

TROUBLE

If the Folder List is not open, click the Toggle Pane button 🗐 on the Standard toolbar.

1. **Start FrontPage, open the marathon Web site from the location where your Web sites are stored, then click the Navigation View button** 🔾Navigation **at the bottom of the Contents pane**

   The Folder List shows the folders and files in the marathon Web site. Navigation view shows the navigation structure, which contains a page icon for index.htm (the site's home page), along with a message about creating navigation buttons. The hyperlinks that appear in the link bar in a shared border are called **navigation buttons**, even though a navigation button might appear as regular text instead of as a button. Page icons in the navigation structure display the page title. You can view the filename and the page title for any Web page in Folders view. You'll change the page title for index.htm in a later lesson.

2. **Click register.htm in the Folder List**

   The register.htm file is selected.

QUICK TIP

If you position a page incorrectly, drag the page icon to the correct location. To remove a page from the navigation structure, right-click the page icon, click Delete, click the Remove page from the navigation structure option button, then click OK.

3. **Drag register.htm from the Folder List and position the pointer as shown in Figure C-4**

   You are adding this page to the navigation structure as a child page of the home page.

4. **With the pointer positioned below the home page, release the mouse button**

   The Registration page icon replaces the message about navigation buttons, and the Registration page becomes a child of the home page.

5. **Drag mail.htm from the Folder List and position it below the Registration page**

   The Mail Registration page becomes a child of the Registration page. The site now has three levels of pages.

6. **Drag events.htm from the Folder List and position it as shown in Figure C-5**

   Two child pages appear below the home page.

QUICK TIP

Clicking a page icon in the navigation structure shows that page's filename on the status bar.

7. **Drag the remaining pages in the Folder List (except for mail_app.doc) and position them as shown in Figure C-6**

   Make sure your pages are positioned exactly as shown in Figure C-6 before continuing. The site's navigation structure is complete. FrontPage will use this information to configure components that are based on the presentation of pages in the navigation structure. Remember that the page icons in the navigation structure show page titles, which might not be the same as the filenames. You can see both filenames and titles for a site's pages by switching to Folders view.

FIGURE C-4: Adding a page to the navigation structure in Navigation view

Toggle Pane button

register.htm page selected

register.htm page being positioned as child page of the home page

Home page (index.htm) is the top-level page

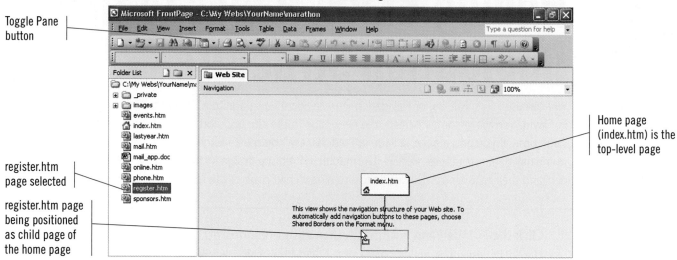

FIGURE C-5: Adding a child page of the home page

events.htm page selected

events.htm page being positioned as child page of the home page

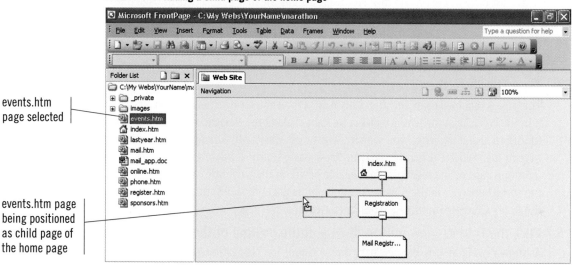

FIGURE C-6: Navigation structure for the marathon Web site

File that is excluded from navigation structure

Completed navigation structure

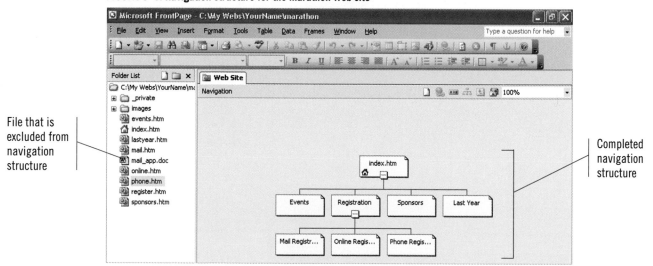

Adding Blank Pages to the Navigation Structure

You can use Page, Folders, or Navigation view to add a new page to a Web site. When you add a new page in Navigation view, you can create the new page in the site and add it to the navigation structure at the same time. If you add a page in Page or Folders view, you must switch to Navigation view to add the page to the navigation structure. 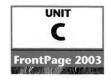 The marathon Web site design includes a page featuring this year's winners and their race times. You decide to add a new child page of the home page for this purpose.

1. **Click the** Toggle Pane button 🔳**, then click the** index.htm page icon

   The Folder List closes, and the home page (index.htm) is selected. Before adding a new page in Navigation view, you need to select the page icon at the level above which you want to add the new page.

   QUICK TIP

   You can use the Zoom list arrow on the Navigation pane to resize the navigation structure.

2. **Click the** New Page button 🔲 **on the Navigation pane**

   A new page is created below the home page. As shown in Figure C-7, the child page that you added appears as the last page in the second row. FrontPage assigns the new page a default page title of "New Page 1" (this number changes if you have already created a new page in the current session).

3. **Right-click the** New Page 1 page icon, **then click** Rename **in the shortcut menu**

   The current page title, "New Page 1," is selected.

4. **Type** This Year, **then press** [Enter]

   The page is renamed using the title "This Year." When you create a new page in Navigation view, you can save it in the Web site by switching views or by right-clicking the Navigation pane and clicking Apply Changes on the shortcut menu. When you switch views or use the Apply Changes command, FrontPage creates a new page in the Web site using the filename "new_page_1.htm" (or a different number, if you have created more than one page in the session) or a filename based on the page title, with an underscore character replacing the space between words. You can create multiple pages in Navigation view. When you switch views or use the Apply Changes command, FrontPage saves all of the pages.

   TROUBLE

   If you see "this_year.htm" as the filename, don't worry. You'll rename the page in the next step.

5. **Click the** Folders View button 📁Folders **at the bottom of the window**

   As shown in Figure C-8, the new page that you added in Navigation view appears in the Contents pane.

6. **Right-click** new_page_1.htm **to open the shortcut menu, click** Rename, **type** thisyear.htm, **then press** [Enter]

   The Rename dialog box opens briefly, and the page's filename changes to "thisyear.htm," matching the file-naming convention of other pages in the site.

FIGURE C-7: New page added to the navigation structure

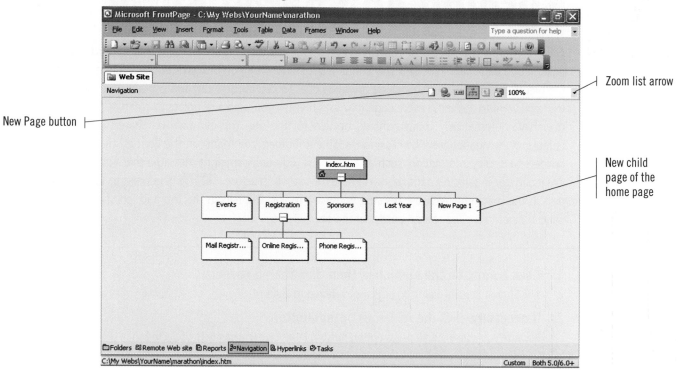

New Page button

Zoom list arrow

New child page of the home page

FIGURE C-8: New page in Folders view

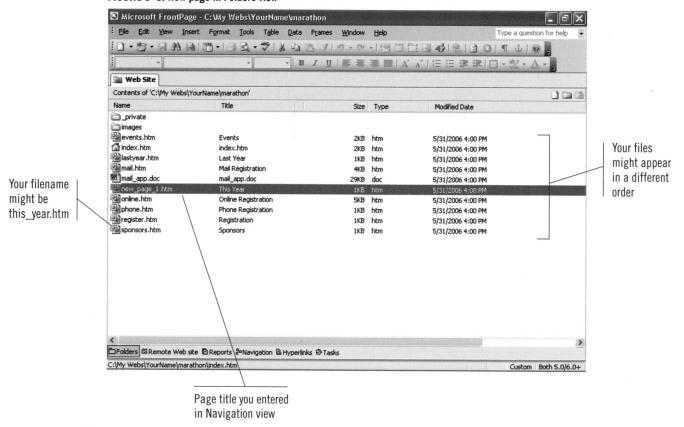

Your filename might be this_year.htm

Your files might appear in a different order

Page title you entered in Navigation view

FrontPage 2003

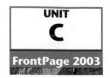

Turning on Shared Borders

A shared border is an area that appears in every page in a Web site that uses it. Shared borders can contain a link bar or a page banner. A **link bar** contains hyperlinks based on the navigation structure. A **page banner** is a picture or text object that includes a page's title. Shared borders can also contain other text and graphics that you want to appear in every page that uses them. If you used a template to create a Web site, FrontPage may have automatically created shared borders for the site. You can turn on shared borders from Page, Folders, or Navigation view by clicking the Shared Borders command on the Format menu. You use shared borders to display information, such as a company logo or a copyright message, that you want to appear in *every* page or in selected pages shown in the navigation structure. You need to turn on shared borders in the marathon Web site because you want to add link bars in the top and left shared borders and a page banner in the top shared border of the site.

STEPS

1. **Click** Format **on the menu bar, then click** Shared Borders
   The Shared Borders dialog box opens, as shown in Figure C-9.

QUICK TIP
If you create a new page in the navigation structure after creating shared borders for all pages in a Web site, FrontPage will apply the shared borders for the Web site to the new page automatically.

2. **If necessary, click the** All pages option button
   Because you chose the All pages option button, FrontPage will create the selected shared borders in every page that you added to the navigation structure.

3. **Click the** Top check box **to select it, then click the** Include navigation buttons check box **to select it**
   The Shared Borders dialog box shows a preview of the top shared border, which includes a page banner and navigation buttons arranged horizontally across the border. These settings are the defaults for the top shared border.

4. **Click the** Left check box **to select it, then click the** Include navigation buttons check box **to select it**
   The preview shows that the left shared border includes navigation buttons arranged vertically down the border.

5. **Click** OK
   The Shared Borders dialog box closes, and the top and left shared borders are added to each page that appears in the navigation structure. You cannot see the shared borders in Folders view.

6. **In Folders view, double-click** register.htm
   The page opens in Design view, where you can see the shared borders. As shown in Figure C-10, the page's title, "Registration," appears as a page banner in the top shared border. A link bar containing links to the home page and to pages at the same level as the current page in the navigation structure appears in the top shared border. A link bar containing links to child pages of the current page appears in the left shared border. Every Web page in the navigation structure uses the same shared borders, but the actual links displayed in each page are different.

QUICK TIP
In a link bar, FrontPage uses the "Home" hyperlink to represent the site's top-level page, even if that page has a different title.

7. **Press and hold** [Ctrl]**, click the** Home **link in the top shared border, then release** [Ctrl]
   The home page opens in Design view. A placeholder appears in the top shared border, instead of a link bar, because the home page does not have any pages at the same level in the navigation structure.

8. **Click the** Web Site tab**, click the** Navigation View **button** ᵈ⁻Navigation **at the bottom of the window, right-click the** index.htm **page icon, then click** Rename **in the shortcut menu**
   The title "index.htm" is selected.

9. **Type** Vail Valley Marathon**, press** [Enter]**, then click the** index.htm page tab **at the top of the window**
   The home page displays the new title.

FIGURE C-9: Shared Borders dialog box

Option to create shared border(s) in all pages that have been added to Navigation view

Option to create shared border(s) in only selected pages

Sample page changes to show the selected shared border(s)

Options to include navigation buttons (links) available only for the top, left, and right shared borders

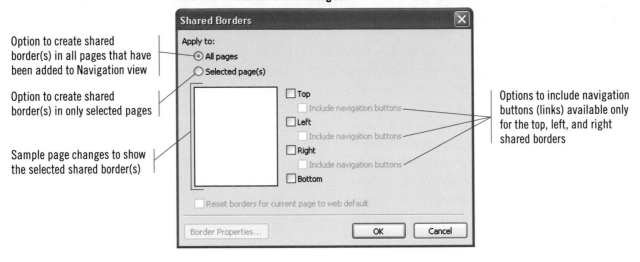

FIGURE C-10: Registration page with shared borders

Inactive hyperlink to the current page

Hyperlink to the home page

Top shared border includes a page banner and a link bar

Link bar in left shared border

Left shared border includes a link bar

Page title (as shown in Navigation view) added as a page banner

Link bar in top shared border

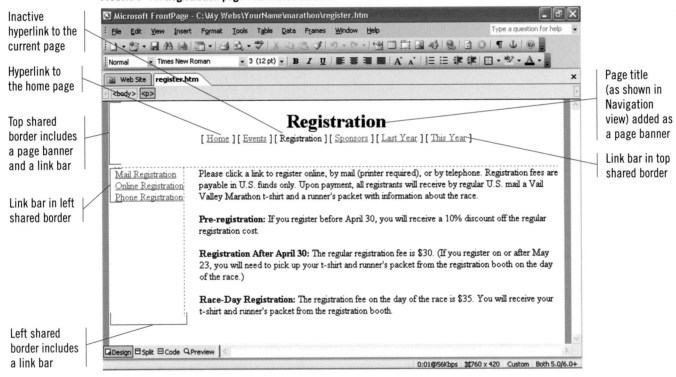

Design Matters

Some things to consider when using shared borders

Selecting the options to include navigation buttons in a Web site's shared borders creates the hyperlinks that connect the pages in a Web site. Shared borders are an excellent way to ensure that every page in the navigation structure is reachable via the hyperlinks created in the site's shared borders. When you use shared borders, however, keep in mind that they can take up a considerable amount of space in a Web page. Users with smaller monitors and lower screen resolutions might need to scroll the pages in your site to view their content. After creating a shared border, you can change its properties, such as font size and spacing, to reduce the amount of space it requires. You can also move and delete pages in the navigation structure to reduce the number of links that appear in the shared border.

Changing Link Bar Properties

When turning on shared borders, if you select the option to include navigation buttons in any or all of the top, left, and right shared borders, FrontPage creates a link bar component using the default settings for that shared border. For the top shared border, the link bar contains hyperlinks to the same-level pages, to the home page, and to the parent page. For the left and right shared borders, the link bar contains hyperlinks to child-level pages. In the navigation structure in Navigation view, same-level pages appear in the same row, the home page is the site's top-level page, and a parent page appears in the row above a child page. After you create the shared borders, you can use the Link Bar Properties dialog box to review and, if necessary, revise the link bar component to display different hyperlinks. ▰▰▱▱ You want to view the default link bar settings for the top and left shared borders.

STEPS

1. **Position the pointer over the text in the top shared border that begins "[Edit the properties..."**
   The pointer changes to 🖼️, indicating that this text is the link bar component.

2. **Right-click the link bar component, then click Link Bar Properties in the shortcut menu**
   The Link Bar Properties dialog box for the link bar in the top shared border opens, as shown in Figure C-11. The Same level option button is selected; this is the default setting for a link bar created in the top shared border. You can also select one, both, or none of the check boxes in the Additional pages section to include or omit these links in the link bar.

> **QUICK TIP**
> In a link bar, FrontPage uses the "Up" hyperlink to represent the parent page of the current page.

3. **Observe the diagram in the dialog box as you click the Child level option button to select it and the Parent page check box to deselect it**
   The diagram changes to show you which hyperlinks you have activated.

4. **Click the Same level option button**
   The link bar in the top shared border includes links to same-level pages and to the home page.

5. **Click the Style tab**
   As shown in Figure C-12, you can change the style and orientation of buttons that appear in link bars. You accept these default settings; you will apply a theme to the Web site in a later lesson.

6. **Click OK**
   These settings are applied to all pages that use the top shared border. You won't see any changes in the link bar's appearance until you apply a theme to this page. Applying the theme will change the appearance of the top shared border to use graphic elements from the theme.

7. **Point to the link bar component in the left shared border so the pointer changes to 🖼️, right-click to open the shortcut menu, then click Link Bar Properties**
   The default setting for a link bar created in the left shared border includes links to child-level pages only. This setting is correct.

8. **Click the Style tab**
   The default style for a left shared border (formatting links enclosed in brackets) is selected. Notice that a description of the currently selected style appears in the Description area.

> **TROUBLE**
> The style's description is "An HTML style where each link is underlined."

9. **Scroll down the Choose a style list box and click the Xxxxx Xxxxx Xxxxx style (the last style in the list), make sure the Vertical option button is selected, then click OK**
   The left shared border is set to display links to child-level pages as underlined text in a vertical arrangement.

FIGURE C-11: Link Bar Properties dialog box for the top shared border

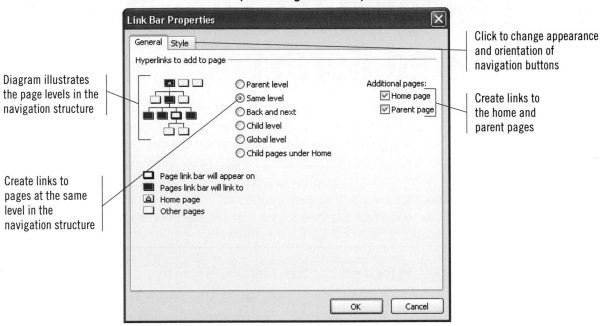

Click to change appearance and orientation of navigation buttons

Diagram illustrates the page levels in the navigation structure

Create links to the home and parent pages

Create links to pages at the same level in the navigation structure

FIGURE C-12: Style tab for the top shared border

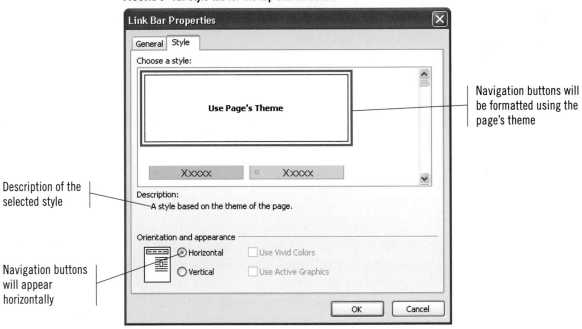

Navigation buttons will be formatted using the page's theme

Description of the selected style

Navigation buttons will appear horizontally

Clues to Use

Using FrontPage link bars to navigate a Web site

When you use FrontPage to create a link bar, you might choose the option in the Link Bar Properties dialog box to include the parent page in the link bar. Remember that the parent page is the page at the next-higher level in the navigation structure. For example, in the marathon Web site, the home page is a first-level page (a parent page) and Registration is a second-level page (a child page). The pages Mail Registration, Online Registration, and Phone Registration are child pages of the Registration page. When you click the Parent page check box in the Link Bar Properties dialog box, FrontPage displays the "Up" hyperlink. Clicking an "Up" hyperlink links to the parent page of the current page. For example, if you click an "Up" hyperlink in the Mail Registration page, which is a third-level page and a child page of the Registration page, then you'll open the parent page, Registration, which is a second-level page.

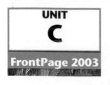

Changing the Content of a Shared Border

After you create shared borders, you can return to the Shared Borders dialog box to make any necessary changes, such as adding or removing navigation buttons or shared borders. In Design view, you can add text, pictures, or other objects to any shared border to present and maintain a consistent appearance in your Web site's pages. For example, you might add a company logo, name, and address to a top shared border to ensure that this information appears in every Web page in the navigation structure. ▰▰▰▰ Jason wants the date and time the site was last updated to appear at the bottom of each page. You decide to add a bottom shared border, text, and a date/time component to display this information.

STEPS

1. **Click Format on the menu bar, then click Shared Borders**
   The Shared Borders dialog box opens.

2. **Make sure that the All pages option button is selected, click the Bottom check box to select it, then click OK**
   FrontPage adds a bottom shared border to every page in the navigation structure.

QUICK TIP
The browser will not display a comment component. You can use comments to insert notes in a Web page. To insert a comment, position the insertion point in the desired location in Design view, click Insert on the menu bar, then click Comment. Type the comment, and then click OK.

3. **Scroll to the bottom of the page**
   As shown in Figure C-13, the bottom shared border contains a comment component, reminding you that this border doesn't contain any content yet.

4. **Point to the comment component so the pointer changes to 🖳, right-click, then click Cut in the shortcut menu**
   The comment is deleted.

5. **With the insertion point in the bottom shared border, press [Shift][Enter], type Last updated, then press [Spacebar]**
   The bottom shared border now contains a blank line and text.

6. **Click Insert on the menu bar, then click Date and Time**
   The Date and Time dialog box opens, as shown in Figure C-14. You use this dialog box to select the date and the time and to specify their formats.

7. **Make sure that the Date this page was last edited option button is selected, click the Date format list arrow, scroll the list, then click the date in the format Wednesday, May 31, 2006 (your date will differ)**
   Your sample date will use the current date; when you update the page in the future, FrontPage will automatically update this information.

8. **Click the Time format list arrow, scroll the list, then click the time in the format 02:00 PM (your time will differ)**
   Your sample time will use the current time; when you update the page in the future, FrontPage will insert the revised time.

9. **Click OK, then click the Save button 🖫 on the Standard toolbar**
   The bottom shared border now displays the current date and time.

FIGURE C-13: Bottom shared border added to the marathon Web site

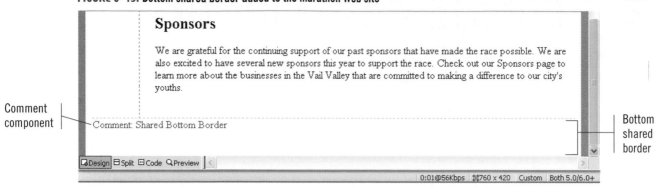

FIGURE C-14: Date and Time dialog box

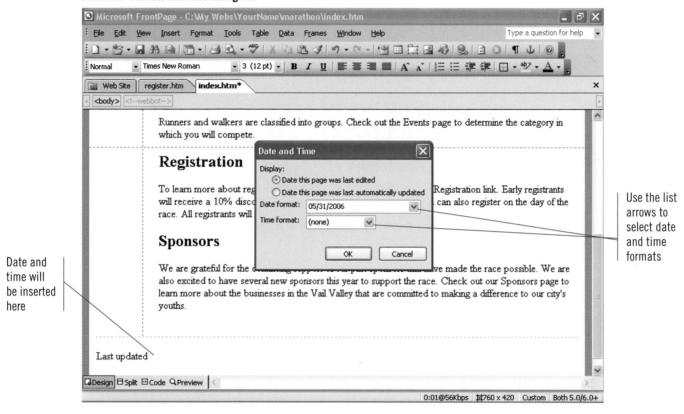

Turning off shared borders for a single Web page

The Shared Borders dialog box provides the option of creating shared borders for all pages in the navigation structure, for only the current page in Page view, or for only those pages selected in Folders or Navigation view. When you need to turn off shared borders for a single page, select the page in Folders or Navigation view, open the Shared Borders dialog box, then clear the check boxes in the Shared Borders dialog box for the selected page.

Sometimes the content of a shared border repeats information that already exists in a home page, such as the company name and address. For example, you can turn off the shared border for the home page (or for any other page) and then manually create a page banner and a link bar to provide page identification and navigation options that match the information displayed by the shared borders of other pages in the site. To create a page banner manually, position the insertion point in the desired location, click Insert on the menu bar, click Page Banner, then complete the information in the dialog box. To create a link bar, position the insertion point in the desired location, click Insert on the menu bar, click Navigation, then complete the information in the dialog box. FrontPage will still update and maintain these components, but they will not appear in a shared border.

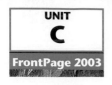

Applying a Theme to a Web Site

When you apply a theme to a Web site, you ensure a consistent, professionally designed appearance in every page in the site. FrontPage provides many themes from which to select. You can change a theme's appearance by changing its **attributes**—active graphics, vivid colors, and background picture. **Active graphics** are theme elements that become animated in the page, such as a hyperlink button changing color when the pointer moves over it. **Vivid colors** are created by an enhanced color set to produce brighter, deeper colors. A **background picture** is a picture that is used as the page's background. After applying a theme, components that use the theme, such as page banners and link bars, will be changed to use the theme's graphics. You apply a theme to the marathon Web site.

STEPS

1. **Press [Ctrl][Home], click Format on the menu bar, then click Theme**

   The Theme task pane opens. The No theme preview in the Web site default theme section indicates that this Web site does not use a theme. The Recently used themes section displays previews of themes that you (or another user) have used recently. The All available themes section displays previews of all themes available on your computer. Themes are arranged alphabetically in each section.

2. **Scroll down the themes list, then click Global Marketing (but do not click the list arrow on the Global Marketing theme)**

   A preview of the Global Marketing theme is temporarily applied to the home page. This theme has a background picture and elements that represent global travel.

3. **Click other themes in the list that you think might be appropriate for the marathon Web site**

   You can preview as many themes as you like. Notice how the various themes use different colors, presentations, and fonts to format pages.

4. **If necessary, scroll up the list of themes, then click Axis in the All available themes section**

   A preview of the Axis theme is temporarily applied to the home page.

5. **Click the Vivid colors check box in the Theme task pane to select it, click the Background picture check box in the Theme task pane to deselect it, then click the Axis theme again**

   As shown in Figure C-15, the theme uses a white background instead of a background picture.

6. **Click the Background picture check box to select it, click the Axis theme, click the list arrow that appears on the Axis theme when you point to it, then click Apply as default theme**

   A message box opens and tells you that applying a theme will permanently replace existing formatting in your pages. Applying a default theme formats every page in the Web site using the theme.

7. **Click Yes**

   If your Web site is stored on a hard drive, FrontPage will apply the theme to the entire Web site quickly. However, if your Web site is stored on a floppy drive or a server, this process could take several minutes.

8. **Click the Save button 🔲 on the Standard toolbar**

9. **Click the register.htm page tab**

   As shown in Figure C-16, this page uses the Axis theme. Notice the appearance of the page banner in the top shared border and the link bars in the top and left shared borders. The link bars appear with the hyperlinks and appearances that you specified in the Link Bar Properties dialog box.

FIGURE C-15: Preview of Axis theme for the home page

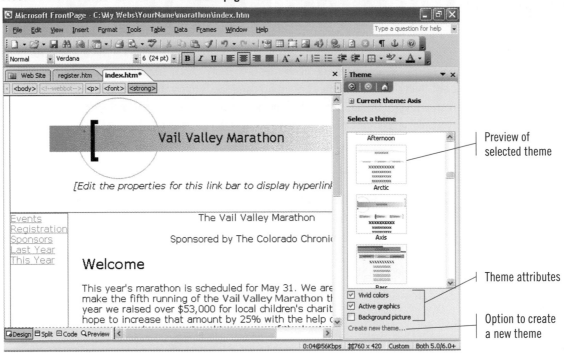

Preview of
selected theme

Theme attributes

Option to create
a new theme

FIGURE C-16: Axis theme applied to the Registration page

Page banner uses
banner picture
from the Axis
theme

Link bar uses
horizontal
navigation button
picture from the
Axis theme

Background
picture from
the Axis theme

Text uses the
fonts from the
Axis theme

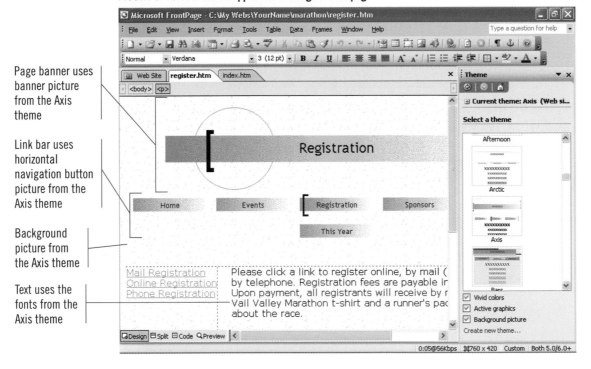

Clues to Use

Changing the theme for individual pages

In most cases, you will apply the same theme to all pages in a Web site. There are times, however, when you might want to apply a different theme to one or more pages. You can select those pages in Folders view by selecting the first page, pressing and holding [Ctrl], selecting the other pages as necessary, and then releasing [Ctrl]. Click Format on the menu bar, then click Theme. Select the desired theme in the Theme task pane, click the list arrow that appears, then click Apply to selected page(s). Each page that you selected in Folders view will use the theme you selected.

Customizing a Theme

After you apply a theme to a Web site, you might want to change the appearance of text, colors, hyperlinks, backgrounds, and other theme elements to more closely match your needs. Customizing a theme is more efficient than simply using the Formatting commands to create a new look; and in some cases, you cannot use the Formatting commands to make changes. When you customize a theme to change the style of headings, for example, you ensure that every occurrence of the heading has the same appearance in the Web site. 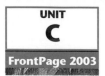 You decide to customize the current theme to use a different font for text that appears in the page banners.

STEPS

1. **Scroll up the themes in the Theme task pane so you can see the Web site default theme section, point to the Axis theme, click the list arrow that appears, then click Customize**

   The Customize Theme dialog box opens. The "What would you like to modify?" section contains three buttons: Colors, Graphics, and Text. You use these buttons to modify the colors, graphics, and text elements of the selected theme.

2. **Click Graphics**

   A second Customize Theme dialog box opens. Even though it's text formatting that you want to change, you click the Graphics button because a page banner is considered a graphic.

   QUICK TIP

   Use the Picture tab to change the page banner picture by browsing for a new graphic.

3. **Click the Item list arrow, click Banner, then click the Font tab**

   As shown in Figure C-17, the Font tab shows the available options for changing the banner. You can change its style, size, and horizontal and vertical alignment. You can also change the default font.

4. **Click Arial in the Font list**

   The theme preview shows the page banner as it will appear with the new Arial font.

5. **Click OK**

   The Customize Theme dialog box shows the customized theme with the Arial font used in the page banner.

6. **Click Save**

   The Save Theme dialog box opens and prompts you to save the customized theme before applying it. Saved themes are available for use in other Web sites. FrontPage suggests using the theme name "Copy of Axis." You could use the suggested name, but using the Web site's name is a good way to identify the theme for future reference, in case you want to apply it to another Web site.

   QUICK TIP

   If you are working in a lab or other public setting, use the information in the Clues to Use box on the next page to delete the Marathon theme from your computer after closing the marathon Web site.

7. **Type Marathon, click OK, click OK in the Customize Theme dialog box, then click Yes in the message box**

   The customized theme is applied to all pages in the marathon Web site. Figure C-18 shows the Registration page with Arial font in the page banner. Notice that the Web site default theme is now "Marathon."

8. **Close the marathon Web site, then exit FrontPage**

FIGURE C-17: Customize Theme dialog box

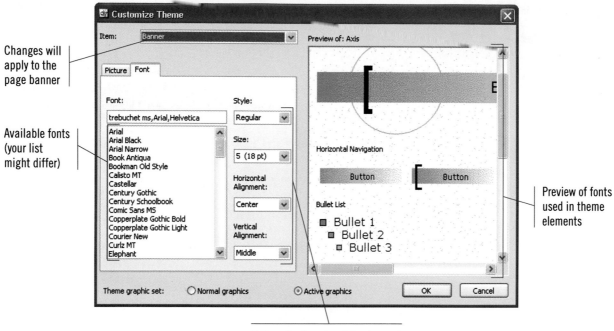

Changes will apply to the page banner

Available fonts (your list might differ)

Preview of fonts used in theme elements

Options for changing style, size, and alignment of text in the page banner

FIGURE C-18: Customized theme applied to the Registration page

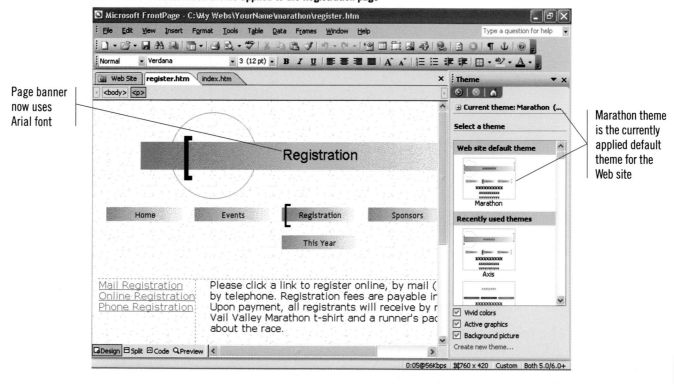

Page banner now uses Arial font

Marathon theme is the currently applied default theme for the Web site

Clues to Use

Deleting a theme

You might need to use a customized Web theme only once. To better manage space on your hard drive, you can delete a Web theme. Be careful, however, because deleting a Web theme is a permanent action. Once you delete a theme you can't apply it to future Web sites. (Web sites that use a deleted theme will still include the theme's elements, however, because the theme's files are stored in the Web site in the _themes folder.) To delete a customized Web theme, make sure that all Web sites are closed, click Format on the menu bar, click Theme, click the list arrow on the theme to delete in the All available themes section of the Theme task pane, click Delete, then click Yes.

Practice

▼ CONCEPTS REVIEW

Refer to Figure C-19 to answer the following questions about customizing a theme.

FIGURE C-19

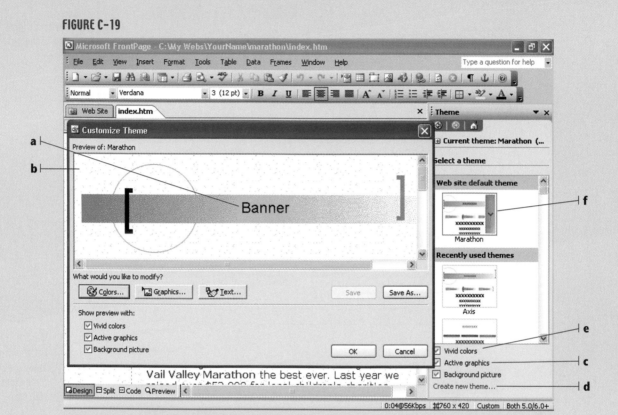

1. Which element do you click to create a new theme?
2. Which element do you click to cause a browser to animate certain features?
3. Which element do you click to enable the theme's brighter, deeper color set?
4. Which line points to the Web site's default theme?
5. Which line points to the theme's background picture?
6. Which line points to the theme's page banner?

Match each of the following terms with the statement that describes its function.

7. Navigation buttons
8. Internal link
9. Link Bar Properties
10. Parent page
11. Shared border
12. Theme
13. External link

a. A collection of coordinated graphics, colors, and fonts applied to individual or all pages in a Web site
b. A hyperlink in a Web page that opens a location in a different Web page or Web site
c. An area in a Web page that can contain components, text, and graphics
d. Hyperlinks that appear in link bars in a shared border
e. The page at the next higher level in Navigation view
f. A hyperlink in a Web page that opens a location in the same Web page
g. Dialog box used to specify and change the hyperlinks to include in a link bar and their appearance

Select the best answer from the following list of choices.

14. **Which shared border(s) can contain navigation buttons?**
    a. Top, left, and right
    b. Top and left
    c. Bottom
    d. Top

15. **The text shown in a page banner is the:**
    a. Page's filename.
    b. Page's title in Navigation view.
    c. First word of text in a page.
    d. First heading in a page.

16. **A shared border can contain:**
    a. Text.
    b. Pictures.
    c. Headings.
    d. All of the above

17. **To turn off a shared border for a Web page, change the settings in:**
    a. The Page Banner dialog box.
    b. The Link Bar Properties dialog box.
    c. The Shared Borders dialog box.
    d. Navigation view.

18. **What is the default link in a link bar component for the top-level page in a Web site?**
    a. Up
    b. Home
    c. Parent
    d. Top

19. **Which one of the following is NOT an attribute that you can change for a Web theme?**
    a. Active graphics
    b. Vivid colors
    c. Shared border
    d. Background picture

20. **To change the font used for a specific theme's page banner, click _____ in the Customize Theme dialog box.**
    a. Colors
    b. Fonts
    c. Text
    d. Graphics

▼ SKILLS REVIEW

1. **Add existing pages to the navigation structure.**
   a. Start FrontPage and use the Empty Web Site template to create a new Web site named **ecomm** in the location where your Web sites are stored.
   b. Select the ecomm Web site's root folder in the Folder List, then import the files encrypt.htm, index.htm, payment.htm, and security.htm into the Web site from the UnitC\SR folder on the drive and folder where your Data Files are stored.
   c. Change to Navigation view. Add the files payment.htm and security.htm to the navigation structure as child pages of the home page.
   d. Add the file encrypt.htm as a child page of the Security Issues page.

FrontPage 2003

2. **Add blank pages to the navigation structure.**
   a. Add three new child pages to the Payment Options page.
   b. Rename the three new child pages **Credit**, **Checks**, and **E-Cash**, respectively. (*Hint:* Rename the child page on the left first, press [Tab] to select the second page, type the new title, press [Tab] and rename the third page, then press [Enter].)
   c. Change to Folders view, then change the filename of the E-Cash page to **ecash.htm**.
   d. Close the Folder List.

3. **Turn on shared borders.**
   a. Open the Shared Borders dialog box.
   b. Make sure the option is selected to apply the shared borders to all pages in the Web site.
   c. Create top, left, and bottom shared borders in all pages in the Web site.
   d. Include navigation buttons in the top and left shared borders.
   e. Close the Shared Borders dialog box.

4. **Change link bar properties.**
   a. Open the home page in Design view.
   b. Edit the link bar in the top shared border so it contains hyperlinks to same-level pages and to the home page, but not to the parent page.
   c. Verify that the link bar style for the top shared border uses the page's theme, then close the Link Bar Properties dialog box. (*Note:* Because there are no pages in the navigation structure at the same level as the home page, the placeholder text will still be visible.)
   d. Edit the link bar in the left shared border so it contains hyperlinks to child-level pages and to the parent page.
   e. Change the link bar style for the left shared border to use the page's theme. (*Note:* The navigation buttons will be displayed as text until you apply a theme.)
   f. Save the home page.

5. **Change the content of a shared border.**
   a. Delete the comment component in the bottom shared border.
   b. Press [Enter], type **This page was last updated by [Your Name] on**, then press [Spacebar].
   c. Insert a component containing today's date in the format Monday, May 15, 2006.
   d. Choose the option to omit displaying a time, close the Date and Time dialog box, then type a period.
   e. Right-align the content of the bottom shared border, then save the home page.

6. **Apply a theme to a Web site.**
   a. Display the Theme task pane.
   b. If necessary, select the options to apply vivid colors, active graphics, and a background picture, then preview the Concrete theme using the home page.
   c. Preview the Evergreen theme using the home page.
   d. Preview the Pixel theme using the home page, then apply it as the default theme for the Web site.
   e. Save the home page, then preview the home page in a browser.
   f. Use the links in the shared borders to navigate all the pages in the site. (*Note:* The Credit, Checks, and E-Cash pages that you added in Navigation view will be blank.)
   g. Close your browser.

7. **Customize a theme.**
   a. Select the Web site's default theme, then choose the option to customize it. (*Hint:* Choose the theme in the Web site default theme section.)
   b. Click Graphics, then select the option in the Item list box to change the horizontal navigation (buttons).
   c. Change the font style of the horizontal navigation buttons used in the theme to bold, 8 points, and Verdana.
   d. Select the option in the Item list box to change the vertical navigation (buttons), then change the font style to bold, 8 point, and Verdana.
   e. Save the theme using the theme name **EComm**, then apply it to all pages in the Web site.
   f. Save the home page, then preview it in your browser. Use the browser to print the Payment Options page.

▼ SKILLS REVIEW (CONTINUED)

g. Close your browser, then close the ecomm Web site.

h. Delete the EComm theme from the All available themes section of the Theme task pane.

i. Close the Theme task pane, then exit FrontPage.

▼ INDEPENDENT CHALLENGE 1

Your family is moving to France this summer as part of an employer-sponsored transfer. You are in charge of selling some of your family's assets that you cannot take with you or put in storage. You decide to put an ad in the local newspaper and refer to a URL so interested buyers can use the Internet to view detailed information about the items. Because you will update the Web site frequently with new items for sale, you decide to use a shared border to ensure that the correct hyperlinks appear in the Web pages.

a. Start FrontPage and use the Empty Web Site template to create a new Web site named **france** in the location where your Web sites are stored.

b. Select the france Web site's root folder in the Folder List, then import the files honda.htm, index.htm, linens.htm, table.htm, and toyota.htm into the france Web site from the UnitC\IC1 folder on the drive and folder where your Data Files are stored.

c. Open the pages that you imported and examine their content. Then, change to Navigation view and add the pages to the navigation structure. (*Hint:* Use each page's contents to determine how to arrange the pages in the navigation structure.)

d. Add top and left shared borders to all pages in the Web site. Both shared borders should include navigation buttons.

e. Open the home page in Design view. Edit the link bar in the top shared border so it contains links to the home page and same-level pages. Confirm that the link style uses the page's theme. (*Note:* Because there are no pages in the navigation structure at the same level as the home page, the placeholder text will still be visible.)

f. Click the blank line below the link bar component in the top shared border, type **Everything must go! Please make an offer today.** Format this text using the Heading 4 style.

g. Edit the link bar in the left shared border so it contains links to child-level pages and to the parent page. Change the link style to use the page's theme.

h. Apply a theme of your choice to the entire Web site. If necessary, select the options to use vivid colors, active graphics, and a background picture.

i. Open the home page in a browser; if prompted to save your changes or replace a file, click Yes. Use the links to examine each page in the Web site, then use the browser to print the Table and Chairs page. Close your browser.

j. Close the france Web site, then exit FrontPage.

▼ INDEPENDENT CHALLENGE 2

You have added all of the necessary pages to the Villages at Kensington Neighbourhood Association Web site. The Web site development team asks you to begin work on creating the hyperlinks that will allow site visitors to navigate the pages in the site. In addition, the team wants you to format the entire site to make it more interesting.

a. Open the **village** Web site from the location where your Web sites are stored. (If you did not create and change this Web site in Units A and B, contact your instructor for assistance.)

b. In Navigation view, change the page title of the home page to **Villages at Kensington**.

c. Create the navigation structure shown in Figure C-20. (*Hint:* Switch to Folders view as needed to associate filenames with page titles; for example, picnic.htm is Canada Day Picnic.)

FIGURE C-20

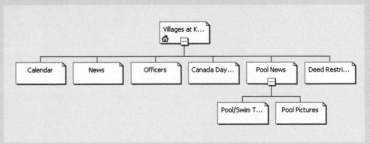

▼ INDEPENDENT CHALLENGE 2 (CONTINUED)

    d. In Navigation view, change the page title of the register.htm page to **Registration Form**. (*Hint:* Click a page icon to view its filename on the status bar.)

    e. Add top and left shared borders to all pages in the Web site. Choose the options to include navigation buttons in both shared borders.

    f. Open the home page in Design view. Verify that the link bar in the top shared border contains links to same-level pages, to the home page, and to the parent page. Verify that the link style uses the page's theme. (*Note:* Because there are no pages in the navigation structure at the same level as the home page, the placeholder text will still be visible.)

    g. Change the properties of the link bar in the left shared border so it contains links to child-level pages and to the parent page. Change the link style to use the page's theme.

    h. Change the default theme for the Web site to Blends. If necessary, select the options to use vivid colors, active graphics, and a background picture. (If you do not have this theme, select another theme of your choice.)

    i. In Folders view, select the register.htm page, then open the Shared Borders dialog box. For the register.htm page only, turn off the top shared border.

    j. With the register.htm page still selected in Folders view, change this page's default theme to No theme. (*Hint:* Click the list arrow for No theme in the All available themes section, then click the option to apply it to the selected page.)

    k. Customize the Web site's default theme so the text in the page banner is bold and the text in the horizontal and vertical navigation buttons is bold and italic. (*Hint:* Click Graphics to change the banner to bold and the horizontal navigation and vertical navigation items to bold italic.) Save the customized theme using the name **Village** and apply it to the Web site.

    l. Open the home page in a browser; if prompted to save your changes or replace a file, click Yes. Print the home page. Click the Pool News link, click the Registration Form link, then print the Registration Form page. (*Note:* You will create a form in this page in another unit.)

    m. Close your browser and the village Web site.

    n. Delete the Village theme from the All available themes section of the Theme task pane, then exit FrontPage.

▼ INDEPENDENT CHALLENGE 3

The Web site for the city of Tryon, North Carolina, now contains several pages. Your next task is to create the site's navigation structure and enhance its appearance.

    a. Open the **tryon** Web site from the location where your Web sites are stored. (If you did not create and change this Web site in Units A and B, contact your instructor for assistance.)

    b. In Navigation view, change the name of the home page to **Tryon, North Carolina**.

    c. Add the pages hotspots.htm, lodging.htm, pictures.htm, and request.htm to the navigation structure as child pages of the home page.

    d. Add the pages b_and_b.htm, camping.htm, and hotels.htm to the navigation structure as child pages of the Places to Stay page.

    e. In Navigation view, change the page title of the Places to Stay page to **Tryon Lodging**.

    f. Add top and left shared borders to all pages in the Web site. Choose the options to include navigation buttons in both shared borders.

    g. Open the home page in Design view. Change the properties of the link bar in the top shared border so it contains links to same-level pages and to the home page. Change the link style to Bars. (*Hint:* The description for this style is "An HTML style where each link is separated by a vertical line.")

    h. Change the properties of the link bar in the left shared border so it contains links to child-level pages and to the parent page. Change the link style to Underlined. (*Hint:* This style is the last one in the list. The description for this style is "An HTML style where each link is underlined.")

    i. Apply the Nature theme as the Web site's default theme. If necessary, select the options to use vivid colors, active graphics, and a background picture.

▼ INDEPENDENT CHALLENGE 3 (CONTINUED)

j. In Folders view, select the request.htm page, then open the Shared Borders dialog box. For this page only, turn off the top shared border.

k. Customize the default Web site's Nature theme by changing the Heading 1 style of text to purple. (*Hint:* Click Colors in the Customize Theme dialog box, click the Custom tab, set the Item list box to Heading 1, then use the Color list arrow to click the purple color.) Save the customized theme using the name **Tryon**, then apply the theme to all pages in the Web site.

l. Open the home page in a browser; if prompted to save your changes or replace a file, click Yes. Use the browser to print the home page and the page that opens when you click the Request Information link. (*Note:* You will create a form in this page in another unit.)

m. Close your browser and the tryon Web site.

n. Delete the Tryon theme from the All available themes section of the Theme task pane, then exit FrontPage.

▼ INDEPENDENT CHALLENGE 4

As the Webmaster for your company, CD Rocks, you are in charge of managing its Web site. CD Rocks sells used and hard-to-find music CDs through its Web site. The Web site development team wants to create a new site with a look and feel similar to current Web sites that music enthusiasts visit, so they will have an easy time navigating your new site. You decide to visit some of these sites and examine elements and features of each.

a. Use your favorite search engine to find Web sites that sell used music CDs. For example, you might search using a question such as **Where can I buy used music CDs on the Web?**

b. Visit at least three sites. For each site, print the home page and one other page that is linked to the home page. On each printed page, see if you can identify the type of navigation options used by that page. For example, does the page use a link bar with links to parent-level and child-level pages, a shared border with navigation buttons, or hyperlinks created manually?

c. Write a brief report in which you comment on each site's visual appearance. Do you think it uses a theme? Why or why not? Do the pages in the site have a consistent appearance? If yes, what makes the appearance consistent?

d. For each page that you printed, comment on the effectiveness of the page's navigation options and appearance. What changes, if any, would you make? How would you use FrontPage to implement them? Why would you make these changes?

e. Attach your completed report to the pages that you printed from each site.

f. Close your browser.

▼ VISUAL WORKSHOP

Use the One Page Web Site template to create a new Web site named **golf** in the location where your Web sites are stored. Add blank pages to the Web site and apply a theme to match the Web page shown in Figure C-21. (*Hint:* The Web site uses top and left shared borders and the Sandstone theme with vivid colors, active graphics, and a background picture. If you do not have this theme, select another one of your choice. The theme's body font has been changed to Times New Roman; save the customized theme using the name **Golf**.) Print the Clubs page using your browser, then close your browser and the golf Web site. Delete the Golf theme from the All available themes section of the Theme task pane, then exit FrontPage.

FIGURE C-21

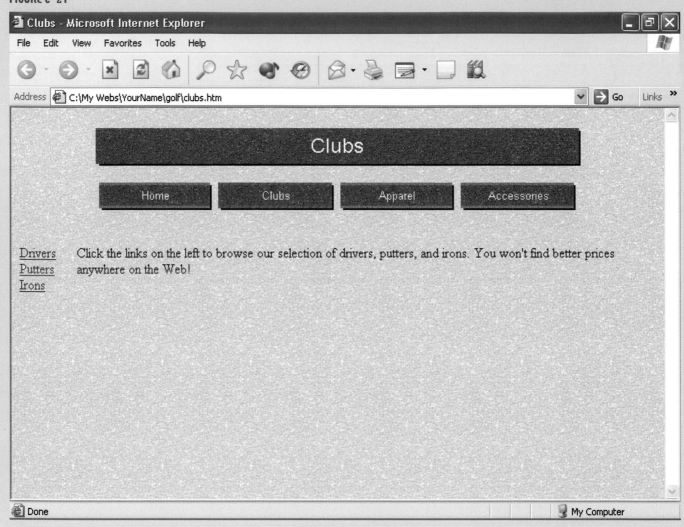

Working with Pictures

OBJECTIVES

Insert a picture
Change a picture's properties
Add text over a picture
Create an image map
Create WordArt
Create a thumbnail picture
Create a photo gallery
Change a photo gallery's properties

Most Web sites contain pictures that enhance the site's appearance, but pictures can add functionality to your site, as well. For example, you can use a picture not only to add visual interest, but also to provide a hyperlink that opens another location. Pictures used in a Web page can be taken with a standard or a digital camera. In addition to photographs, you can add graphic elements such as clip-art images, WordArt, drawings, and shapes to your Web pages. When your Web page contains a related collection of pictures, such as pictures in a product catalog, you can create a photo gallery in which to store them. Now that the marathon Web site contains several pages and uses link bars and a theme to connect and format those pages, you are ready to begin working on the pictures that will appear in the site. Jason Tanaka, manager of the Vail Valley Marathon, has provided you with a picture of last year's marathon winners, a map of the race route, and photos of the beautiful scenery runners will see during the competition. He asks you to add these pictures to the Web site.

Inserting a Picture

In FrontPage, a **picture** might be a photograph that you scanned or took using a digital camera, a clip-art image, or a shape or image that you created using the Drawing toolbar. You can also format text as a picture. Pictures used in Web pages are usually saved in one of three popular file formats: **GIF**, which displays pictures with up to 256 colors in a compressed format that supports animation; **PNG**, which displays pictures with up to 16 million colors in a compressed format; and **JPEG (JPG)**, which is used for photographs and other high-quality digital images. While pictures add visual interest to your Web pages, you can also use them as hyperlinks that open other Web pages. When you insert a picture in a Web page, the picture file is separate from the Web page itself and must be saved. To save the picture as part of the Web site, you **embed** it in the site. You usually save all picture files in the **images folder**, which FrontPage automatically creates when you create a new Web site. 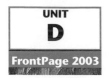 Jason asks you to include a picture of the top male and female finishers in last year's marathon in the Last Year Web page. The file containing this picture is stored in JPG format.

STEPS

1. **Start** FrontPage, **then open the** marathon **Web site from the location where your Web sites are stored**

2. **In Folders view, double-click** lastyear.htm

   The Last Year Web page opens in Design view and includes top, left, and bottom shared borders. The page is formatted using a theme. The insertion point is blinking to the left of the word "We" on the first line in the page.

3. **Click the** Insert Picture From File button 🖼 **on the Standard toolbar**

   The Picture dialog box opens.

4. **Navigate to the drive and folder where your Data Files are stored, open the** UnitD folder, **then double-click** finisher.jpg

   The picture appears in the Web page to the left of the word "We" in the first paragraph.

TROUBLE

If the Pictures toolbar doesn't open automatically, click View on the menu bar, point to Toolbars, then click Pictures. If necessary, drag the title bar of the Pictures toolbar and dock it below the Formatting toolbar.

5. **Click the** picture **to select it**

   When you select a picture, sizing handles appear on the picture's corners and sides, as shown in Figure D-1. The Pictures toolbar might open automatically when a picture is selected. The Pictures toolbar contains buttons for editing pictures.

6. **Click the** Save button 🖫 **on the Standard toolbar**

   The Save Embedded Files dialog box opens, as shown in Figure D-2. You use this dialog box to rename a selected picture, to change the folder in which to save a selected picture, and to change the action (save or overwrite a file). You can also click Picture File Type in this dialog box to change the picture's file format (GIF, JPEG, PNG-8, or PNG-24), quality (for JPEG pictures only), and transparency (for GIF pictures only).

7. **Click** Change Folder

   The Change Folder dialog box opens, displaying the folders in the marathon Web site.

QUICK TIP

FrontPage might select the images folder for you automatically. If "images/" appears in the Folder column, the images folder is already selected.

8. **Click the** images folder, **then click** OK

   The entry in the Folder column changes to "images/".

9. **Click** OK

   FrontPage saves the Last Year Web page in the Web site and saves the finisher.jpg picture in the Web site's images folder.

FIGURE D-1: Picture inserted in the Last Year Web page

Pictures toolbar docked below the Formatting toolbar

Sizing handles for picture

Selected picture

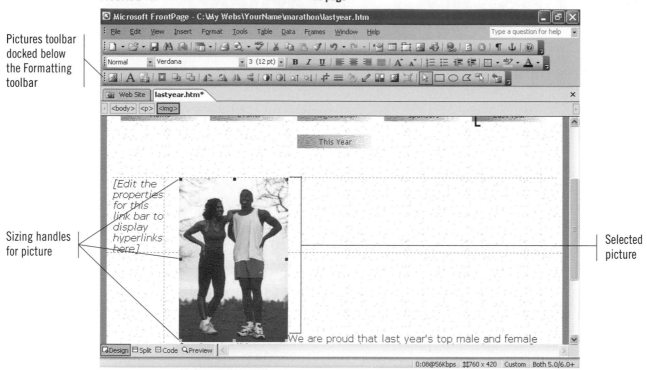

FIGURE D-2: Save Embedded Files dialog box

Embedded picture's filename

No folder specified

Action set to "Save"

Click to rename the selected picture file

Preview of picture

Click to change the selected picture's quality and file format

Click to change the folder in which to save the selected picture

Click to change the action

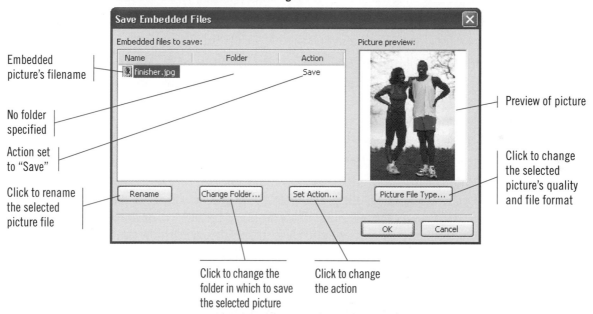

FrontPage 2003

Changing a Picture's Properties

After you insert a picture in a Web page, you can use the buttons on the Pictures toolbar to change many of the picture's characteristics. For example, you can increase and decrease the contrast and brightness in the picture or change its colors. For any picture, you can change its position, the way that text flows around it, and its orientation—that is, flip it vertically or horizontally, or rotate it right or left. You can also click and drag a sizing handle on a selected picture to increase or decrease the picture's size. Jason doesn't like the way the picture appears in the Last Year Web page. He asks you to change the picture so the text in the page wraps around the picture's left side. You also decide to decrease the picture's size and increase its contrast and brightness.

STEPS

1. **Make sure the picture is selected and that the Pictures toolbar is open**

2. **Click Format on the menu bar, then click Position**

   The Position dialog box opens, as shown in Figure D-3. When you insert a picture in a page, the default wrapping and positioning styles are set to None. You can set a picture so that adjacent text wraps to the left or right of the picture, or so that the picture is positioned absolutely or relative to other objects. An **absolutely positioned picture** is placed precisely in a page using coordinates; a **relatively positioned picture** is placed precisely using text in the page to specify the location.

3. **In the Wrapping style section, click the Right button, then click OK**

   The picture moves to the right side of the page, and the text wraps around the left side of the picture.

4. **Position the pointer on the lower-left sizing handle of the picture so it changes to ↗, drag ↗ up and to the right to resize the picture as shown in Figure D-4, then release the mouse button**

   The picture's size is reduced, and the text in the page wraps around the left side of the picture. The Picture Actions button appears below the picture.

QUICK TIP
You can also click the Resample button on the Pictures toolbar to resample a picture.

5. **Point to the Picture Actions button, click the list arrow that appears, then click the Resample Picture To Match Size option button**

   The Picture Actions button disappears. FrontPage reduces the file size of the picture to match the current display size of the picture. When you reduce the size of a picture, **resampling** it removes extra pixels so the picture downloads more quickly. Resampling a picture also improves the clarity of the picture.

6. **With the picture selected, click the More Contrast button on the Pictures toolbar, then click the More Brightness button on the Pictures toolbar**

   The colors in the picture become sharper and brighter.

7. **Click the Save button on the Standard toolbar**

   Because you made changes to the picture, the Save Embedded Files dialog box opens. The images folder is selected, and the action is set to overwrite the file already saved in the Web site's images folder.

8. **Click OK**

   FrontPage overwrites the finisher.jpg file in the images folder and saves the Last Year Web page.

9. **Click the Close button for the lastyear.htm page**

   The Last Year Web page closes.

FIGURE D-3: Position dialog box

Text wrapping options →

Positioning style options →

Options for positioning a picture →

Change these values to resize a picture →

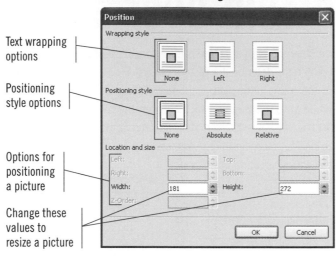

FIGURE D-4: Wrapping style set to "Right"

More Contrast button →

Text flows around the left side of the picture (your text might wrap differently) →

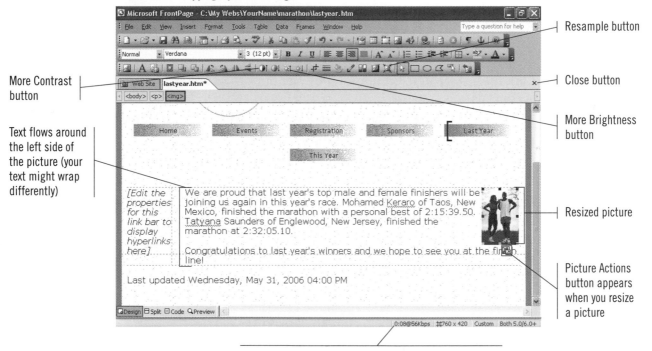

→ Resample button

→ Close button

→ More Brightness button

→ Resized picture

→ Picture Actions button appears when you resize a picture

Estimated download time in seconds using a 56.6 Kbps modem

Estimating download times for Web pages

An important consideration when inserting pictures in Web pages is the amount of time that they will require to download from the server. Larger pictures take more time to download from the server than smaller, resampled pictures. You can decrease a picture's size, and subsequently its download time, by using the sizing handles that appear on a selected picture. After resizing a picture, use the Picture Actions button 🖼 or the Resample button 🖼 on the Pictures toolbar to resample it. FrontPage will change the picture's file size to match the picture's display size. Another advantage of clicking the Resample button is that the overall quality of the picture improves, regardless of whether you increased or decreased its size.

You can check the amount of time that it will take to download a Web page from the server by viewing the Estimated Time to Download pane on the status bar in Design view. The default setting shows download times in seconds using a modem or network connection. You can change the default transmission speed setting by clicking the Estimated Time to Download pane on the status bar and then clicking another connection speed on the menu that appears. If a page will take longer than 30 seconds to download using a 56.6 Kbps modem, you might consider reducing the size of the pictures in the page or splitting the page's content into separate pages that will download more quickly.

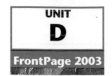

Adding Text over a Picture

One of the neat things you can do with a picture is to change its properties so that colors are washed out, and then add text over the picture to describe the picture's function or to create an interesting visual effect. When you **wash out** a picture, the colors in the picture appear with less intensity and brightness. You can also change a picture to black-and-white or to **grayscale**, which changes the picture to use shades of gray. One of the marathon's sponsors, the Vail Valley Conservation Society, doesn't have a logo that you can include in the Sponsors Web page. You decide to use FrontPage to create a simple graphic image from a picture you found to associate with the Vail Valley Conservation Society.

STEPS

1. **In Folders view, double-click** sponsors.htm
   The Sponsors Web page opens in Design view.

2. **Press [End], then press [Enter]**
   A new paragraph is created.

3. **Click the** Insert Picture From File button 🖼 **on the Standard toolbar; if necessary, open the** UnitD folder, **then double-click** vvcs.wmf
   The picture is inserted in the page.

4. **Click the** picture **to select it, click the** Color button 🎨 **on the Pictures toolbar, then click** Wash Out
   The colors in the picture are washed out, appearing with less intensity than the colors in the original image.

5. **Click the** Text button 🅰 **on the Pictures toolbar**
   A warning message appears, explaining that the picture will be converted to GIF format because some special effects are available only for pictures saved in the GIF format.

6. **Click** OK
   FrontPage converts the picture to GIF format and creates a text box in the center of the picture, as shown in Figure D-5.

7. **Type** Vail Valley Conservation Society, **select the text you typed, click the** Font Size list arrow **on the Formatting toolbar, click** 4 (14 pt), **click the** Font Color list arrow 🅰▾ **on the Formatting toolbar, then click the** Navy **color in the Standard Colors section**

8. **Click anywhere outside the picture to deselect the text**
   The text appears over the picture and is center-aligned automatically. Because you washed out the colors in the picture, the text is readable, as shown in Figure D-6.

TROUBLE
If the images folder is not selected, click Change Folder, click the images folder, then click OK.

9. **Click the** Save button 💾 **on the Standard toolbar, make sure that the picture will be saved in the images folder, then click** OK
   FrontPage saves the picture in the Web site's images folder and saves the Sponsors Web page.

FIGURE D-5: Adding text over a picture

Font Size list arrow

Text button

Font Color list arrow

Color button

Text box over picture

Selected picture

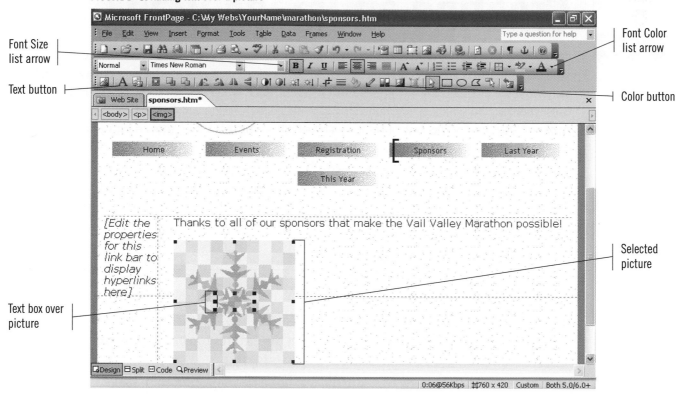

FIGURE D-6: Text added over picture

14-point navy text

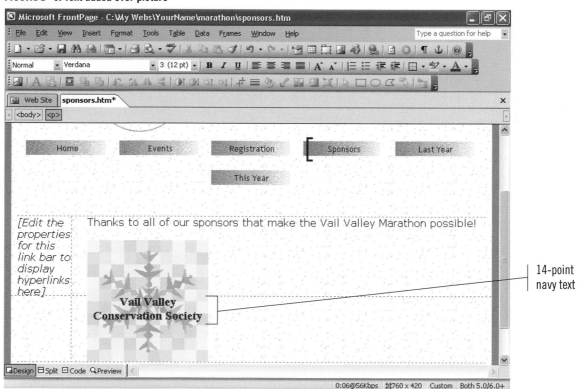

Creating an Image Map

You can use pictures not only to create visual interest in your Web pages, but also to create links to other Web pages and Web sites. An entire picture, or part of a picture, can serve as a hyperlink to a location in the same Web site or a different site, just as a text hyperlink does. When you select the picture before creating the hyperlink, the entire picture functions as a hyperlink; clicking any part of the picture opens the hyperlink's target. Another way of creating a hyperlink in a picture is to create an **image map**, a picture that contains one or more hotspots. A **hotspot** is an area of a picture that, when clicked, opens the hyperlink target. A hotspot can have a rectangular, circular, or polygonal shape. To create a hotspot, you use the pointer to draw a shape on the picture, then you use the Insert Hyperlink dialog box to specify the hyperlink target. Jason wants to format the "Vail Valley Conservation Society" text in the picture as a hyperlink that opens the Web site for that organization. You will create a rectangular hotspot to accomplish this goal.

STEPS

1. **Click the picture to select it**
   Sizing handles appear around the picture, and a box encloses the text you added over the picture.

2. **Click the Rectangular Hotspot button ▢ on the Pictures toolbar, then point to the picture**
   The pointer changes to ✐, which you use to draw the hotspot.

3. **Click the upper-left inside corner of the text box over the picture, drag the pointer down to the lower-right inside corner of the text box (see Figure D-7), then release the mouse button**
   The Insert Hyperlink dialog box opens. The hotspot will include only the text.

4. **If necessary, click the Existing File or Web Page button 🖾 on the Link to bar**
   The insertion point appears in the Address text box.

QUICK TIP
You do not need to type the http:// in URLs, as FrontPage adds this protocol for Web pages automatically.

5. **Type www.vailvalleyconservationsociety.org, then click OK**
   The Insert Hyperlink dialog box closes, and the target of the hotspot is the URL for the Vail Valley Conservation Society Web site.

6. **Click the Save button 🖫 on the Standard toolbar, then click the Show Preview View button 🔍Preview at the bottom of the Contents pane**
   The Sponsors Web page appears in Preview view.

QUICK TIP
The Vail Valley Conservation Society is fictitious.

7. **If necessary, scroll down the page, then point to the Vail Valley Conservation Society text**
   As shown in Figure D-8, the pointer changes to 👆, and the target of the hotspot—the URL of the Vail Valley Conservation Society Web site—appears on the status bar, both indicating that clicking the hotspot will connect to the Vail Valley Conservation Society Web site.

8. **Click the Show Design View button 🖾Design, then click the Close button for the sponsors.htm page**
   The Sponsors Web page closes.

FIGURE D-7: Creating a hotspot in a picture

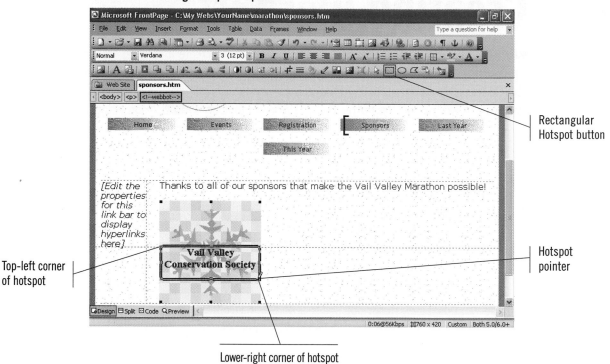

Rectangular Hotspot button

Hotspot pointer

Top-left corner of hotspot

Lower-right corner of hotspot

FIGURE D-8: Preview of the Sponsors Web page

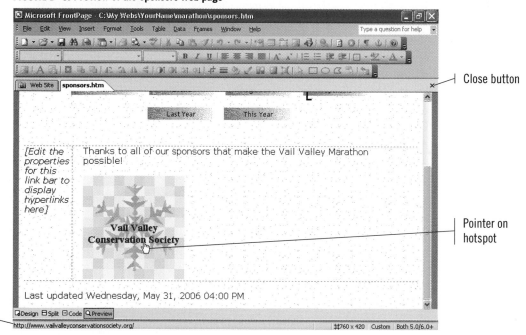

Close button

Pointer on hotspot

Target of the hotspot

Design Matters

Highlighting and working with hotspots

Sometimes it is difficult to identify the location of a hotspot on a picture because the hotspot might be drawn over an existing line or the picture might be too dark to display the hotspot's box. To identify hotspots in Design view, click a picture to select it, then click the Highlight Hotspots button 🔲 on the Pictures toolbar. FrontPage will change the entire picture to a solid color (usually white) and identify the picture's hotspot with an outline or a different solid color (usually black). To turn off the highlighting of hotspots, click 🔲 again, or click anywhere outside a selected picture. To verify the target of a hotspot, click the hotspot in the picture, then click the Insert Hyperlink button 🔲 on the Standard toolbar. FrontPage opens the Insert Hyperlink dialog box, where you can inspect the hyperlink's target or make any necessary changes to it. To remove a hotspot, click it to select it, then press [Delete].

Creating WordArt

WordArt is an object that uses text and special effects to create a picture. You create a WordArt object using existing or new text; shorter phrases and single words work best. FrontPage provides many style choices for formatting text, and after creating a WordArt object, you can change its colors, direction, style, and content easily using the buttons on the WordArt toolbar. ███████ Jason wants the "Sponsored by The Colorado Chronicle" text to stand out more on the home page. You decide to change this text to a WordArt object.

STEPS

1. **In Folders view, double-click** index.htm
   The home page opens in Design view.

2. **Select the text** Sponsored by The Colorado Chronicle

3. **Click** Insert **on the menu bar, point to** Picture, **then click** WordArt
   The WordArt Gallery dialog box opens, as shown in Figure D-9. You can click any style in the list to apply it to the selected text. Some of the styles use colors and cause the text to move in different directions.

4. **Click the style in** row 2, column 1, **then click** OK
   The Edit WordArt Text dialog box opens, as shown in Figure D-10. You can use this dialog box to change the font, font size, font style (bold or italic), and content of the text, or you can accept the default settings.

5. **Click** OK
   The Edit WordArt Text dialog box closes, the WordArt toolbar opens, and the text is formatted using the default settings for the WordArt style you selected. The WordArt object is selected, as indicated by the sizing handles that appear around it. You realize that the WordArt object is currently too large to be effective.

6. **Click the** Edit Text button Edit Text... **on the WordArt toolbar, click the** Size list arrow, **scroll up the list, click** 16, **then click** OK
   The font size in the WordArt object is reduced to 16 points. See Figure D-11.

7. **Click anywhere outside the WordArt object to deselect it, then click the** Show Preview View button Preview **at the bottom of the Contents pane**
   The text "Vail Valley Marathon" appears twice—once in the page banner and again in the page. Having this text appear twice is unnecessary.

8. **Click the** Show Design View button Design, **select the text** The Vail Valley Marathon **above the WordArt object, then press** [Delete]
   The text and the line on which it appears are deleted.

9. **Click the** Save button 💾 **on the Standard toolbar, then click the** Close button **for the** index.htm page
   FrontPage saves the home page and the WordArt object. WordArt is a picture, but you don't save it as an embedded file in the Web site as you would for other pictures. The files that create a WordArt object in a Web page are stored in a new folder that FrontPage creates in the Web site. This folder's name is the page's file-name plus an underscore and the word "files" (in this case, index_files).

FIGURE D-9: WordArt Gallery dialog box

WordArt style in
row 2, column 1

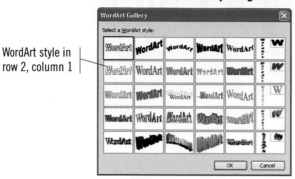

FIGURE D-10: Edit WordArt Text dialog box

Click the Font list arrow
to change the font

Click the Font Size list arrow
to change the font size

Text in the
WordArt object

Click the Bold button or the Italic
button to change the font style

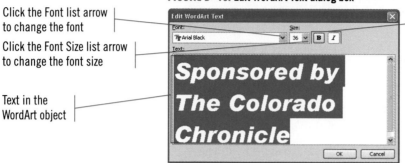

FIGURE D-11: Resized WordArt object

WordArt toolbar (yours
might appear in a
different location)

Edit Text button

Sizing handles for
the WordArt object

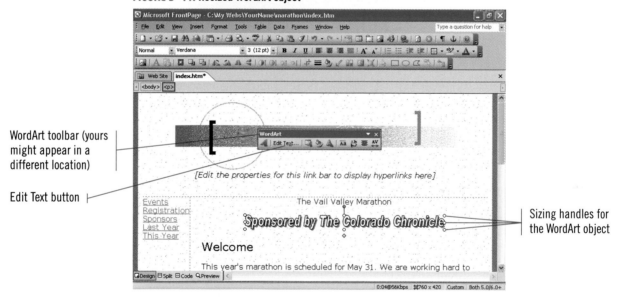

Clues to Use

Inserting drawings and shapes

FrontPage includes tools that let you create simple drawings and shapes in your Web pages. To insert a drawing, click Insert on the menu bar, point to Picture, then click New Drawing. The Drawing and Drawing Canvas toolbars open, along with a canvas on which to draw objects. You use the buttons on the Drawing toolbar to create boxes, lines, arrows, text, and other objects on the canvas. You use the buttons on the Drawing Canvas toolbar to change the size of the canvas. After you are finished drawing, click anywhere outside the canvas to deselect it.

To insert a shape in a Web page, click Insert on the menu bar, point to Picture, then click AutoShapes. The Drawing and AutoShapes toolbars open. You can use the buttons on the AutoShapes toolbar to insert lines, basic shapes, block arrows, a flowchart, stars and banners, callouts, and additional shapes (available on the Clip Art task pane) in a Web page. To insert a shape, click the button on the AutoShapes toolbar for the general category (such as Basic Shapes), then click the desired shape on the palette (or task pane) that opens. Use the pointer to draw the shape, then click anywhere outside the shape to deselect it.

FrontPage 2003

Creating a Thumbnail Picture

Because large pictures can take a long time to download, it's important to use them sparingly in a Web site. However, in some cases, you might need to include pictures that show detailed information, such as map images. When you must include large, complex pictures in a Web page, but want to keep the download time of the page in which they appear to a minimum, you can create a thumbnail picture. A **thumbnail picture** is a small version of a larger picture that, when clicked, activates a hyperlink and opens the original, larger picture. When a thumbnail picture appears in a Web page, it reduces the download time for the page when compared to including the full-sized picture. Users who need to view the original, larger picture can click the thumbnail picture to open a new page containing the full-sized picture. FrontPage creates the thumbnail picture and the hyperlink to the original image automatically. ▰▰▰ Jason gives you a map of the race's route to include in the Events Web page. To minimize the download time for this page, you will create a thumbnail picture of the map.

STEPS

1. **In Folders view, double-click** events.htm
   The Events Web page opens in Design view.

2. **Press** [Ctrl][End]
   The insertion point moves to the bottom of the page, where you will insert the picture.

3. **Click the** Center button ≣ **on the Formatting toolbar, click the** Insert Picture From File button 🖾 **on the Standard toolbar, if necessary open the** UnitD folder, **then double-click** map.gif
   The picture is inserted and centered on the line.

4. **Click the** picture **to select it, then click the** Auto Thumbnail button 🖾 **on the Pictures toolbar**
   FrontPage creates the thumbnail picture, as shown in Figure D-12, and creates the hyperlink to the full-sized original picture.

   > **QUICK TIP**
   > You can edit the filenames supplied by FrontPage by selecting the file, clicking Rename, then typing the new filename.

5. **Click the** Save button 🖫 **on the Standard toolbar**
   As shown in Figure D-13, the Save Embedded Files dialog box shows that you'll be saving two files. The first file, map_small.gif, is the thumbnail picture that FrontPage created. The second file, map.gif, is the original picture that you inserted. FrontPage creates the thumbnail file using the original filename plus "_small."

6. **Make sure that the pictures will be saved in the images folder, then click** OK
   FrontPage saves the pictures in the Web site's images folder and saves the Events Web page.

7. **Click the** Preview button 🔍 **on the Standard toolbar, scroll down the page, then point to the** thumbnail picture
   The pointer changes to 🖑, and the path to the original picture that you saved in the Web site's images folder appears on the status bar.

   > **QUICK TIP**
   > To return to the Events Web page when viewing the picture in a browser, click the Back button.

8. **Click the** thumbnail picture
   The full-sized picture opens, replacing the Events Web page.

9. **Close your browser, then click the** Close button **for the** events.htm **page**
   The Events Web page closes.

FIGURE D-12: Thumbnail picture created

Auto Thumbnail
button

Sizing handles
for the thumbnail
picture

Thumbnail
picture of
larger map.gif
picture

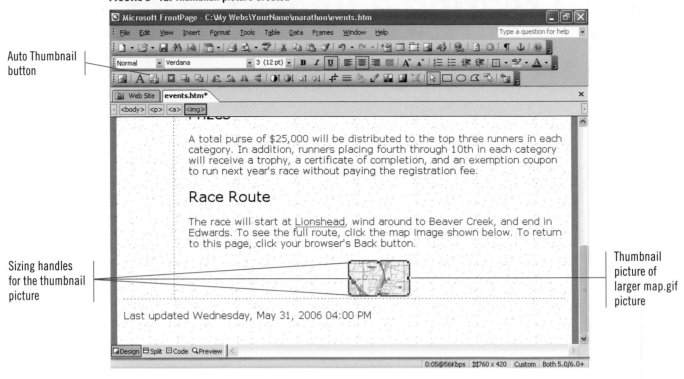

FIGURE D-13: Saving the thumbnail and full-sized pictures

Thumbnail picture
filename

Full-sized picture
filename

No preview is available
because multiple
images are selected

Pictures will be saved
in the images folder

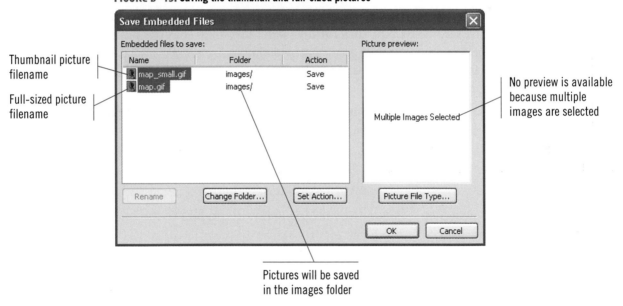

Design Matters

Enhancing a thumbnail picture

To enhance a thumbnail picture, consider changing the thumbnail's properties to wash out the colors, then add text over the thumbnail picture to describe its purpose or function. For example, you might use the Text button on the Pictures toolbar to add the text "Map Route" over the thumbnail picture you created in the Events Web page. In addition, instead of using the default hyperlink created by FrontPage to the full-sized picture, you could change the thumbnail's hyperlink target to a new Web page that includes a link bar and descriptive text along with the full-sized picture. Then the user doesn't need to click the browser's Back button to return to the page containing the thumbnail picture. Instead, he or she could use the link bar to move to any desired page.

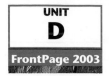
Creating a Photo Gallery

A **photo gallery** is a FrontPage component that displays pictures, thumbnail pictures, photo captions, and photo descriptions. You can use a photo gallery to display multiple pictures related to a specific category. The advantage of using a photo gallery instead of inserting pictures individually in a page is that the photo gallery organizes your pictures and provides predefined layout options for their placement, arrangement, and appearance in the page. For example, you might choose a photo gallery layout that displays thumbnail pictures; when a user clicks a thumbnail in the photo gallery, the full-sized picture appears, along with its caption and description. Or, you might select a layout that displays pictures in a collage. You want to create a new Web page and a photo gallery to include pictures of the beautiful scenery runners will encounter in the Vail Valley.

STEPS

QUICK TIP

If you click the Create a new normal page button on the Standard toolbar, FrontPage creates a new Web page and opens it in Design view.

1. **In Folders view, right-click any blank area, point to** New **on the shortcut menu, then click** Blank Page
   FrontPage creates a new page in the Web site. The default filename, new_page_1.htm, is selected.

2. **Type** photos.htm, **press [Tab], type** Marathon Pictures, **then press [Enter]**
   The new page now has the filename photos.htm and the title Marathon Pictures.

3. **In Folders view, double-click** photos.htm
   The Marathon Pictures page opens in Design view. The placeholders at the top and left side of the page remind you to add this page to the Web site's navigation structure.

QUICK TIP

Remember that you can adjust your view if necessary by using the Zoom list arrow on the Navigation toolbar.

4. **Click the** Web Site tab **at the top of the Contents pane, click the** Navigation View **button** 몹Navigation, **turn on the Folder List, position the** photos.htm **file to the right of the** This Year Web page, **turn off the Folder List, then click the** photos.htm tab
   The page now includes the page banner and a link bar in the top shared border. The placeholder text appears in the left shared border because this page has no child pages. The insertion point is blinking on the first line of the Web page.

5. **Click** Insert **on the menu bar, point to** Picture, **then click** New Photo Gallery
   The Photo Gallery Properties dialog box opens, as shown in Figure D-14.

6. **Click** Add, **click** Pictures from Files, **if necessary open the** UnitD folder, **then double-click** vail1.jpg
   The vail1.jpg picture appears in the preview box. It will be the first picture in the photo gallery.

7. **Repeat Step 6 to add the** vail2.jpg **and** vail3.jpg **files to the photo gallery, then click** OK
   The photo gallery, which contains three pictures, appears in the Marathon Pictures Web page. See Figure D-15. The photos are arranged using the default layout.

8. **Click the** Save button **on the Standard toolbar, make sure that the three pictures will be saved in the images folder, then click** OK

9. **Click the** Preview button **on the Standard toolbar, then click the** second picture **in the photo gallery**
   The full-sized picture opens. FrontPage automatically created the thumbnail pictures and linked them to the full-sized images you added to the photo gallery.

FIGURE D-14: Photo Gallery Properties dialog box

Add button

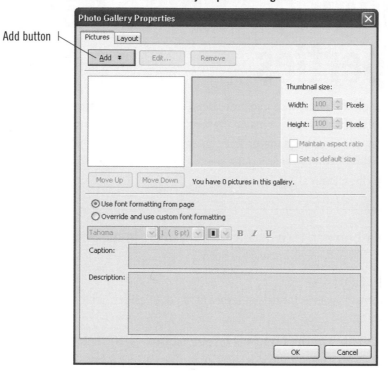

FIGURE D-15: Photo gallery added to the Marathon Pictures Web page

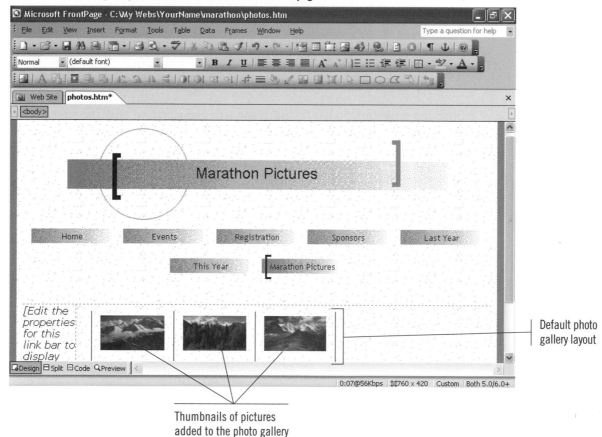

Default photo gallery layout

Thumbnails of pictures added to the photo gallery

Changing a Photo Gallery's Properties

After creating a photo gallery, you might decide to add, delete, or rearrange pictures. You might also decide to add captions and descriptions, change the font and style of captions and descriptions, or use a different photo gallery layout to arrange the pictures. In any case, changing the properties of a photo gallery is an easy process. After examining the photo gallery, you decide to consider other layout options and add captions to the pictures.

STEPS

1. **Close your browser, then double-click anywhere in the** photo gallery
   The Photo Gallery Properties dialog box opens.

2. **Click the** Layout tab
   The Horizontal Layout is the default layout for a photo gallery. Table D-1 describes the other photo gallery layouts you can use.

3. **Click** Slide Show **in the Choose a layout list box, then click the** Pictures tab
   The photo gallery changes to the Slide Show layout. The vail1.jpg file is selected in the list box on the Pictures tab.

   QUICK TIP
   You could also enter a description of this picture by typing one in the Description text box.

4. **Click in the** Caption text box, **then type** Clouds in the Mountain Tops
   The picture now includes a caption, as shown in Figure D-16.

5. **Click** vail2.jpg **in the list box, click in the** Caption text box, **then type** Summer is Beautiful in the Vail Valley
   Selecting a picture in the list box lets you enter a caption or a description for it.

6. **Click** vail3.jpg **in the list box, click in the** Caption text box, **type** The Rocky Mountains, **then click** OK
   The photo gallery, which appears black because it is selected, appears with the new layout and captions.

7. **Click the** Save button 🖫 **on the Standard toolbar, then click the** Preview button 🔍 **on the Standard toolbar**

8. **Scroll down the page so you can see the photo gallery and the caption, then point to each** thumbnail picture **in turn and click it**
   Figure D-17 shows the full-sized picture and caption for the third picture.

9. **Close your browser, close the marathon Web site, then exit FrontPage**

FIGURE D-16: Caption added to vail1.jpg picture

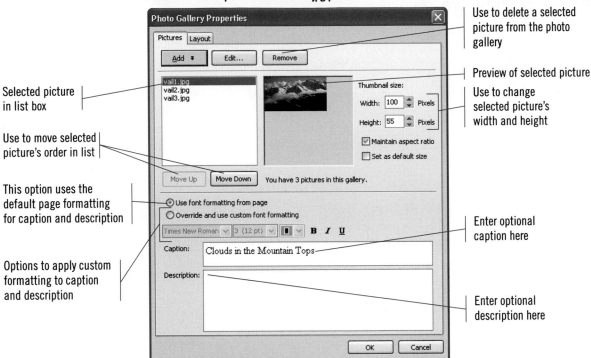

Use to delete a selected picture from the photo gallery

Selected picture in list box

Preview of selected picture

Use to change selected picture's width and height

Use to move selected picture's order in list

This option uses the default page formatting for caption and description

Options to apply custom formatting to caption and description

Enter optional caption here

Enter optional description here

FIGURE D-17: Marathon Pictures Web page in a browser

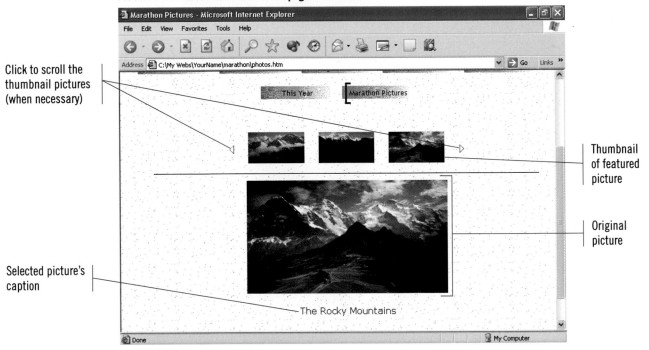

Click to scroll the thumbnail pictures (when necessary)

Thumbnail of featured picture

Original picture

Selected picture's caption

TABLE D-1: Photo gallery layout options

layout	description
Horizontal Layout	Thumbnail pictures appear in rows, with optional captions and descriptive text below each picture
Montage Layout	Thumbnail pictures appear in a collage; optional captions appear when the pointer points to a picture; no descriptions are allowed
Slide Show	Thumbnail pictures appear in a row; when you click a thumbnail, the original picture appears below the thumbnails with its optional caption and description below it
Vertical Layout	Thumbnail pictures appear in columns, with optional captions and descriptive text to the right of each picture

Practice

▼ CONCEPTS REVIEW

Refer to Figure D-18 to answer the following questions about working with pictures.

FIGURE D-18

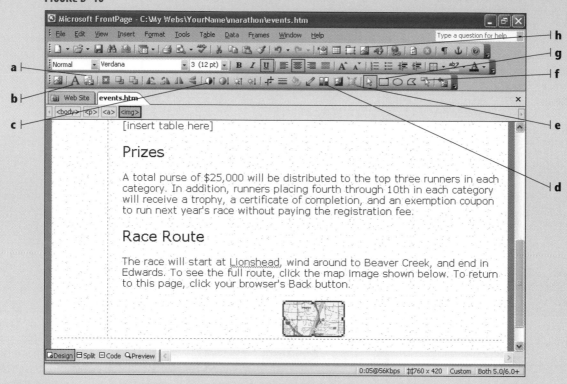

1. Which button creates a thumbnail picture?
2. Which button adds text over a selected picture?
3. Which button lets you insert a picture in a Web page?
4. Which button increases the contrast of a selected picture?
5. Which button displays the hotspots in a picture?
6. Which button resizes a picture to match its display size?
7. Which button creates a rectangular hotspot in a picture?
8. Which button lets you change the colors in a selected picture?

Match each of the following terms with the statement that describes its function.

9. Background picture
10. GIF
11. Hotspot
12. JPG
13. Thumbnail
14. Wash out
15. WordArt

a. An effect that results in less intense and less bright colors in the selected image
b. A defined area in a picture that, when clicked, activates a hyperlink
c. A file format for pictures with up to 256 colors
d. A file format for pictures that is used for photographs and high-quality digital images
e. A picture object created using text
f. A picture that is applied behind text and other objects in a Web page
g. A small version of a picture that contains a hyperlink to a larger version of the same picture

Select the best answer from the following list of choices.

16. **In FrontPage, a picture might be:**
    a. Applied to the background of a Web page.
    b. A digital photograph or a scanned photograph.
    c. A shape, such as a smiley face.
    d. All of the above

17. **You can use the Position dialog box to:**
    a. Change the way text flows around a picture.
    b. Change the colors in a picture.
    c. Rename a picture.
    d. All of the above

18. **Which one of the following buttons would you click to change a selected picture's colors?**
    a. [button]
    b. [button]
    c. [button]
    d. [button]

19. **To see the hotspots in a picture in a Web page, click _____ on the Pictures toolbar.**
    a. [button]
    b. [button]
    c. [button]
    d. [button]

20. **Which of the following photo gallery layouts does not permit the use of descriptions?**
    a. Slide Show
    b. Montage
    c. Vertical
    d. Horizontal

▼ SKILLS REVIEW

1. **Insert a picture.**
   a. Start FrontPage and use the One Page Web Site template to create a new Web site named **resume** in the location where your Web sites are stored.
   b. Turn on the Folder List, make sure the root folder of the resume Web site is selected, then import the file index.htm from the UnitD\SR folder on the drive and folder where your Data Files are stored into the Web site. (*Hint:* Overwrite the existing file with the same filename in the Web site.) Turn off the Folder List, then open the file index.htm in Design view.
   c. On the first line of the document, select the text **Your Name**, then type your first and last names.
   d. Position the insertion point at the end of the **Experience** heading, then insert the picture globe.gif from the UnitD\SR folder.
   e. Save the picture in the Web site's images folder.

2. **Change a picture's properties.**
   a. Select the globe.gif picture.
   b. Use the lower-left sizing handle of the globe.gif picture to reduce the picture's size by approximately 50%.
   c. Resample the picture to match its display size.
   d. Increase the picture's contrast by clicking the appropriate toolbar button once.

   e. Increase the picture's brightness by clicking the appropriate toolbar button twice.

   f. Set the picture's wrapping style to Right.

   g. Save the page and overwrite the existing globe.gif file in the images folder.

3. Add text over a picture.

   a. Select the globe.gif picture.

   b. Wash out the colors in the picture.

   c. Add the text **Click here to view samples** over the globe.gif picture.

   d. Change the font size of the text you added over the globe.gif picture to 10 points.

   e. Change the font color of the text you added over the globe.gif picture to purple. Your globe picture should look similar to the one shown in Figure D-19. (*Note:* Your globe.gif picture will be smaller.)

   f. Save the page and overwrite the globe.gif picture in the images folder.

4. Create an image map.

   a. Select the picture by clicking the text that appears on it.

   b. Draw a rectangular hotspot just inside the picture's outer perimeter, so the hotspot includes the entire picture and the text box.

   c. Create a hyperlink from the hotspot to the URL **www.mywebsite.com**.

   d. Deselect the picture, then change to Preview view. Point to the picture to verify the URL for the hotspot on the status bar. (*Note:* Do not click the link.)

   e. Return to Design view, then save the page.

5. Create WordArt.

   a. Select your name on the first line of the Web page. Make sure that you select only the text, and not the line break character at the end of the line.

   b. Change your name to a WordArt object. Select a WordArt style of your choice.

   c. Edit the text used in the WordArt object to 16 points and a font of your choice.

   d. Save the page.

6. Create a thumbnail picture.

   a. Scroll to the bottom of the page, then click to the left of the word **Excellence** in the last line of the page.

   b. Insert the storm.jpg picture from the UnitD\SR folder.

   c. Change the picture to a thumbnail.

   d. Save the storm.jpg and thumbnail pictures in the images folder using the default filenames.

   e. Preview the page in a browser, click the thumbnail picture, then close your browser.

   f. Return to Design view, print the index.htm page, then close it.

7. Create a photo gallery.

   a. Create a new blank Web page in the resume Web site using the filename **photos.htm** and the title **Photo Gallery**.

   b. Open the page in Design view, type your first and last names on the first line, and on a new line insert a photo gallery.

   c. Insert the following pictures, stored in the UnitD\SR folder, in the photo gallery: fall.jpg, lake.jpg, and snow.jpg.

   d. Save the Photo Gallery page, and save the pictures you added to the photo gallery in the images folder.

   e. Preview the Photo Gallery page in a browser, then click each picture in the photo gallery. (*Hint:* Use your browser's Back button to return to the photos.htm page.)

   f. Close your browser.

▼ SKILLS REVIEW (CONTINUED)

8. **Change a photo gallery's properties.**
   a. Open the Photo Gallery Properties dialog box.
   b. Add the caption **Fall in New England** to the fall.jpg picture.
   c. Add the caption **Lake Wonataka** to the lake.jpg picture.
   d. Add the caption **Snowstorm** to the snow.jpg picture.
   e. Change the photo gallery layout to Vertical Layout.
   f. Save the Photo Gallery Web page, preview it in a browser, then use the browser to print the page.
   g. Close your browser, close the resume Web site, then exit FrontPage.

▼ INDEPENDENT CHALLENGE 1

The city of Nassau Bay needs to add a page to its Web site that identifies the materials the city's sanitation department can recycle from the curbside. The Marketing Department will advertise the new recycling program and provide the URL to the page to help residential customers know which materials they can recycle. The marketing manager asks you to create the Web page.

a. Start FrontPage, then use the Empty Web Site template to create a new Web site named **recycle** in the location where your Web sites are stored.

b. Import the FP D-1.htm file from the UnitD\IC1 folder on the drive and folder where your Data Files are stored into the root folder of the recycle Web site.

c. Use Folders view to change the filename of the page to **index.htm**, then open the page in Design view.

d. Change the text on the first line of the page to a WordArt object. (Make sure that you select only the text and not the paragraph mark at the end of the line.) Select a WordArt style of your choice, change the default font to one of your choice, and change the font size to 16 points.

e. Change the centered heading on the last line of the page to the same WordArt style and font that you created for the heading at the top of the page, but use a 14-point font size. (Make sure that you select only the text and not the entire line.)

f. Replace the text **Your Name** in the second paragraph with your first and last names.

g. Click to the left of the word **Need** in the second paragraph, then insert the recycle.gif picture from the UnitD\IC1 folder.

h. Change the wrapping style of the recycle.gif picture so the text in the second paragraph wraps to the left of the picture. (*Hint:* Use the pictures on the Appearance tab to determine which text wrapping style to select.)

i. Reduce the picture's size by approximately 50%. Resample the picture to match its display size.

j. Insert the speckles.gif file from the UnitD\IC1 folder as the page's background picture.

k. Change the recycle.gif picture to transparent, so the page's background shows through the picture. (*Hint:* Select the picture, click the Set Transparent Color button 🖉 on the Pictures toolbar, then click ✎ on the white color in the center of the picture.)

l. Save the page, save the picture files in the Web site's images folder, then preview the page in a browser. Use the browser to print the page, then close your browser.

m. Use FrontPage to print the HTML document for the page, return to Design view, close the recycle Web site, then exit FrontPage.

▼ INDEPENDENT CHALLENGE 2

The Villages at Kensington Neighbourhood Association Web site now has a professional appearance and contains several pages. Your next task is to insert pictures in the Pool Pictures page and to add other graphics as necessary to enhance the site's appearance.

a. Start FrontPage and open the village Web site from the location where your Web sites are stored. (If you did not create and change this Web site in Units A through C, contact your instructor for assistance.)

b. Open the poolpics.htm page in Design view.

▼ INDEPENDENT CHALLENGE 2 (CONTINUED)

c. Insert a photo gallery on the first line of the page (but not in a shared border). Add the following pictures from the UnitD\IC2 folder on the drive and folder where your Data Files are stored into the photo gallery: pool1.jpg, pool2.jpg, pool3.jpg, and pool4.jpg.

d. For each picture in the photo gallery, create an appropriate caption using a custom format of Arial, 14-point, blue, bold font, then add a one- or two-sentence description. The descriptions for each photo should use the default font formatting.

e. Change the default photo gallery layout to Vertical Layout, with two pictures displayed in each row.

f. Save the pictures in the Web site's images folder.

g. Preview the Pool Pictures Web page in a browser, then examine each picture, caption, and description that you added. Print the page, then close your browser.

h. Open the news.htm page in Design view. Click to the left of the word **It's** in the first paragraph, then insert the firework.gif picture from the UnitD\IC2 folder. Resize the picture so it is approximately two inches high and two inches wide, resample the picture to match its display size, then position the picture so text wraps to its left. Save the page, and save the picture file in the Web site's images folder.

i. Change the firework.gif picture to transparent so the page's background shows through the picture. (*Hint:* Select the picture, click the Set Transparent Color button ✐ on the Pictures toolbar, then click ✎ on the beige color in the picture.)

j. Save the page, overwriting the existing firework.gif file, preview the page in a browser, then print it.

k. Close your browser, close the village Web site, then exit FrontPage.

▼ INDEPENDENT CHALLENGE 3

The Web site for the city of Tryon, North Carolina, contains several pages, shared borders to link those pages, and a theme to enhance the site's overall appearance. Your next task is to insert pictures in the Photo Gallery Web page and to add other graphics as necessary to enhance the site's appearance.

a. Start FrontPage and open the tryon Web site from the location where your Web sites are stored. (If you did not create and change this Web site in Units A through C, contact your instructor for assistance.)

b. Open the pictures.htm page in Design view.

c. On a blank line below the text in the page (but not in a shared border), insert a photo gallery. Add the nine pictures saved in the UnitD\IC3\photo folder on the drive and folder where your Data Files are stored to the photo gallery. (*Hint:* You can add all nine files in one step by selecting the first file in the File Open dialog box, pressing and holding [Shift], clicking the last picture, releasing [Shift], then clicking Open.)

d. Use the previews of the pictures in the Photo Gallery Properties dialog box to arrange the pictures in the order that seems appropriate to you. Use the Move Up and Move Down buttons in the Photo Gallery Properties dialog box to organize the pictures. Select the Slide Show photo gallery layout.

e. For each picture in the photo gallery, create an appropriate caption and a one- or two-sentence description. Format the caption for each photo using a customized format of your choice. (Make sure the customized caption formatting complements the existing text in the page.) The descriptions for each photo should use the default page formatting.

f. Save the pictures in the Web site's images folder.

g. Preview the Photo Gallery Web page in a browser, then examine each picture, caption, and description that you added. Select any picture in the photo gallery, print the page, then close your browser.

h. Open the hotspots.htm Web page in Design view. Insert the following pictures from the UnitD\IC3 folder in the Web page in appropriate places: golf.jpg, dining.jpg, and govt.jpg. (*Hint:* Read the text in the page to determine where to insert the pictures.) Use positioning to make the text wrap around the pictures to enhance their appearance in the page. If you think it would improve their appearance, use the buttons on the Pictures toolbar to enhance the pictures; use the mouse pointer to resize the pictures as necessary, then resample them to match their display sizes in the page. Save the page, and save the picture files in the Web site's images folder.

i. Preview the hotspots.htm page in a browser, then print it.

j. Close your browser, close the tryon Web site, then exit FrontPage.

▼ INDEPENDENT CHALLENGE 4

Marilyn Gregory is a kindergarten teacher who is working on a home page for her class. Mrs. Gregory wants to include several pictures in the home page containing hyperlinks that open Web sites with educational resources related to phonics, early reading, science, and math. She wants to make the home page as visually pleasing as possible, so she decides to search the Internet to locate Web sites that provide free or inexpensive graphics that she can use. She wants to focus on finding graphics relevant to young children, so she will search for things such as images of fruits, crayons, and interesting shapes. Figure D-20 shows two examples of images that Mrs. Gregory might use.

a. Use your favorite search engine and the keywords **free Web graphics** to search for possible graphics for the Web page. You might use Excite, Infoseek, MSN, AltaVista, or another search engine of your choice.

FIGURE D-20

b. Examine the sites that your search returns, read their descriptions, and then open three sites that look like they might provide buttons and other graphics, such as fruits, crayons, and shapes that could easily be used as hotspots. You might be able to search the site specifically for these types of pictures. For each site that you visit, print the home page and a page that describes the site's policy for using its graphics in your own work. (*Hint:* This page might be titled **Terms**, **Terms of Use**, **Usage Policy**, or something similar. You can usually find a hyperlink to this type of page at the bottom of a site's home page.)

c. After you find three sites that might provide the graphics that Mrs. Gregory needs, close your browser. (Do *not* download graphics from any site.)

d. Write a brief report on the types of graphics that you found. Which types of graphics would make the best image maps? How would you use the tools in FrontPage to modify the graphics that you found to make them more appropriate for use as image maps?

e. Examine each site's usage policy and answer the following questions for each site that you visited: Are the graphics at the site free of charge to everyone, or just for certain types of uses? What is the fee, if any, for commercial use? Can you distribute the site's graphics to other users? What is the penalty for violating the site's usage policy?

f. When you are finished, make sure that your name appears in your report. Submit your report and the printouts from the browser to your instructor.

▼ VISUAL WORKSHOP

Use the One Page Web Site template to create a new Web site named **academy** in the location where your Web sites are stored. Open the home page (index.htm) and create the content shown in Figure D-21. Use Folders view to change the page's title. The images and background picture are saved as driving.jpg, putting.jpg, and hands.gif, respectively, in the UnitD\VW folder on the drive and folder where your Data Files are stored. The heading was created using WordArt—experiment with different font sizes so your WordArt object matches the one shown in Figure D-21. When you are finished, use FrontPage to print the HTML document for the page, preview the page in a browser and print it, then close your browser, the academy Web site, and FrontPage.

FIGURE D-21

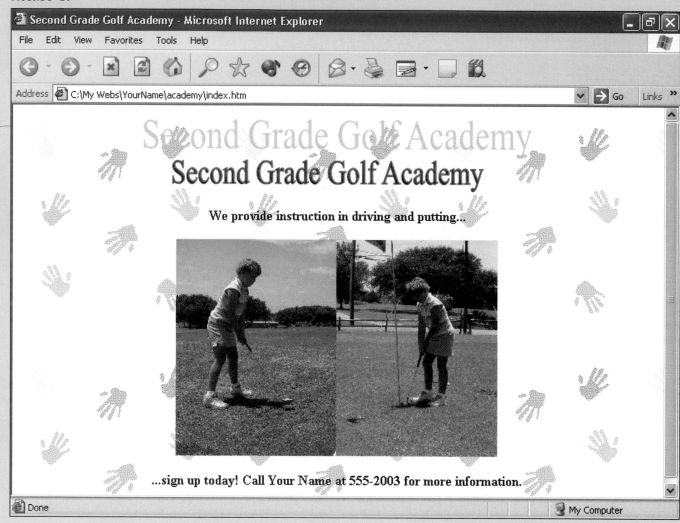

Creating a Table

OBJECTIVES

Add a table to a Web page
Change table properties
Enter table data and resize cells
Insert and delete cells
Merge and split cells
Insert a picture in a cell
Align and format cells
Apply an AutoFormat to a table

Tables are an effective way to present information in Web pages because they allow you to organize information in rows and columns. Tables are also an important design element in Web pages because they help you control the way content appears in the page. For example, if you need to position text and pictures in a page, you can use a table to ensure that every user of the page sees information in the same way. If you use [Spacebar] or [Tab] to align data, a browser might not display the data as you intended. After creating a table, you can use the tools in FrontPage to change the table's alignment, organization, and appearance. Jason Tanaka, manager of the Vail Valley Marathon, wants to include a list of the running categories and their related age groups in the Events Web page. You decide to create a table to store this data to provide runners with an easy way of identifying the category in which they should compete.

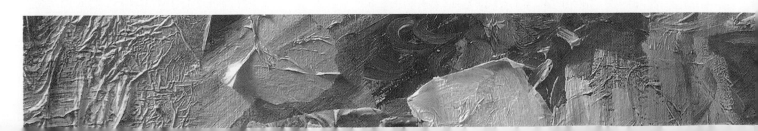

Adding a Table to a Web Page

You may already be familiar with tables that you can create using a word-processing program, such as Microsoft Word. A **table** consists of one or more rows of cells that organize and arrange data. A **cell** is the smallest component of a table. Table cells are similar to cells that you may have used in a spreadsheet program, such as Microsoft Excel. A cell can contain text or a picture or even another table, called a **nested table**. When you need to organize and arrange data in a Web page, your design might include a table to store the data. Using a table ensures that all Web browsers will display the data as you intended it to appear. Before using FrontPage to create a table, it is a good idea to sketch the table's appearance on paper so you know what size table you need.  Jason wants to provide the running categories and their related age groups in the Events Web page. You will format this information using a table.

STEPS

1. **Start** FrontPage, **open the** marathon **Web site from the location where your Web sites are stored, then if necessary change to** Folders view
   The marathon Web site contains 10 Web pages and a Word document.

2. **Double-click** events.htm **in the Contents pane**
   The Events Web page opens in Design view.

3. **If necessary, scroll down the page, then select the text** [insert table here]
   You will insert the table and replace the selected text. Figure E-1 shows a sketch of the table for the Events page.

4. **Click** Table **on the menu bar, point to** Insert, **then click** Table
   The Insert Table dialog box opens. You use this dialog box to specify the table's size, alignment, width, and other features.

> **QUICK TIP**
> You can click the Insert Table button on the Standard toolbar and then click the cell in the table grid that represents the table size you need to create a table.

5. **Select the value in the** Rows list box, **type** 4, **press** [Tab] **to move to the Columns list box, then type** 5
   The table will have four rows and five columns.

6. **Click the** Alignment list arrow, **then click** Center
   The table will be centered in the Web page.

7. **Select the text in the** Specify width text box, **type** 90, **then make sure that the** In percent option button **is selected**
   The setting in the Specify width text box formats the table as a percentage of the width of the browser window. The table's actual size will vary based on the width of the browser window in which it appears, but it will always be 90% of the browser window's width. You can also set the table's width using a fixed number of pixels, so the table will always be the same width, regardless of the monitor and the resolution that is used to view it. The table settings are now complete, as shown in Figure E-2.

> **TROUBLE**
> If the Tables toolbar doesn't open automatically, click View on the menu bar, point to Toolbars, then click Tables; if necessary, drag the toolbar to dock it below the Formatting toolbar.

8. **Click** OK
   A centered table with four rows and five columns appears in the page, as shown in Figure E-3. Your table and cell borders might differ. The Tables toolbar might open automatically when a table is selected.

FIGURE E-1: Sketch of the table for the Events Web page

<insert logo here>	Young Adult	Adult	Master	Senior
Men	Under 18	19-35	36-55	Over 55
Women	Under 18	19-41	42-57	Over 57
Wheelchair and Disabled	Under 18	19-40	41-65	Over 65

FIGURE E-2: Insert Table dialog box

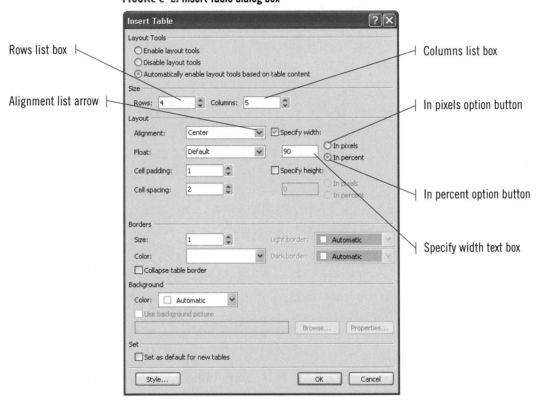

Rows list box

Alignment list arrow

Columns list box

In pixels option button

In percent option button

Specify width text box

FIGURE E-3: Centered table added to the Events Web page

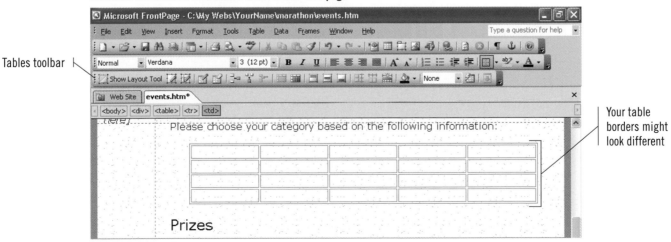

Tables toolbar

Your table borders might look different

Please choose your category based on the following information:

Prizes

FrontPage 2003

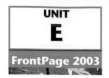

Changing Table Properties

When you first create a table, the Insert Table dialog box provides many options for setting the table's appearance. After seeing the table in the Web page, you might decide to change its appearance to match your needs more closely. The default table settings include specifications for cell padding, cell spacing, and borders. **Cell padding**, which is measured in pixels, is the distance between the contents of a cell and the inside edge of the cell. **Cell spacing**, which is also measured in pixels, is the distance between table cells. Increasing the cell spacing increases the distance between the borders that surround each cell. A table actually has two types of borders: a table border and cell borders. The **table border** is the outside border of the table. A **cell border** is the border around each individual cell. You can change the color and size of the table and cell borders. When you increase the border size, the border becomes thicker. You can also add a caption to your table. A **caption** is an optional title that appears above or below a table. ▰▰▰▰ You want to make the table easier to read, so you decide to change the default settings for the cell padding and the cell spacing. You also want to add a caption above the table to identify its contents.

STEPS

QUICK TIP

To change a cell's properties, right-click the cell, then click Cell Properties on the shortcut menu.

1. **Right-click any cell in the table, then click** Table Properties **on the shortcut menu**

   The Table Properties dialog box opens. This dialog box includes the same options as the Insert Table dialog box.

2. **Select the value in the** Cell padding list box, **then type** 3

   Setting the cell padding value to 3 increases the amount of space between the data in each cell and the cell's inside border.

3. **Press** [Tab] **to move to the** Cell spacing list box, **then type** 1

   Setting the cell spacing value to 1 decreases the amount of space between the table's cells.

QUICK TIP

Valid cell spacing and cell padding values are integers between 0 and 100.

4. **If necessary, click the** Collapse table border check box **to add a check mark**

   The completed Table Properties dialog box appears in Figure E-4.

5. **Click** OK

   The Table Properties dialog box closes, and the table appears with the new settings.

6. **Click** Table **on the menu bar, point to** Insert, **then click** Caption

   The insertion point is blinking on a new line above the table, indicating the default position for a caption. By default, the caption uses the Normal style for text and is centered above the table. You can change the caption's formatting before or after you type it, just like any other text.

QUICK TIP

To change a caption's position, right-click it, then click Caption Properties on the shortcut menu.

7. **Click the** Style list arrow **on the Formatting toolbar, click** Heading 3, **then type** Marathon Categories

   As shown in Figure E-5, the new caption appears above the table and uses the formatting for the Heading 3 style as defined by the page's theme. Although it looks like normal text, the caption is formatted using the HTML tag for a table caption.

8. **Click the** Save button 🖫 **on the Standard toolbar**

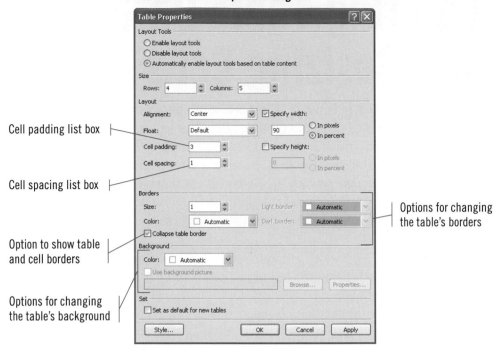

Cell padding list box

Cell spacing list box

Option to show table and cell borders

Options for changing the table's background

Options for changing the table's borders

FIGURE E-5: Caption added to table

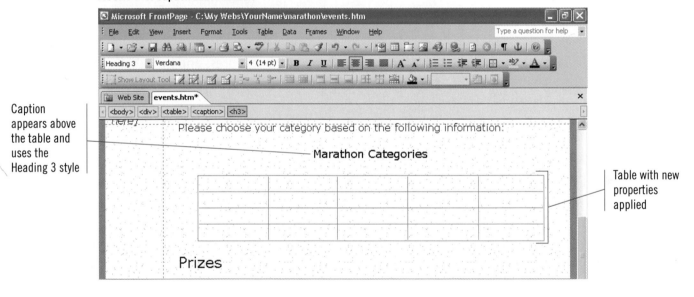

Caption appears above the table and uses the Heading 3 style

Table with new properties applied

Clues to Use

Changing the border colors of tables and cells

To change the border color of a table or of selected cells, follow these steps. Right-click anywhere in the table or in the cell(s) to which you want to apply the border color, click either Table Properties (to apply the border color to all cells in a table) or Cell Properties (to apply the border color to only the cell(s) you have selected) on the shortcut menu, click the Color list arrow in the Borders section, then choose a color or create a custom color. You can create a three-dimensional effect for tables and cells by choosing complementary light and dark border colors. A light border color is applied to a cell's top and left borders; a dark border color is applied to a cell's bottom and right borders.

If the Color, Light border, and Dark border options in the Table Properties or Cell Properties dialog box are dimmed, then the Web page uses a theme or a cascading style sheet that specifies and controls the border color of the selected table or selected cells. The options will also be dimmed if you deselected the option to collapse the table border in the Table Properties dialog box.

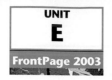
Entering Table Data and Resizing Cells

After creating the initial table structure and setting the table's properties using the information in your sketch, you can start entering data in the table's cells. To enter data in a cell, click in it to position the insertion point, then type the data. To move to the next cell to the right, press → or [Tab]. To move up, down, or left in a table, press the corresponding arrow key or use the mouse to click in the desired cell. Just like in a word-processing program, pressing [Tab] in the last cell of the last row of a table creates a new table row. After entering data in your table, you might find it necessary to resize the table, rows, or columns to present the data best. ▰▰▰▰▰ You are ready to enter data in the table. You will also resize the table.

STEPS

1. **Click in the** row 1, column 1 cell

   The insertion point appears in the first cell. When you create a table, the default alignment for individual cells is set to left. You can identify the cell's alignment because the insertion point appears at the left side of the cell.

2. **Type** logo, **press** [Tab], **type** Young Adult, **then press** [Tab]

   Text appears in the first two cells of the table, and the insertion point is in the third cell. As you type in each cell, the widths of the columns change to accommodate the data you enter.

3. **Type** Adult, **press** [Tab], **type** Master, **press** [Tab], **type** Senior, **press** [Tab], **type** Men, **press** [Tab], **then type** Under 18

   You completed the first row of the table and typed the data in the first two cells of the second row.

4. **With the insertion point in the row 2, column 2 cell, press and hold** [Shift], **click in the** row 4, column 2 cell, **then release** [Shift]

   The second, third, and fourth cells in column 2 are selected.

5. **Click the** Fill Down button ▣ **on the Tables toolbar**

   The value "Under 18" now appears in each selected cell. When your table contains repetitive data, you can use the Fill Down or Fill Right buttons on the Tables toolbar to copy one value to selected cells below or to the right of the current cell.

6. **Use Figure E-6 to enter the remaining data in the table**

   Your table should look like Figure E-6. Your word wrap might differ.

7. **Position the pointer at the top of the first column so it changes to ↓, then click**

   The first column is selected. Although you don't have to select a column before resizing it, by doing so you ensure that you are resizing a column and not an individual selected cell or other table element.

8. **Position the pointer on the** right border **of the selected column so it changes to ↔, drag the border to the left (see Figure E-7), then release the** mouse button

   The width of the first column decreases. Notice that the width of the second column increased to accommodate the first column's new size. As you make changes to the size of one column, the sizes of other columns change.

9. **Select the** second column **in the table, press and hold** [Shift], **select the** last column, **then release** [Shift]

   Columns 2 through 5 are selected.

10. **Click the** Distribute Columns Evenly button ▦ **on the Tables toolbar, then click the** Save button ▣ **on the Standard toolbar**

    The columns are resized to equal widths.

FIGURE E-6: Data entered into the table

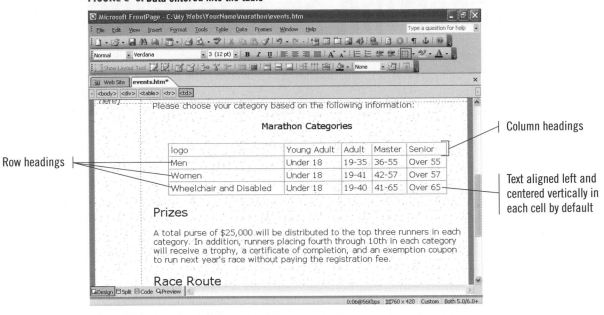

Row headings

Column headings

Text aligned left and centered vertically in each cell by default

FIGURE E-7: Increasing the width of the first column

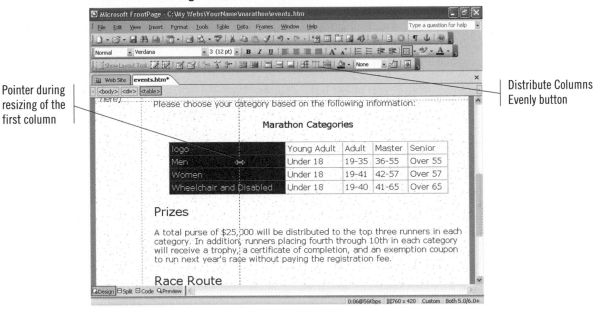

Pointer during resizing of the first column

Distribute Columns Evenly button

Removing table borders

Using a table ensures a consistent appearance for data when it is viewed using different Web browsers and at different screen resolutions and sizes. Sometimes you might need to control the arrangement of data but won't want it to appear as a table, with borders (gridlines) around the entire table and around each individual cell. In this case, you can still format data using a table to gain the advantage of controlling the way data is displayed, but remove the borders so the user doesn't see them. To remove a table's borders, right-click anywhere in the table, click Table Properties on the shortcut menu, then change the value in the Size list box in the Borders section to 0. In FrontPage, the table's borders will change to dotted

lines, as shown in Figure E-8, providing you with a way to identify the individual cells in the table. However, when you view the table in your Web browser, the table's borders will be invisible.

FIGURE E-8

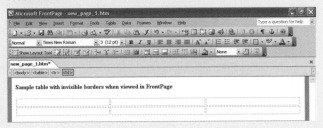

Inserting and Deleting Cells

After creating a table and entering data into it, you might need to add or delete columns and rows, change the way cells are displayed, and use different colors to format the table's appearance. You can use buttons on the Tables toolbar to make these types of changes to an existing table. The marathon officials decide to replace the separate Wheelchair and Disabled categories with a new Wheelchair/Disabled subcategory, which will appear in each of the gender categories. To make this change, you need to delete the last row of the table and create a new column.

STEPS

1. **Position the pointer on the left edge of the last row so it changes to ➡, then click**
   The selected columns are deselected, and the last row is selected.

2. **Click the Delete Cells button 🔳 on the Tables toolbar**
   The last row is deleted. To insert a new column or row, you first need to select a row or column adjacent to the location in which you will insert the new row or column.

3. **Position the pointer at the top of the last column so it changes to ⬇, then click**
   The last column is selected.

4. **Click Table on the menu bar, point to Insert, click Rows or Columns, make sure that the Columns and Right of selection option buttons are selected, then click OK**
   A new column is inserted to the right of the selected column, as shown in Figure E-9.

5. **Click in the first cell of the new column, type Wheelchair/, press [Shift][Enter], type Disabled, press ▼, type All ages, press ▼, then type All ages**
   As you type "Wheelchair/" the column's width changes to match the width of the text. Pressing [Shift][Enter] in a table cell creates a new line in the cell.

6. **Select columns 1 through 6, click the Distribute Columns Evenly button 🔳 on the Tables toolbar, then click in any cell to deselect the columns**
   As shown in Figure E-10, the columns now have equal widths.

7. **Right-click the table to open the shortcut menu, click Table Properties, select the value in the Specify width text box, type 90, click the In percent option button, then click OK**
   When you distribute columns evenly, FrontPage resizes the table's width to pixels, so you changed it back to 90% of the browser window width.

8. **Click the Save button 🔳 on the Standard toolbar**
   FrontPage saves the Events Web page.

FIGURE E-9: New column added to table

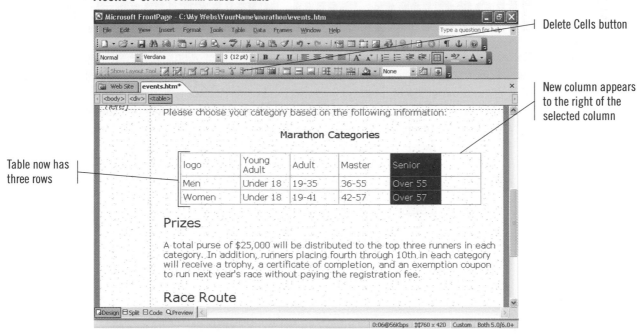

Delete Cells button

New column appears to the right of the selected column

Table now has three rows

FIGURE E-10: Resized columns

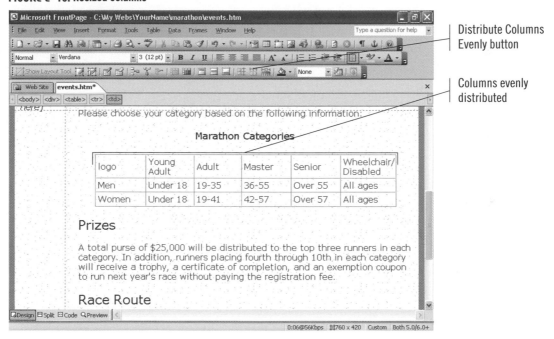

Distribute Columns Evenly button

Columns evenly distributed

FrontPage 2003

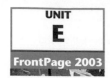
Merging and Splitting Cells

Columns and rows are made up of individual cells. Sometimes your table design might use cells that span several columns or rows to create column or row headings. To make adjustments to the default appearance of a cell, you can split and merge cells. **Splitting** is the process of dividing a single cell into two or more columns or rows. **Merging** is the process of combining two or more cells in a column or row into a single cell. ▓▓▓ Jason wants to include a reminder in the table so runners will know how to select a category. He also wants to remind runners that the top 10 finishers in each category will earn prizes. Because he wants each sentence to span the full width of the table, you will need to create a new row, combine the cells in the new row into a single cell, then split the single cell into two rows.

STEPS

QUICK TIP

Clicking the Insert Rows button 🖥️ on the Tables toolbar inserts a new row *above* the selected row. To insert a row *below* a selected row, you must use the Rows or Columns command on the Table/Insert menu.

1. **Select the last row of the table, click Table on the menu bar, point to Insert, then click Rows or Columns**

   The Insert Rows or Columns dialog box opens, as shown in Figure E-11. Because you selected a row before opening this dialog box, the Rows option button is selected automatically.

2. **Make sure that the Below selection option button is selected, then click OK**

   A new row with six cells appears below the selected row.

3. **Select the new last row, click the Merge Cells button 🖥️ on the Tables toolbar, then click in the selected cell**

   As shown in Figure E-12, the individual cells in the last row are combined into a single cell that spans the width of the table. The insertion point appears in the new cell.

4. **Type Note: Please register in the age group for your age as of May 31.**

   The text spans the merged cell.

5. **Select the last row of the table (which contains one cell), then click the Split Cells button 🖥️ on the Tables toolbar**

   The Split Cells dialog box opens, as shown in Figure E-13. You can split the selected row into two or more columns or two or more rows.

6. **Click the Split into rows option button, then click OK**

   The selected row is split into two rows, which adds a new row at the bottom of the table. The new row contains merged cells because the row you selected for splitting contained merged cells.

7. **Click in the new last row, then type Prizes awarded to the top 10 finishers in each category!**

8. **Click the Save button 🖥️ on the Standard toolbar**

FIGURE E-11: Insert Rows or Columns dialog box

Rows option button inserts one or more rows

Columns option button inserts one or more columns

Above selection option button inserts a row above the selected row(s)

Number of rows list box

Below selection option button inserts a row below the selected row(s)

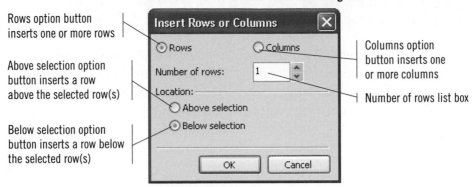

FIGURE E-12: Merged cell in table

Merge Cells button

Insertion point in merged cell

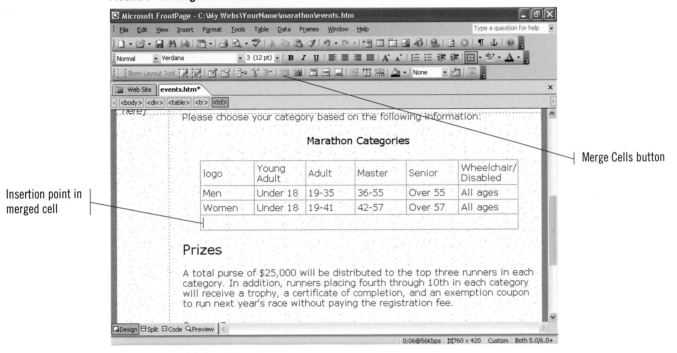

FIGURE E-13: Split Cells dialog box

Split Cells button

Split into columns option button

Number of columns (or rows) to create

Split into rows option button

Cell to split

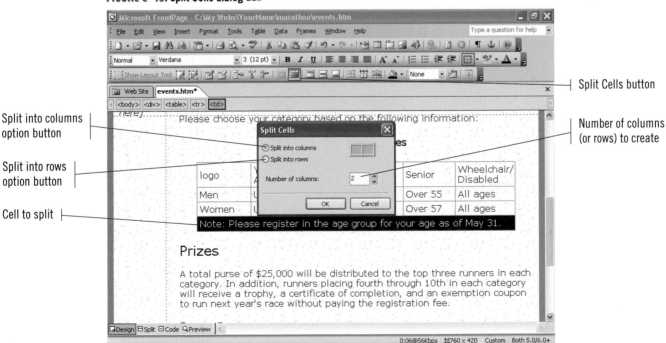

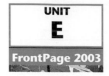

Inserting a Picture in a Cell

When you insert a picture in a table cell, FrontPage automatically resizes the cell that contains the picture to accommodate the picture's size. If the picture is too small or too large for your needs, you can click it and use a sizing handle to increase or decrease the picture's size. When you insert a picture in a table cell, you can change the picture using the same methods for changing other pictures that you insert in a Web page. For example, you might add special effects to the picture, wash out the picture, or use the picture as a hyperlink that opens another Web page. ░░░░░ Jason asks you to add the Vail Valley Marathon logo to the first cell of the table.

STEPS

1. **Select the text logo in the row 1, column 1 cell**
   You will replace this text with a picture.

2. **Click the Insert Picture From File button 🖾 on the Standard toolbar, open the UnitE folder from the drive and folder where your Data Files are stored, then double-click vvm_logo.gif**
   The logo is inserted in the cell, as shown in Figure E-14. Notice that the cell's size increased to accommodate the picture. You can resize this picture and change its characteristics just like any other picture you insert in a Web page.

   TROUBLE
   If the Pictures tool-bar doesn't open when you select the picture, click View on the menu bar, point to Toolbars, then click Pictures.

3. **Click the picture to select it, then click the Bevel button 🖾 on the Pictures toolbar**
   The beveled edges add a raised appearance to the picture.

4. **With the picture still selected, click the Insert Hyperlink button 🖾 on the Standard toolbar, in the Insert Hyperlink dialog box scroll the list of files if necessary and click index.htm, then click OK**
   The picture now contains a hyperlink to the site's home page.

5. **Click the Save button 🖫 on the Standard toolbar, make sure that FrontPage will save the vvm_logo.gif file in the images folder, then click OK**
   The table's content is complete.

6. **Click the Preview button 🔍 on the Standard toolbar, then scroll down the page and view the table**
   As shown in Figure E-15, the table is centered in the page and uses 90% of the available width of the browser window.

   TROUBLE
   If you don't see the Restore Down but-ton on the browser's title bar, click Maximize button to display it.

7. **Click the Restore Down button 🗗 on the browser's title bar, then scroll as needed to view the table**
   The table is resized to 90% of the new browser window size, based on the settings you set in an earlier lesson.

8. **Click the Maximize button 🗖 on the browser's title bar, then click the logo in the first table cell**
   The home page opens.

9. **Close your browser**

FIGURE E-14: Picture added to first table cell

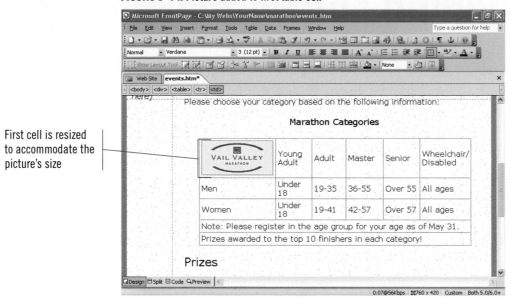

First cell is resized to accommodate the picture's size

FIGURE E-15: Events Web page in a browser

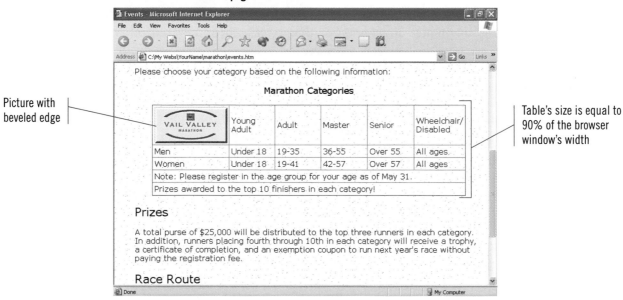

Picture with beveled edge

Table's size is equal to 90% of the browser window's width

Clues to Use

Using a background picture for a table

In addition to inserting pictures in the individual cells of a table, you can use a background picture for the entire table, as shown in Figure E-16. When using a background picture in a table, make sure that the text typed in the cells is still readable when viewed against the background picture. You can experiment with washed-out images and different font colors to produce the results you need. To add a background picture to a table, follow these steps. Right-click any cell in the table, click Table Properties on the shortcut menu, click the Use background picture check box in the Background section, click Browse, browse to and select the image file to use, click Open, then click OK. After inserting the background picture, you'll need to save it as an embedded picture file in the Web site's images folder, just as you would for any other picture file. Netscape Navigator does not support background pictures for tables, so the Use background picture feature is disabled if you configured your Web site to include Navigator as a supported browser.

FIGURE E-16

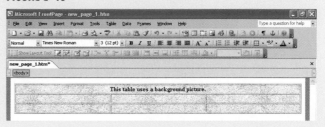

Aligning and Formatting Cells

As you have learned, the alignment of a table and the alignment of individual cells in the table can differ. The table itself can have only one alignment: right, left, or center. But the content of individual cells in the table can be right- or left-aligned, centered, or justified. Your table design might call for centered alignment for headings, right alignment for financial data, and left alignment for row headings. In addition, you can format the data in a table using any of the text formatting tools available in FrontPage. █████▓ When you created the Marathon Categories table, you set the table's alignment to center. You decide to change the formatting of the column and row headings and the alignment of selected cells to improve the table's appearance.

STEPS

TROUBLE

If the Pictures toolbar is still open, click View on the menu bar, point to Toolbars, then click Pictures.

1. **Click in the** row 1, column 2 cell **(with the content "Young Adult"), press and hold** [Shift], **click the** last cell in the first row, **then release** [Shift]
   The cells in columns 2 through 6 of the first row are selected.

2. **Click the** Center button ▤ **on the Formatting toolbar, then click the** Bold button **B** **on the Formatting toolbar**
   The data in the selected cells changes to center alignment and bold.

3. **Click in the** row 2, column 1 cell **(with the content "Men"), hold down the** mouse button, **drag the pointer down one cell, then release the** mouse button
   You selected the cells in column 1, rows 2 and 3 using the mouse.

4. **Click** **B**
   The data in the selected cells changes to bold.

5. **Select the** cells in rows 2 and 3 **and** columns 2 through 6, **then click** ▤
   The data in the selected cells changes to center alignment, as shown in Figure E-17.

6. **Select the** last two rows **in the table, then click** ▤
   The data in these cells changes to center alignment.

7. **Click the** Font Size list arrow **on the Formatting toolbar, then click** 2 (10 pt)
   The size of the selected text changes to 10 points.

8. **Click in the** last row, **click the** Borders button list arrow ▦ ▾ **on the Formatting toolbar, then click the** Top Border button ▤
   The top border is removed from the last row. The table now has the new formatting and alignment, as shown in Figure E-18.

9. **Click the** Save button ▦ **on the Standard toolbar**

FIGURE E-17: Table cells formatted and aligned

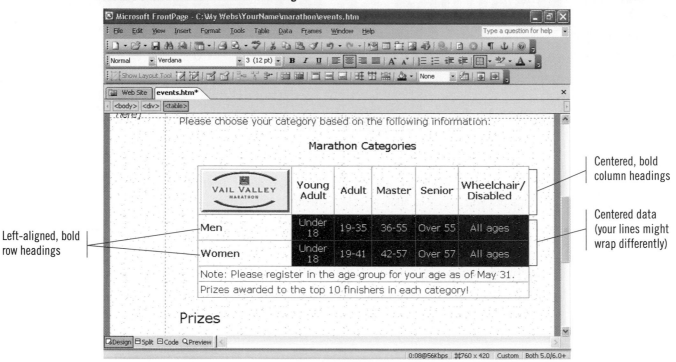

Centered, bold column headings

Centered data (your lines might wrap differently)

Left-aligned, bold row headings

FIGURE E-18: Completed table

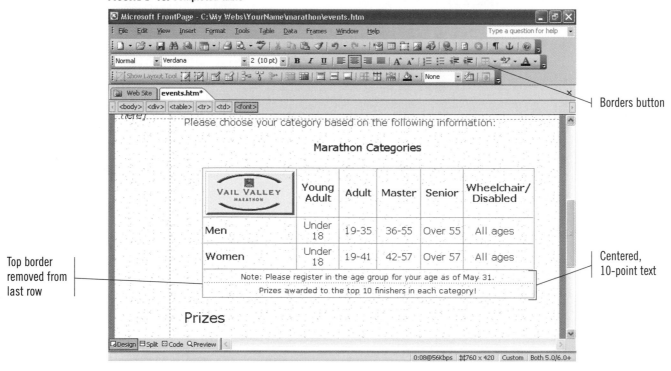

Borders button

Top border removed from last row

Centered, 10-point text

Applying an AutoFormat to a Table

When you apply a **Table AutoFormat**, FrontPage enhances the table with a predefined combination of colors, colored borders, and special effects. A Table AutoFormat might be simple, colorful, classic, or three-dimensional. After applying an AutoFormat, you can use the Table Properties dialog box to customize the AutoFormat even more to produce your own customized table appearance. You are satisfied with the table's content, alignment, and picture. You could continue enhancing the table using the tools in FrontPage but you decide to apply a Table AutoFormat to save time.

STEPS

1. **With the insertion point positioned in any table cell, click the Table AutoFormat button on the Tables toolbar**

   The Table AutoFormat dialog box opens, as shown in Figure E-19. You use this dialog box to select and preview the available Table AutoFormats. The two sections at the bottom of the dialog box—Formats to apply and Apply special formats—contain check boxes that you can select or deselect to change the way formats (borders, font, shading, and color) and special formats (heading rows, last row, first column, and last column) are applied to certain areas of the table. If you select the AutoFit check box, FrontPage will condense the table to make it as small as the data it contains.

2. **Click Simple 2 in the Formats list**

   The preview changes to show a simple table format, with lines added to emphasize the column and row headings.

3. **Click Classic 2 in the Formats list**

   This format uses color for the column and row headings.

4. **Scroll down the Formats list and click List 8**

   This format uses color to format alternate rows in the table.

5. **Scroll up the Formats list and click Colorful 2**

   This format will complement the Vail Valley Marathon logo's colors and has an easy-to-read appearance.

6. **Click OK**

   The AutoFormat is applied to the table.

7. **Click the Save button on the Standard toolbar, then click the Preview button on the Standard toolbar**

   The Events Web page opens in your browser.

8. **Scroll down the page so you can see the table**

   The completed table appears in Figure E-20.

9. **Close your browser and the marathon Web site, then exit FrontPage**

FIGURE E-19: Table AutoFormat dialog box

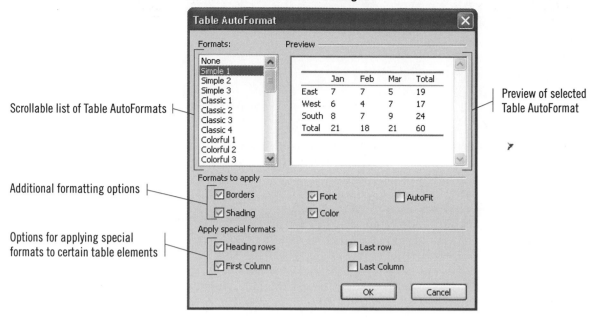

Scrollable list of Table AutoFormats

Preview of selected Table AutoFormat

Additional formatting options

Options for applying special formats to certain table elements

FIGURE E-20: Completed Events Web page

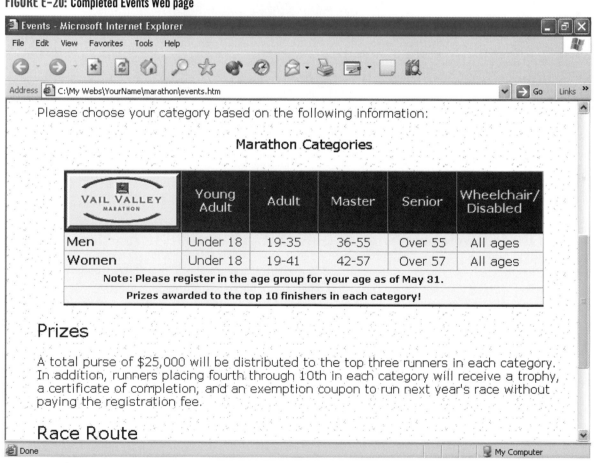

FrontPage 2003

Practice

▼ CONCEPTS REVIEW

Label each element in the Microsoft FrontPage window shown in Figure E-21.

FIGURE E-21

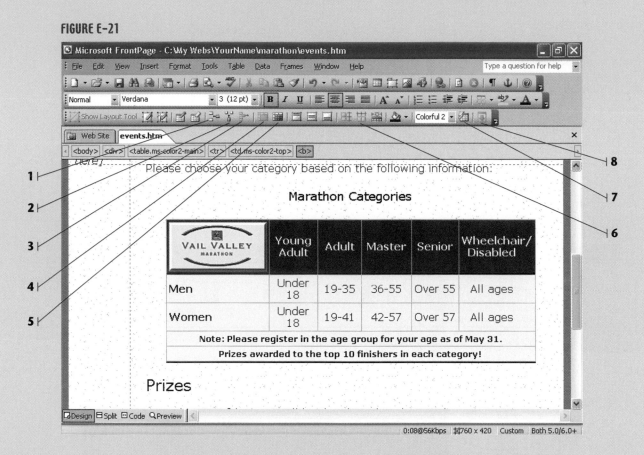

Match each of the following terms with the statement that describes its function.

9. **Caption**

10. **Cell**

11. **Cell padding**

12. **Cell spacing**

13. **Merging cells**

14. **Splitting cells**

15. **Table**

a. The process of dividing a single cell into two or more columns or rows

b. The distance between table cells, measured in pixels

c. An object with one or more rows and columns that is used to organize and arrange data

d. The distance between the contents of a cell and the inside edge of a cell, measured in pixels

e. Optional text that identifies a table

f. The smallest component of a table

g. The process of combining two or more cells in a column or row into a single cell

Select the best answer from the following list of choices.

16. **How do you center an existing table in a Web page?**
    a. Select the entire table, then click the Center button on the Formatting toolbar.
    b. Right-click anywhere in the table, then click Center Table on the shortcut menu.
    c. Right-click anywhere in the table, click Table Properties on the shortcut menu, click the Alignment list arrow, click Center, then click OK.
    d. You cannot center a table in a Web page.

17. **To increase the distance between cells in a table, you need to change the cells':**
    a. Padding.
    b. Border.
    c. Alignment.
    d. Spacing.

18. **To decrease the distance between a cell's contents and the inside border of the cell, you need to change the cell's:**
    a. Padding.
    b. Border.
    c. Alignment.
    d. Spacing.

19. **Applying complementary light and dark border colors in a table will create a:**
    a. Three-dimensional effect.
    b. Solid cell border.
    c. Border around the outside of the table.
    d. None of the above

20. **To distribute the selected rows evenly in a table, click _____ on the Tables toolbar.**
    a.
    b.
    c.
    d.

21. **To delete a selected cell from a table, click _____ on the Tables toolbar.**
    a.
    b.
    c.
    d.

▼ SKILLS REVIEW

1. **Add a table to a Web page.**
   a. Start FrontPage and use the Empty Web Site template to create a new Web site named **menu** in the location where your Web sites are stored.
   b. Create a new Web page named **index.htm** and titled **Friday's Menu**.
   c. Insert a table with three rows and two columns that is centered on the page.
   d. Specify a width of 85% of the browser window's size.
   e. On a new line below the table, type your first and last names.

2. **Change table properties.**
   a. Use the Table Properties dialog box to change the cell padding to 2, the cell spacing to 3, and the table's border size to 3.
   b. Insert a table caption using the text **Friday's Menu**. Change the caption to the Heading 2 style.
   c. Save the page.

3. **Enter table data and resize cells.**
   a. In the first row, type **Breakfast** in the first cell and **Lunch** in the second cell.
   b. In the first cell in the second row, type **Breakfast tacos with egg, potato, and cheese**, create a new line in the cell, then type **Orange juice**. (*Hint:* Press [Shift][Enter] to create a new line in a cell.)
   c. In the second cell in the second row, type **Chicken fried steak**, create a new line, type **Mashed potatoes with country gravy**, create a new line, type **Green beans**, create a new line, then type **Roll**. (*Note:* The data in row 2, column 1 will be vertically centered in the cell.)
   d. Use the pointer to decrease the width of the first column by approximately 50%.
   e. Save the page.

4. **Insert and delete cells.**

   a. Insert a new column to the left of the **Breakfast** column.

   b. Insert a new row above the first row in the table.

   c. Delete the last row in the table.

   d. Distribute the columns evenly.

   e. Reset the table's width to 85% of the browser window's size.

5. **Merge and split cells.**

   a. Merge the cells in the first row into a single cell.

   b. In the merged cell, type **The cafeteria will close at 2:00 P.M. today for the Memorial Day weekend.**

   c. Split the first cell in the second row into two columns. (*Hint*: Click in the cell, then split the cell into two columns.)

   d. In the first cell of the second row, type **Friday**. In the second cell of the second row, type **May 24**.

   e. Save the page.

6. **Insert a picture in a cell.**

   a. In the first cell of the third row, insert the menu.gif picture from the UnitE\SR folder on the drive and folder where your Data Files are stored.

   b. Save the picture in the Web site's images folder.

7. **Align and format cells.**

   a. Change the text in the first cell of the table (the merged cell) to 14 points, bold, italic, yellow, and centered.

   b. Change the first cell in the second row (**Friday**) to 14 points, bold, and centered.

   c. Apply the formatting that you applied to the first cell in the second row to the rest of the cells in the second row. (*Hint*: You can use the Format Painter to copy and paste the formatting.)

   d. Save the page, preview and print the page in your browser, then close your browser.

8. **Apply an AutoFormat to a table.**

   a. Apply the Column 3 Table AutoFormat to the table.

   b. Save the page, preview and print the page using your browser, then close your browser.

   c. Close the menu Web site, then exit FrontPage.

▼ INDEPENDENT CHALLENGE 1

You work at Partners for Good Health, a professional association of physicians specializing in internal medicine and general practice. During the winter months, the office answers many calls a day from patients who are unsure about their symptoms and need to be diagnosed with a cold or the flu. Doctors prefer that patients with colds use over-the-counter medications and bed rest to treat their symptoms. Doctors usually want to see those patients with the flu because the flu can lead to serious complications, including pneumonia. The office manager asks you to prepare a Web page to be posted on the office's Web site so patients can use it as a resource for analyzing their illnesses and as a basis for making office appointments. Figure E-22 shows a sketch of the page that you will create.

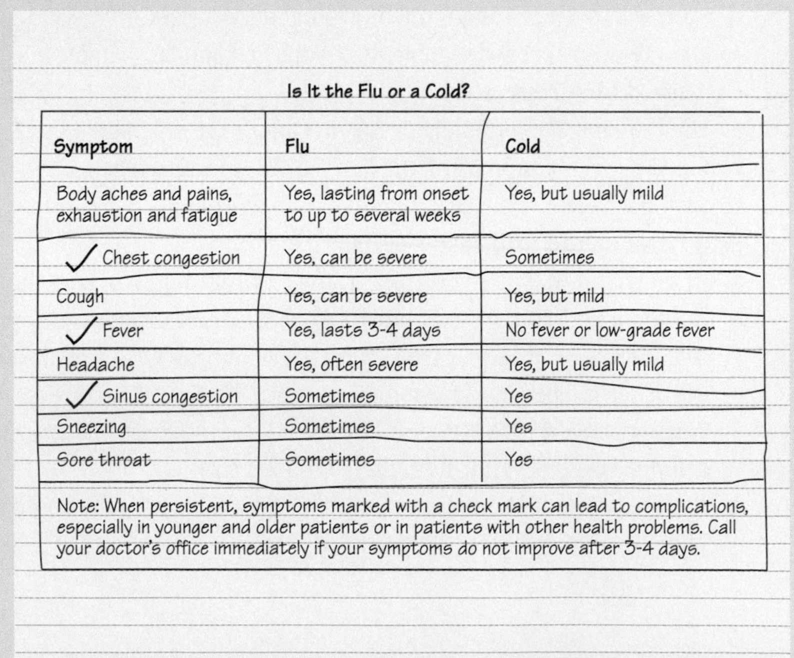

   a. Start FrontPage, then use the One Page Web Site template to create a new Web site named **health** in the location where your Web sites are stored.

FIGURE E-22

Is It the Flu or a Cold?

Symptom	Flu	Cold
Body aches and pains, exhaustion and fatigue	Yes, lasting from onset to up to several weeks	Yes, but usually mild
✓ Chest congestion	Yes, can be severe	Sometimes
Cough	Yes, can be severe	Yes, but mild
✓ Fever	Yes, lasts 3-4 days	No fever or low-grade fever
Headache	Yes, often severe	Yes, but usually mild
✓ Sinus congestion	Sometimes	Yes
Sneezing	Sometimes	Yes
Sore throat	Sometimes	Yes

Note: When persistent, symptoms marked with a check mark can lead to complications, especially in younger and older patients or in patients with other health problems. Call your doctor's office immediately if your symptoms do not improve after 3-4 days.

▼ INDEPENDENT CHALLENGE 1 (CONTINUED)

b. In Folders view, change the title of the home page (index.htm) to **Is It the Flu or a Cold?**

c. In Design view, create the table shown in Figure E-22, including the caption and formatting (bold text and center alignment). (*Note:* Your word wrap might differ.) The table is centered on the page, uses 95% of the width of the browser window, and has a cell padding value of 3 and a cell spacing value of 2. You can use any method for creating the table.

d. The picture is located in the UnitE\IC1 folder on the drive and folder where your Data Files are stored. Insert the picture saved as check.gif in the appropriate cells. Save the picture in the Web site's images folder.

e. Apply the Colorful 3 Table AutoFormat to the table. For cells with the darker background color applied to them, change the font color to white.

f. Save the page, preview and print the page in a browser, then close your browser.

g. Use FrontPage to print the HTML document for the page, close the health Web site, then exit FrontPage.

▼ INDEPENDENT CHALLENGE 2

When the Calendar and Officers pages in the Web site for the Villages at Kensington Neighbourhood Association were originally created, the author of these pages used the spacebar to create an effect to simulate columns of data. After examining these pages, you realize that a table would give you greater control over the format and alignment of this data. You decide to change the lists of information in these two pages to a table.

a. Start FrontPage, open the village Web site from the location where your Web sites are stored, then if necessary change to Folders view. (If you did not create and change this Web site in Units A through D, contact your instructor for assistance.)

b. Open the Calendar Web page in Design view. Notice that the data in the page appears in rows and columns, separated by multiple space characters.

c. Use the mouse to select the four paragraphs appearing in the document (beginning with **Date** on the first line and ending with **P.M.** on the last line), click Table on the menu bar, point to Convert, then click Text to Table.

d. In the Convert Text To Table dialog box, make sure that the Paragraphs option button is selected, then click OK. A table containing four rows and one column now holds the data.

e. Change the table's structure so the table has four rows and three columns. Each heading (**Date**, **Event**, and **Location/Time**) should appear in its own column. Use drag-and-drop or cut-and-paste to move the existing data in the remaining three rows in column 1 into the correct table cells, based on the column headings. If necessary, format the text in the first row in the Heading 2 style.

f. For each cell in the table, delete the extra space characters that appear at the end of the cell's contents. (*Hint:* You can press [End] to move to the end of the cell's contents and use [Backspace] as necessary to delete the extra spaces, or click at the end of the cell's contents and then press [Delete] multiple times.)

g. Change the table's properties so it is centered on the page, uses 85% of the browser window's width, has cell padding and cell spacing values of 3 each, and has a border size of 2. Make sure the table is set to collapse the table border.

h. Change the table's background color to light yellow (with a hex value of {FF, FF, CC}). (*Hint:* Click the Color list arrow in the Background section of the Table Properties dialog box, then use the More Colors dialog box to locate the correct light yellow color.)

i. Change the alignment of the cells in the first row to center. Then evenly distribute the columns in the table and reset the table's width to 85% of the browser window's width.

j. Save the Calendar Web page, preview and print the page in a browser, then close your browser.

k. Open the Officers Web page in Design view. Convert the data in the page to a table with five rows and three columns, and the same properties that you applied to the table in the Calendar Web page. The first row of the table (containing the data **The current officers are:**) should appear in a single cell that spans the width of the table. When you are finished, save the page, preview and print it in a browser, then close the browser.

l. Close the village Web site, then exit FrontPage.

▼ INDEPENDENT CHALLENGE 3

Nick Dye, the city manager of Tryon, North Carolina, is excited to see the Web site coming together. The site now includes pictures, a theme, and several pages of content. Nick wants to include some links to local campgrounds, hotels, and bed-and-breakfast inns to provide Web site visitors with information about these lodging options. He has gathered a list of camp-grounds and asks you to add this information to the Camping Web page. He will collect additional information for the Bed-and-Breakfast and Hotels Web pages so you can finish these pages later.

   a. Start FrontPage, open the tryon Web site from the location where your Web sites are stored, then if necessary change to Folders view. (If you did not create and change this Web site in Units A through D, contact your instructor for assistance.)

   b. Open the camping.htm page in Design view. On a new line below the existing paragraph, insert a table with four columns and three rows. Set the table's properties so the table uses 100% of the browser window's width, is centered on the page, has cell padding and cell spacing values of 2 each, and has a border size of 2. Make sure the table is set to collapse the table border.

   c. In the first row, insert the following data in the row's four cells: **Campground Name, Address, Phone Number, Pets Allowed?** Change these cells to bold and center alignment.

   d. In the second row of the table, enter the following data: **Saluda River Park, 53907 Saluda Highway, 828-555-5433, Yes**. In the third row of the table, enter the following data: **River Campground, 765 West Tryon Drive, 828-555-4577, Yes**.

   e. Insert a new column to the right of the Pets Allowed? column. Then insert the following data in each cell of the new column: **RV Hookup?, Yes, No**. Change the RV Hookup? text to bold and centered.

   f. Split the last row of the table into two rows, merge the cells in the new row, then type **This list is not complete; check back soon for updates.** Change the alignment of the text in the merged cell to centered, and change the font size of the text to 10 points.

   g. Apply a Table AutoFormat of your choice to the table. Make sure that the table's content is readable.

   h. Save the page, preview and print it in a browser, then close your browser.

   i. Close the tryon Web site, then exit FrontPage.

▼ INDEPENDENT CHALLENGE 4

Scoliosis is a condition that causes a side-to-side curvature of the spine. For many teenagers and adults, surgery is the only method to correct the spinal imbalance caused by these curves and to prevent further progression of the curve. Christine Cherico was diagnosed with adolescent idiopathic scoliosis at the age of 13. As a teenager and young adult, Christine did not have any problems as a result of her spinal curvature. However, for the past year she has had increasing pain and is considering spinal fusion surgery. She wants to gather as much information as possible about scoliosis to help her understand her options. To make this information available to other people with scoliosis, she decides to create a Web page with links to important sites. Organizing the links in a table will make it easy for others to use the page.

   a. Start FrontPage, use the One Page Web Site template to create a new Web site named **research** in the location where your Web sites are stored, then open the home page (index.htm) in Design view.

   b. Start your Web browser and use your favorite search engine to search for sites using the keyword **scoliosis**. Use the descriptions provided by the search engine to open sites from reputable sources, such as research institutions, hospitals, and national foundations. Identify four sites you think would be useful to people diagnosed with scoliosis.

   c. In Design view, add the title **Scoliosis Resources** at the top of the page, and then change this text to the Heading 1 style and center alignment.

   d. Insert a table with two columns and five rows in the page. Set the table's properties so it is 600 pixels wide and centered on the page. Choose the option to collapse the table border.

   e. In the first cell of the first row, type **Resource**. In the second cell of the first row, type **Description**.

f. In rows 2 through 5 of the table, type the name of a site you viewed in the Resource column and a brief description of the site in the Description column. Format the site's name as a hyperlink that opens the Web site's home page. (*Hint:* Copy the URL of each Web site that appears in the browser's address field, then paste it into the Insert Hyperlink dialog box.)

g. Add a Table AutoFormat of your choice to the table, then save the home page.

h. Preview the home page at 640 × 480 resolution and leave the browser window open. Then preview the home page at 800 × 600 resolution. What do you notice about the tables? Describe your findings and explain why the difference(s) occur.

i. In the 800 × 600 browser window, click the hyperlinks in the first column to open the home pages of the sites you selected. Use your browser's Back button to return to the research Web site. When you have examined each site, close the browser windows.

j. In Design view, type your name below the table, and then print the HTML document for the home page in FrontPage. Save the home page, close the research Web site, and then exit FrontPage.

▼ VISUAL WORKSHOP

Start FrontPage, then use the One Page Web Site template to create a new Web site named **zones** in the location where your Web sites are stored. Create the content for the home page (index.htm) shown in Figure E-23. Use Folders view to change the page's title. The pictures are saved as tomato.gif, jalapeno.gif, and cilantro.gif in the UnitE\VW folder on the drive and folder where your Data Files are stored. Use the skills you learned in this unit to create the table. (*Hint:* The table and each cell in the table use the centered alignment. The table's width is set to 90%. Use the previews to apply the correct Table AutoFormat.) When you are finished, save the pictures in the images folder, use FrontPage to print the HTML document for the page, preview the page in a browser and print it, close your browser, close the zones Web site, then exit FrontPage.

FIGURE E-23

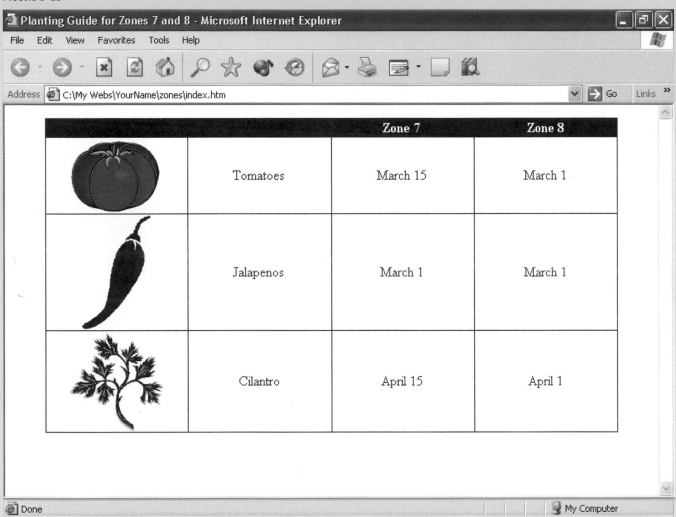

Creating a Frames Page

OBJECTIVES

Understand frames
Create a frames page using a template
Set pages to open in a frames page
Create a new page in a frames page
Set multiple pages to open in a frame
Create a new frame in a frames page
Delete a frame from a frames page
Set frame properties

Frames help you organize your Web site's content. A frames page contains two or more windows (or frames), each displaying a separate Web page. In addition, the Web page appearing in each frame can contain its own scroll bars, so users can scroll the pages that appear in the frames as necessary to view the content.  Jason Tanaka, manager of the Vail Valley Marathon, wants to change the page in the marathon Web site that identifies the marathon's sponsors so that each sponsor has a full page while the other sponsors' names remain visible. You will use a frames page to provide maximum visibility for the marathon's sponsors.

Understanding Frames

A **frames page**, or a **frameset**, is a single Web page that divides the browser window into two or more windows, each containing a separate, scrollable page. A frames page doesn't contain content—it contains only the specifications to create the frames within it. Figure F-1 shows a frames page in a browser. You use a frames page when you want each frame to display content independent of the other frames in the frames page. When you open a frames page in a browser, first the browser opens the frames page, then it opens the pages set to open in the individual frames. If the frames page contains three frames, your browser is really displaying four separate Web pages—the frames page and one page in each of the three frames. Before deciding to create a frames page in the marathon Web site, you need to consider the pros and cons of using frames pages in a Web site and learn more about frames page templates.

DETAILS

- ### Advantages of using frames pages in a Web site
  Displaying multiple pages at the same time in a frames page allows you to provide uniform information, such as navigation options, a company logo, or company information, in one frame while the contents of other frames change. Hyperlinks in one frame might link to other pages in the Web site; hyperlinks in another frame might open pages in a different frame. In addition, you can set a page displayed in a frame so that it never changes, such as when the page displays company and address information, thereby ensuring that this information is always visible. A frames page can load faster than a Web page that doesn't contain frames because the pages that open in a frames page usually do not use shared borders and other components that take more time to load.

- ### Disadvantages of using frames pages in a Web site
  Some browsers cannot display frames pages. If your site's potential users are using older browser versions that cannot display frames pages, you might change your Web site plan to avoid using them. Another option is to create an additional page for users who cannot view frames. FrontPage automatically displays a No Frames page in these situations, and you can add links to this page so users can access the pages contained in the frames page. Another concern when using frames pages is that the page in the main frame appears in less space than what is provided by a full browser window. As a result, if the page in the main frame contains a lot of text, your site's visitors might need to use the scroll bars to scroll the page's contents, which can be distracting. Finally, frames pages can be overwhelming to many Internet users. If a frames page is poorly designed, it can distract site visitors instead of help them navigate your Web site.

- ### Using frames page templates
  Figure F-2 shows an empty frames page created by the Nested Hierarchy frames page template, which is one of many frames page templates available in FrontPage. Although the number of frames and layouts created by each frames page template varies, the way you work with a frames page is consistent for all frames page templates. The frames page shown in Figure F-2 will have four pages associated with it: the frames page itself and one page appearing in each of its three frames.

  When a frame is selected, a blue border appears inside the frame's border. In Figure F-2, the frame on the left is selected. After creating the frames page, two buttons appear in each frame. The Set Initial Page button lets you set an existing Web page to open in the frame when the frames page opens in a browser. You use the New Page button to create a new page and at the same time set it to open in the frames page. Pages used in a frames page are just like any other Web pages that you might create, but most are designed to be used only in the frames page. Each Web page appearing in a frames page has a filename and a title, just like any other Web page, but only the title of the frames page appears in the browser's title bar when the frames page is open.

  When the content of a Web page displayed in a frame exceeds the space available, scroll bars appear on the frame, allowing users to scroll the page in the frame just like any other Web page. Scrolling the page in one frame doesn't affect the pages in the other frames.

FIGURE F-1: Frames page in a browser

Frames page title

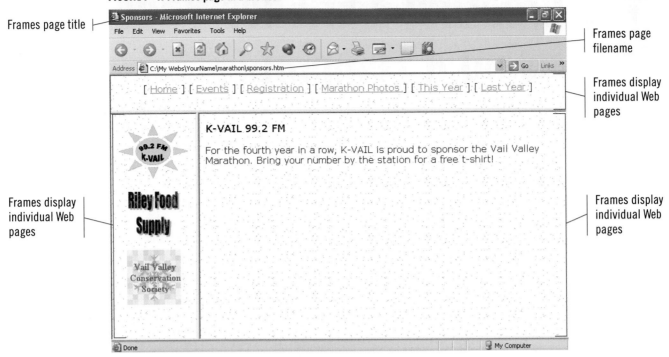

Frames page filename

Frames display individual Web pages

Frames display individual Web pages

Frames display individual Web pages

FIGURE F-2: Frames page created by the Nested Hierarchy frames page template

Selected frame

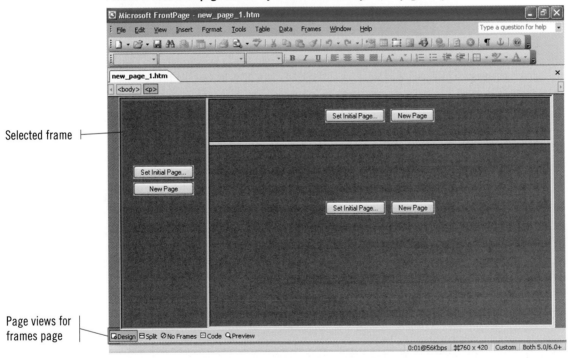

Page views for frames page

Clues to Use

Creating "No Frames" pages for browsers that can't display frames

When a browser cannot display a frames page, it displays a page without frames that contains a message. When you create a frames page in FrontPage, FrontPage automatically creates a **No Frames page**, which by default provides a message that says "This page uses frames, but your browser doesn't support them." You can change the information in the No Frames page by clicking the Show No Frames View button at the bottom of the Contents pane and then editing the existing message or creating a new one. You can also create hyperlinks from the No Frames page to open the individual pages contained in the frames page in a full browser window.

Creating a Frames Page Using a Template

The easiest and fastest way to include a frames page in a Web site is to create it using a template. A **frames page template** is a Web page that contains the specifications for the individual locations and sizes of the frames in a frames page. When you create a frames page using a template, FrontPage assigns each frame in the page a name (such as "top" or "contents") and creates its initial size and location in the frames page. FrontPage includes many different frames page templates to create frames pages with two, three, and four frames. The templates include different orientations for the frames. For example, some frames pages contain frames arranged vertically or horizontally in the frames page or a combination of both. You should select the frames page template that most closely matches the arrangement of information you have planned.  You want to include some promotional material for each of the marathon's three main sponsors. You decide to present this information using a frames page.

STEPS

1. **Start** FrontPage, **open the** marathon **Web site from the location where your Web sites are stored, then if necessary change to Folders view**

2. **Click** View **on the menu bar, click** Task Pane, **click the** Other Task Panes list arrow, **then click** New

---
TROUBLE

Your list of frames page templates in the Page Templates dialog box might differ.

---

3. **In the New page section of the New task pane, click** More page templates, **then in the Page Templates dialog box click the** Frames Pages tab

   The Frames Pages tab shows the available frames page templates. When you select an icon, its description and preview appear on the right, as shown in Figure F-3. Each gray box in the preview represents a frame.

4. **Click each template icon on the Frames Pages tab to view its description and preview**

   Some of the templates provide frames arranged vertically, horizontally, or both.

QUICK TIP

You'll set the pages that open in the frames in the next lesson.

---

5. **Click the** Banner and Contents template icon, **then click** OK

   A new Web page is created using the Banner and Contents frames page template, as shown in Figure F-4. The buttons at the bottom of the Contents pane display options for frames pages. The Show Design View button lets you edit the frames page. The Show Split View button shows the HTML document for the frames page and the frames page in Design view at the same time. The Show No Frames View button displays the No Frames page, the Show Code View button displays the HTML document for the frames page, and the Show Preview View button shows the frames page in Preview view.

QUICK TIP

The title you set for a frames page appears in the browser's title bar when the frames page appears in a browser.

---

6. **Click the** Save button 🔲 **on the Standard toolbar**

   The Save As dialog box opens, as shown in Figure F-5. The thick, dark blue border around the frames page indicates that you will be saving the frames page and not a page in a frame. The default filename is selected in the File name text box.

7. **Type** sponsors.htm

8. **Click** Change title, **type** Sponsors **in the Page title text box, then click** OK

9. **Click** Save, **then click** Yes **to replace the file**

   The frames page is saved using the filename sponsors.htm and the title "Sponsors," overwriting the existing version of the Sponsors page in the Web site.

FIGURE F-3: Frames page templates

Selected frames page template icon

Description of selected template

Preview of selected template

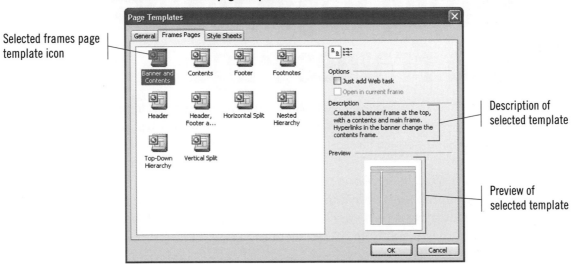

FIGURE F-4: Frames page created using the Banner and Contents frames page template

Banner frame

Contents frame

Main frame

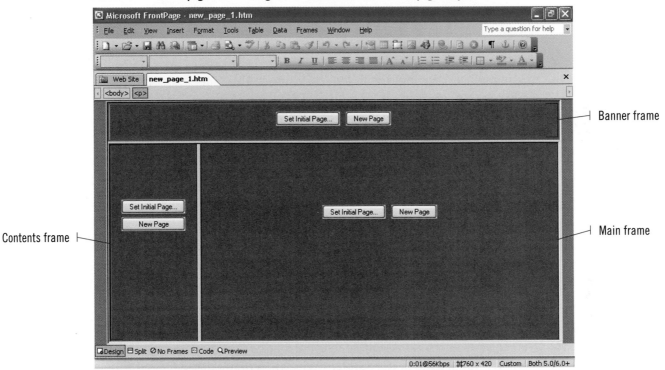

FIGURE F-5: Save As dialog box

Default page title

Thick, dark blue border indicates that you are saving the frames page

Opens the Change title dialog box

Default filename

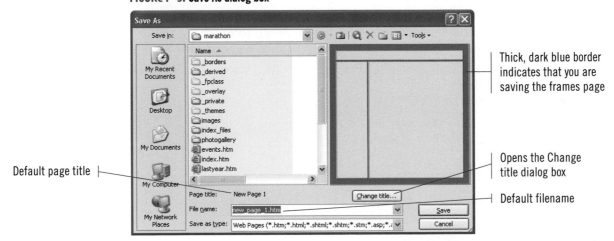

FrontPage 2003

Setting Pages to Open in a Frames Page

When you create a frames page, each frame contains two buttons: Set Initial Page and New Page. You click the Set Initial Page button in the desired frame to open an existing Web page in the frame. You click the New Page button in the desired frame when you want to create a new Web page in a frame. Because the pages that open in a frames page are often developed with the sole purpose of appearing in a frames page, you usually don't add pages appearing in a frames page to the Web site's navigation structure. However, you can add a frames page to the navigation structure when you want to include the frames page in the Web site's components that are dependent on Navigation view, such as shared borders or link bars. Jason has provided you with pages to use in two of the three frames in the frames page. You need to set these pages to open in the appropriate frames.

STEPS

1. **Click in the contents frame (but not a button in the contents frame) to select it**

   As shown in Figure F-6, a dark blue border appears inside the contents frame, indicating that it is selected.

QUICK TIP

You can also select sequentially listed files by clicking the first file in the list, pressing and holding [Shift], clicking the last file in the list, then releasing [Shift].

2. **Turn on the Folder List and make sure the Web site's root folder is selected, click File on the menu bar, click Import, click Add File, open the UnitF folder on the drive and folder where your Data Files are stored, press and hold [Ctrl], click banner.htm, contents.htm, kvail.gif, riley.gif, riley_pg.htm, vvcs_pg.htm, and vvcs_sm.gif, release [Ctrl], click Open, click OK, then click kvail.gif in the Folder List**

3. **With kvail.gif selected, press and hold [Ctrl], click riley.gif, click vvcs_sm.gif, release [Ctrl], then drag the selected files to the images folder in the Folder List; when the pointer changes to ⚓, release the mouse button**

   The three picture files are moved to the images folder, where all picture files for the marathon Web site are stored.

4. **Close the Folder List**

5. **Click Set Initial Page in the contents frame**

   The Insert Hyperlink dialog box opens. To open a page in a frame, you create a hyperlink to it.

6. **Double-click contents.htm in the list**

   You set the contents.htm page to open in the contents frame, as shown in Figure F-7. This frame now contains a logo for each of the marathon's three major sponsors.

7. **Click Set Initial Page in the banner frame, then double-click banner.htm in the list**

   The Banner page opens in the banner frame. It contains a link bar with hyperlinks to child pages of the home page.

8. **Click the Save button 🖫 on the Standard toolbar**

   FrontPage saves the frames page, which now contains the specifications that open the banner.htm and contents.htm pages in the banner and contents frames. You will set the content of the main frame in another lesson.

FIGURE F-6: Contents frame selected

Dark blue border indicates a selected frame

Banner frame

Contents frame

Main frame

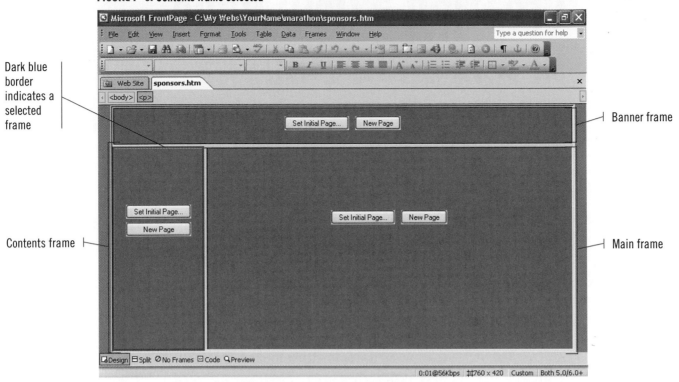

FIGURE F-7: Web page in the contents frame

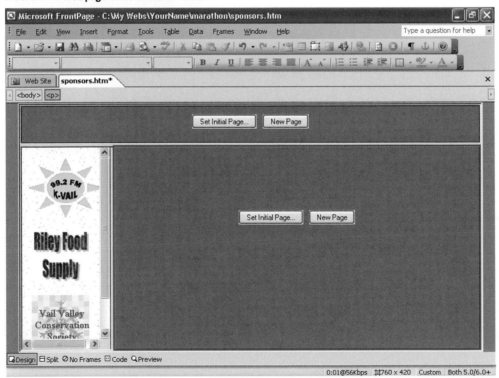

Creating a New Page in a Frames Page

When you open the frames page in a browser, the browser opens a page in each frame. For example, when the Sponsors frames page is opened in a browser, the banner frame is set to display the banner.htm page and the contents frame is set to display the contents.htm page. The initial page that opens in each frame might be one that already exists in your Web site, or it might be a new page that you create. Creating a new page in a frames page is similar to creating other pages in a Web site. When you use the New Page button to create a new page in a frame, you must save the page with a filename and a page title, just like you do when creating other pages. A new page that you create and set to open in a frames page appears in the Folder List with other pages. You need to create a new page for K-VAIL, a local radio station. You will set this page to open initially in the third frame of the frames page, the main frame.

STEPS

1. **Click** New Page **in the main frame**

   A new page opens in the main frame. The page uses the background picture from the Web site's theme.

2. **Click the** Style list arrow **on the Formatting toolbar, then click** Heading 3

3. **Type** K-VAIL 99.2 FM, **then press** [Enter]

   The text uses the Heading 3 style from the theme.

4. **Type** For the fourth year in a row, K-VAIL is proud to sponsor the Vail Valley Marathon. Bring your number by the station for a free t-shirt!

   The page now contains a heading and text, as shown in Figure F-8.

5. **Click the** Save button ⊞ **on the Standard toolbar**

   The Save As dialog box opens. As shown in Figure F-9, the main frame is dark blue in the sample frames page, identifying the page you are saving. The Save command will save this page in the Web site and also will save the Sponsors frames page. If you had made other changes to the pages in the other frames, those pages would be saved as well.

6. **If necessary, select the text in the File name text box, type** k-vail_pg.htm, **click** Change title, **type** K-VAIL, **click** OK, **then click** Save

   The K-VAIL Web page is saved in the marathon Web site, as is the Sponsors frames page. Now the Sponsors frames page is set to open a Web page in each of its three frames.

FIGURE F-8: New Web page created in the main frame

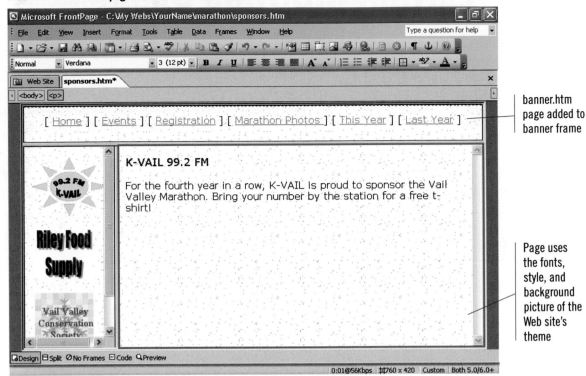

banner.htm page added to banner frame

Page uses the fonts, style, and background picture of the Web site's theme

FIGURE F-9: Saving a new Web page

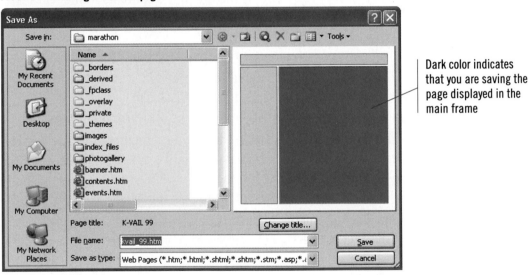

Dark color indicates that you are saving the page displayed in the main frame

---

Clues to Use

Saving multiple pages in a frames page

The steps in this lesson teach you how to create and save a single page in a single frame. You can also create new pages in two or more frames without having to save the frames page between creating the new pages. If you create more than one new page in a frames page, clicking Save opens the Save As dialog box. One of the frames in the Save As dialog box will be a darker color, indicating the page that you are saving. For the selected page, type a filename

in the File name text box, click Change title and type the page's title, click OK, then click Save. FrontPage saves the page and keeps the Save As dialog box open, but now the sample frames page in the dialog box changes the color of the next page you are saving to dark blue. Repeat the steps to save the second new page. After you have saved all of the new pages that you created in the frames page, the Save As dialog box closes.

Setting Multiple Pages to Open in a Frame

When creating a hyperlink in a frames page, you need to decide how to open the link's target page. You can set a link in any frame to open a new page in the same frame, in a different frame, in a new browser window, or in the same browser window (which replaces the frames page). When you set a link's target page to open in a frame, you are setting a frame target, or a target frame. A **target frame** is the frame in which to open a new Web page. Table F-1 describes some common frame targets you can use. ▰▰▰ The contents frame contains the logos of sponsors of the Vail Valley Marathon. You want Web site visitors to be able to read more about each sponsor by clicking a logo. To accomplish this goal, you decide to create a hyperlink from each picture in the contents frame to open its corresponding page in the main frame.

STEPS

QUICK TIP

Links in a contents frame usually open pages in the main frame of the frames page.

1. **Click the K-VAIL picture in the contents frame to select it, click the Insert Hyperlink button 🖳 on the Standard toolbar, when the Insert Hyperlink dialog box opens click k-vail_pg.htm (open) in the list box, then click Target Frame**

   The Target Frame dialog box opens, as shown in Figure F-10. The target "Page Default (main)" is already selected in the Common targets list box.

2. **Click OK, then click OK in the Insert Hyperlink dialog box**

   The K-VAIL picture is a hyperlink that opens the target page (k-vail_pg.htm) in the main frame.

QUICK TIP

By default, FrontPage configures hyperlinks created in the contents frame to open target files in the main frame, but it's still a good idea to check the settings.

3. **Click the Riley Food Supply picture in the contents frame, click 🖳, scroll down the list of files and click riley_pg.htm, click Target Frame, make sure Page Default (main) is selected, click OK, then click OK**

   The Riley Food Supply picture is a hyperlink that opens the target page (riley_pg.htm) in the main frame.

4. **Click the Vail Valley Conservation Society picture in the contents frame, then repeat Step 3 to set it to open the vvcs_pg.htm file in the main frame**

   Each picture is a hyperlink that opens its target page in the main frame.

QUICK TIP

Links in a banner frame usually open pages in a full browser window, replacing the frames page.

5. **Click the Save button 🖫 on the Standard toolbar, click the Preview button 🔍 on the Standard toolbar, click each picture in the contents frame, then click the Registration hyperlink in the banner frame**

   The Registration page replaces the frames page, which is the action that you want to occur.

6. **Click the Sponsors hyperlink, then click the Home hyperlink in the banner frame**

   As shown in Figure F-11, the Home hyperlink isn't set correctly.

7. **Close your browser, right-click the Home hyperlink in the banner frame, click Hyperlink Properties on the shortcut menu, then click Target Frame**

   As shown in Figure F-12, the contents frame is the current target of the Home hyperlink.

8. **Click Whole Page in the Common targets list box, click OK, then click OK again**

9. **Click 🖫, click 🔍, then click the Home hyperlink**

   The Home hyperlink now correctly closes the frames page and opens the home page.

FIGURE F-10: Target Frame dialog box

Clicking a frame in the Current frames page section sets that frame as the target

Name of target frame appears here when you select a target frame

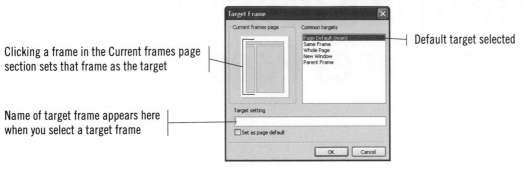

Default target selected

FIGURE F-11: Sponsors page in a browser

Home hyperlink in the banner frame

Home page incorrectly opening in the contents frame instead of in the full browser window

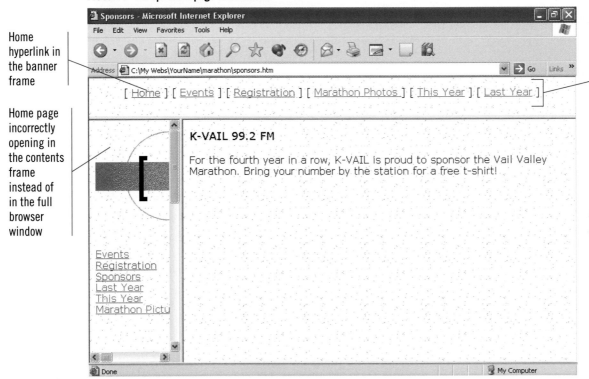

Hyperlinks in the banner frame should close the frames page and open pages in the same browser window

FIGURE F-12: Target for the Home hyperlink in the banner frame

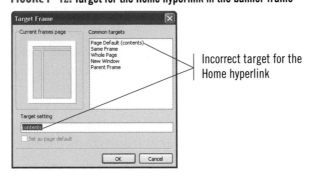

Incorrect target for the Home hyperlink

TABLE F-1: Common frame targets

frame target	description
Page Default *(frame name)*	The target of the hyperlink is the default frame specified by the frames page template, where *frame name* indicates the frame in which to open the page
Same Frame	The target of the hyperlink opens in the same frame as the page containing the hyperlink
Whole Page	The target of the hyperlink replaces the frames page and opens in a full browser window
New Window	The target of the hyperlink opens the page in a new browser window

Creating a New Frame in a Frames Page

After you create a frames page, you might need to create another frame in it. For example, you might add a small frame to contain a company logo or name. When you need to create a new frame in a frames page, you can **split** an existing frame into two frames. You can split frames horizontally or vertically, depending on your needs. ▰▰▰ Jason wants the Vail Valley Marathon logo to appear at the top of the frames page. Instead of adding it to the page in the banner frame, you decide to split the banner frame to create a new frame. In the new frame, you will create a page containing the logo.

STEPS

TROUBLE

You might not see the blue border unless you first click in another frame and then click in the banner frame.

1. **Close your browser**

2. **If necessary, click in the banner frame to select it**
   The banner frame is selected, as indicated by its dark blue border.

QUICK TIP

To resize a frame, click and drag its border to the new location.

3. **Press and hold [Ctrl], position the pointer on the left border of the banner frame so it changes to ◄──►, hold down the mouse button and drag the left border to the right (see Figure F-13), release the mouse button, then release [Ctrl]**
   A new frame is created in the upper-left corner of the frames page, as shown in Figure F-13.

4. **Click New Page in the new frame, click the Insert Picture From File button 🖼 on the Standard toolbar, if necessary open the images folder of the marathon Web site, then double-click vvm_logo.gif**
   The picture is inserted in the new frame.

5. **Click the picture in the new frame, use the scroll bars as needed and the pointer to reduce the picture's size (see Figure F-14), click the Picture Actions button 🖳, then click the Resample Picture To Match Size option button**
   As shown in Figure F-14, the picture fits in the frame.

QUICK TIP

A Web site can have multiple pages with the same page title, but Web pages cannot have the same filenames unless they are saved in different folders within the Web site.

6. **Click the Save button 💾 on the Standard toolbar, save the new page as vvm.htm and with the title Vail Valley Marathon Logo, then if necessary click OK to overwrite the vvm_logo.gif picture in the images folder**

7. **Click the Preview button 🔍 on the Standard toolbar**
   The Sponsors frames page now contains the new frame.

FIGURE F-13: New frame added to frames page

In Step 3, drag pointer to here

New frame

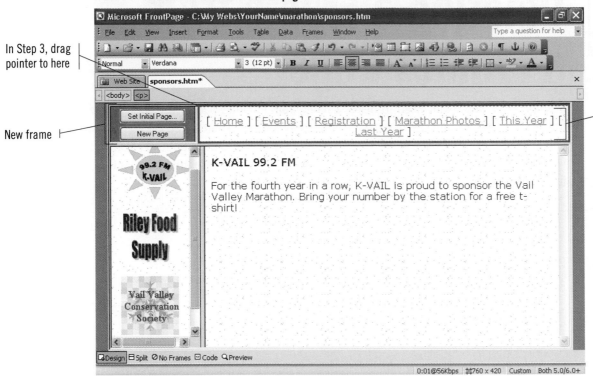

Banner frame is narrower to make room for the new frame

FIGURE F-14: Picture added to new frame

Resized and resampled picture

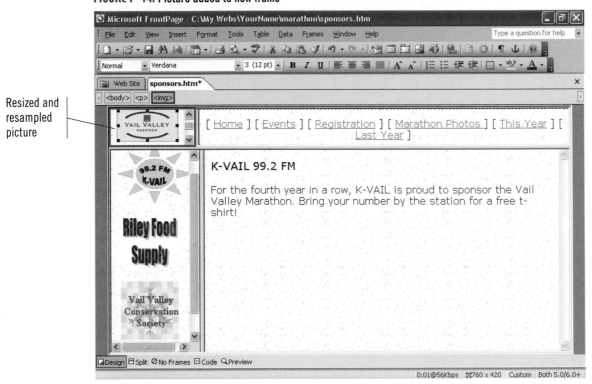

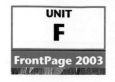

Deleting a Frame from a Frames Page

In some cases, you might need to delete a frame from a frames page. When you delete a frame from a frames page, you are only deleting the HTML tag that *creates* the frame. You are not deleting the Web page that appears in the frame. If you need to delete the page itself, you must do so in Folders view. ▒▒▒▒▒ After viewing the frames page in a browser, Jason decides the Vail Valley Marathon logo is too small to be effective. He asks you to delete the frame that holds the logo and its file.

STEPS

1. **Close your browser**

2. **If necessary, click in the frame in the upper-left corner to select it**

3. **Click Frames on the menu bar**
   The Frames menu, as shown in Figure F-15, contains options for working with frames. Table F-2 provides a description of the Frames menu commands.

4. **Click Delete Frame**
   The frame is deleted from the frames page. The banner frame, which is the frame that you split to create the deleted frame, returns to its original size automatically.

5. **Click the Save button 🖫 on the Standard toolbar**
   FrontPage saves the revisions to the frames page, which once again contains three frames.

6. **Click the Web Site tab at the top of the Contents pane**
   The Vail Valley Marathon Logo page still exists in the marathon Web site, even though you deleted the frame that contained this page from the frames page.

7. **Right-click vvm.htm in the Contents pane, click Delete on the shortcut menu, then click Yes**
   The Vail Valley Marathon Logo Web page is deleted from the marathon Web site.

TABLE F-2: Frames menu commands

command	description
Split Frame	Opens a dialog box in which you can split a selected frame into rows or columns, instead of using the mouse
Delete Frame	Deletes the currently selected frame from the frames page, but does not delete the page displayed in that frame from the Web site
Open Page in New Window	Opens the Web page in the selected frame as a regular Web page, without the frames page
Save Page	Saves the Web page in the currently selected frame, without saving any changes that you may have made to the frames page itself
Save Page As	Saves the Web page in the currently selected frame using a different filename
Frame Properties	Opens the Frame Properties dialog box, which contains options for setting the frame's size, initial page, and other options

FIGURE F-15: Frames menu for the selected frame

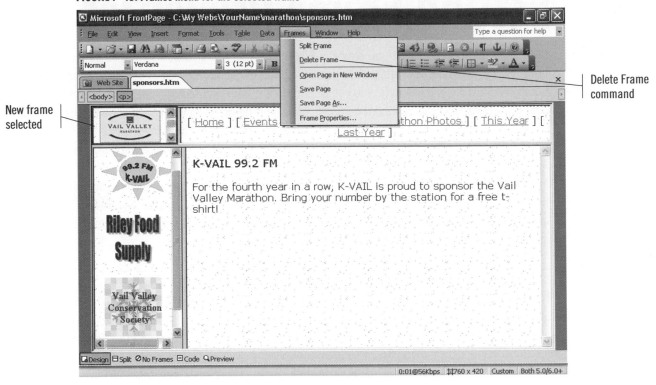

New frame selected

Delete Frame command

Printing a frames page in a browser

As you browse the Internet, you'll visit many Web sites that use frames pages to organize the way that you view Web pages. Printing a frames page is different from printing a Web page that does not use frames. Each browser handles printing a frames page differently. In Internet Explorer, you have the option of printing the page as it appears in the browser, printing only the page displayed in the selected frame, or printing the page in each frame on a separate sheet of paper. To print a frames page in these different ways, click the Print command on the File menu, which opens a Print dialog box similar to the one shown in Figure F-16. (Your dialog box might look different.)

There are two other options in the Internet Explorer Print dialog box that you might find useful when printing Web pages. If you add a check mark to the Print all linked documents check box, you will print the page that appears in the browser window and all pages that are linked to that page. For example, you might print the home page and all pages that open using links on the home page. Use this option carefully, however, as some pages contain many links. If you

add a check mark to the Print table of links check box, you will print the page that appears in the browser window and a separate sheet that lists all of the documents that are linked to that page.

FIGURE F-16: Print dialog box in Internet Explorer

Setting Frame Properties

Just like any other object that you create in FrontPage, you can change the properties and behavior of a frames page and its frames: You can change the default frame name (such as contents, banner, or main) to make it easier for you to identify, you can set a different Web page to open in the frame when the frames page first opens, you can change the frame's width and height, and you can change the frame's margins. The **frame margin** is the amount of space between the inside border of the frame and the text or picture(s) in the frame. The default setting for a frame is to permit users to resize the frame in the browser by dragging the frame's border with the pointer. You can turn off this option using the Frame Properties dialog box for the selected frame. You can also set the frames page so it does not display borders. Finally, you have three options for displaying the scroll bars in a frame: If Needed, Never, and Always. ▓▓▓▓ You change the Sponsors frames page to hide its borders. In addition, you set the k-vail_pg.htm page so the scroll bar never appears in the browser.

STEPS

1. **Click the** sponsors.htm tab, **select the** contents frame, **click** Frames **on the menu bar, then click** Frame Properties

   As shown in Figure F-17, the Frame Properties dialog box opens. Some settings in this dialog box affect only the selected frame; others affect each frame in the frames page.

   QUICK TIP
   You should turn off the display of scroll bars in a frame only when you are certain that users won't need to scroll the page.

2. **Click the** Show scrollbars list arrow, **click** Never, **then click** OK

   The vertical scroll bar no longer appears in the contents frame.

3. **Select the** main frame, **click** Frames **on the menu bar, then click** Frame Properties

   The Frame Properties dialog box opens again. The Initial page text box shows the k-vail_pg.htm page, which confirms that the K-VAIL Web page opens in the main frame when the frames page opens.

4. **Click** Frames Page, **then if necessary click the** Frames tab

   The Page Properties dialog box opens, as shown in Figure F-18. The Show Borders check box is selected, which means that the borders between frames will show up in the browser.

5. **Click the** Show Borders check box **to clear it**

   The Frame Spacing value automatically changes to zero because the frame's borders will no longer be displayed. **Frame spacing** is the thickness of the frame's borders when they appear in the frames page. Increasing the frame spacing value creates a thicker border.

   QUICK TIP
   When you select a frame with hidden borders in Design view, the dark blue border appears around the frame.

6. **Click** OK, **then click** OK **in the Frame Properties dialog box**

   The frames page now has hidden frame borders.

7. **Click the** Save button 💾 **on the Standard toolbar, then click the** Preview button 🔍 **on the Standard toolbar**

   The completed frames page opens in the browser, as shown in Figure F-19.

8. **Use the links in the contents and banner frames to navigate the Web site**

   The links in the contents frame open pages in the main frame; the links in the banner frame open pages in the full browser window. Clicking the Sponsors hyperlink in pages appearing in the full browser window opens the frames page again.

9. **Close your browser and the marathon Web site, then exit FrontPage**

FIGURE F-17: Frame Properties dialog box

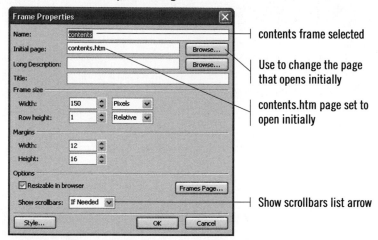

contents frame selected

Use to change the page that opens initially

contents.htm page set to open initially

Show scrollbars list arrow

FIGURE F-18: Frames tab of the Page Properties dialog box

Deselect to change the frames page to use invisible borders

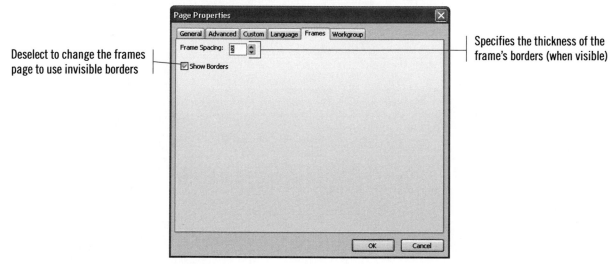

Specifies the thickness of the frame's borders (when visible)

FIGURE F-19: Completed frames page

Frame borders are hidden

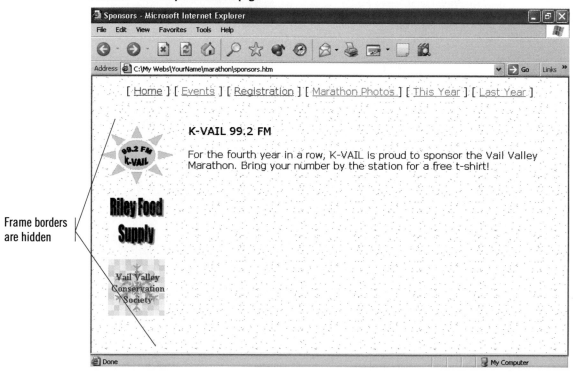

FrontPage 2003

Practice

▼ CONCEPTS REVIEW

Label each element in the Microsoft FrontPage window shown in Figure F-20.

FIGURE F-20

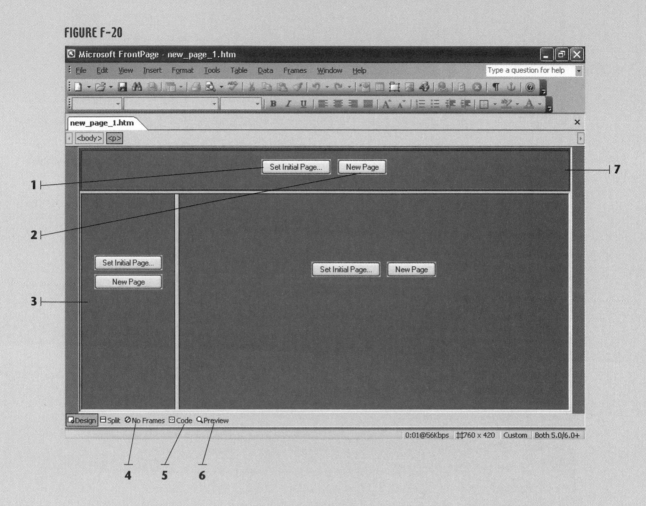

Match each of the following terms with the statement that best describes its function.

8. **Frame margin**

9. **Frame spacing**

10. **No Frames page**

11. **Set Initial Page**

12. **Target frame**

a. A Web page that opens when a user's browser cannot display a frames page

b. The amount of space between the inside border of a frame and the text or picture in the frame

c. The frame in which a corresponding hyperlink opens

d. The thickness of a frame's borders

e. The button you click to specify the page in a Web site that should open in a frame in a frames page

Select the best answer from the list of choices.

13. **An advantage of using a frames page is:**
    a. It provides a way to display two or more Web pages at the same time.
    b. It provides an efficient way to display long Web pages containing a lot of text.
    c. It lets you keep some information readily visible in one frame while information in another frame changes.
    d. Both a and c are correct

14. **When a frames page with two frames appears in the browser, how many pages is the browser displaying?**
    a. One
    b. Two
    c. Three
    d. Four

15. **To view the HTML document for a frames page in FrontPage, change to _____ view.**
    a. Design
    b. No Frames
    c. Code
    d. Preview

16. **How can you tell when a frame is selected in Design view?**
    a. Its border is gray.
    b. Its border is blue.
    c. Its content is selected.
    d. Its HTML document appears in the frame.

17. **In frames pages created by the Banner and Contents frames page template, hyperlinks in the banner frame usually open Web pages in the:**
    a. Contents frame.
    b. Main frame.
    c. Banner frame.
    d. Full browser window, outside the frames page.

18. **In frames pages created by the Banner and Contents frames page template, hyperlinks in the contents frame usually open Web pages in the:**
    a. Contents frame.
    b. Main frame.
    c. Banner frame.
    d. Full browser window, outside the frames page.

19. **Which of the following targets starts a second browser window in which to open Web pages?**
    a. Same Frame
    b. Whole Page
    c. New Window
    d. Page Default

20. **Frame spacing is:**
    a. The amount of space between the frame's border and the content of the frame.
    b. The amount of space that appears between frames in a frames page.
    c. The thickness of the frame's borders.
    d. None of the above

▼ SKILLS REVIEW

1. **Create a frames page using a template.**
   a. Start FrontPage, then use the Empty Web Site template to create a new Web site named **rates** in the location where your Web sites are stored.
   b. Create a new frames page using the Contents frames page template. In this frames page, the frame on the left is the contents frame and the frame on the right is the main frame.
   c. Save the frames page as **rates.htm** and with the title **Seasonal Rates**.
   d. Select the main frame.

2. **Set pages to open in a frames page.**
   a. Import the weekday.htm file from the UnitF\SR folder on the drive and folder where your Data Files are stored into the root folder of the rates Web site.
   b. In the main frame, set the weekday.htm page to open initially.
   c. Save the frames page.

▼ SKILLS REVIEW (CONTINUED)

3. **Create a new page in a frames page.**
   a. In the contents frame, create a new page.
   b. Type **Weekday Rates** on the first line of the new page. Press [Enter], then type **Weekend Rates**.
   c. Save the new page as **contents.htm** and with the title **Contents**.

4. **Set multiple pages to open in a frame.**
   a. In the contents frame, select the text **Weekday Rates**.
   b. Create a hyperlink from the selected text to open the weekday.htm page in the main frame.
   c. Create a new normal Web page, then type **Weekend Rates** on the first line, change this text to the Heading 1 style and to center alignment, and then on a new left-aligned line, type **The nightly rate for Friday, Saturday, and Sunday is $199.99**. Save this page as **weekend.htm** and with the title **Weekend Rates**, then close the page.
   d. Create a hyperlink using the **Weekend Rates** text in the contents frame to open the weekend.htm page in the main page.

5. **Create a new frame in a frames page.**
   a. Use the pointer to split the contents frame at the bottom to create a new frame in the lower-left corner of the frames page. The new frame should be approximately two inches high.
   b. Create a new page in the new frame. In the new page, type **THE DUNES** on the first line and **888-555-3822** on the second line. Save the new page as **dunes.htm** and with the title **The Dunes**.
   c. Use the pointer to split the contents frame at the top to create a new frame in the upper-left corner of the frames page. The new frame should be approximately two inches high.
   d. Create a new page in the new frame. In the new page, type **Always fun in the sun!**
   e. Save the new page as **sun.htm** and with the title **Our Motto**.

6. **Delete a frame from a frames page.**
   a. If necessary, select the frame containing the sun.htm page.
   b. Delete the selected frame.
   c. In Folders view, delete the sun.htm page from the Web site.
   d. Save the frames page.

7. **Set frame properties.**
   a. Change the properties of each frame so that it never displays scroll bars.
   b. For the frames page, change the frame spacing value to **6**. (*Hint:* With the Frame Properties dialog box open for any selected frame, click Frames Page. You only need to set this property once.)
   c. Save the frames page and then preview it in a browser.
   d. Use the browser to print the frames page as it appears with the Weekend Rates page displayed in the main frame.
   e. Close your browser and the rates Web site, then exit FrontPage.

▼ INDEPENDENT CHALLENGE 1

Ella Jacobsen is the director and owner of a preschool. She wants to use her Web site to provide parents with information about state-mandated tests for three- and four-year-old children who attend the preschool. She asks you to help her create a frames page to make it easy for parents to get the information they need by selecting a link corresponding to the child's age. After you create the frames page, Ella will provide the content. For now you enter placeholder text so she can preview the page's appearance.

   a. Start FrontPage, then use the Empty Web Site template to create a new Web site named **school** in the location where your Web sites are stored.
   b. Use the Vertical Split frames page template to create a new Web page. Save the frames page using the filename **tests.htm** and the title **Tests for Preschool Children**.
   c. In the left frame, create a new Web page. In this page, type the following information on separate lines: **Required tests for three-year-old children** and **Required tests for four-year-old children**.
   d. In the right frame, create a new Web page. In this page, type **Hearing and vision tests are required by law.**

e. Save the page in the left frame as **ages.htm** and with the title **Ages**, and save the page in the right frame as **threes.htm** and with the title **Three-Year-Olds**. (*Hint:* You are prompted to save each new Web page. Click Save after saving the first page, enter the filename and the title for the second page, then click Save again to save the second page. The dark blue frame in the preview identifies which page you are saving.)

f. Click the Create a new normal page button on the Standard toolbar. In the new page that opens, type **Speech tests, vision screening, and hearing tests are required.** Save the page with the filename **fours.htm** and the title **Four-Year-Olds**, then close the page.

g. In the left frame, create a hyperlink for the **Required tests for three-year-old children** text that opens the threes.htm page in the right frame. (*Hint:* To set a page to open in the right frame, click the right frame in the Current frames page section. FrontPage displays **right** in the Target setting text box after you select the right frame.)

h. In the left frame, create a hyperlink for the **Required tests for four-year-old children** text that opens the fours.htm page in the right frame.

i. Use the pointer to decrease the width of the left frame by approximately 50%.

j. Create a new frame in the upper-left corner of the frames page by splitting the left frame. The frame should be approximately one inch high and contain a new page with the text **River Valley Preschool**.

k. Save the frames page, then save the page in the new frame using the filename **river.htm** and with the title **River Valley Preschool**.

l. Preview the frames page in a browser, test the hyperlinks, then print the frames page as displayed by the browser with the fours.htm page appearing in the right frame. Close your browser.

m. Delete the frame that contains the name of the preschool, save your changes, then print the HTML document for the frames page.

n. Close the school Web site, then exit FrontPage.

▼ INDEPENDENT CHALLENGE 2

After evaluating the Web site for the Villages at Kensington Neighbourhood Association, you decide to convert the Deed Restrictions Web page to a frames page, where each major topic included in the longer Deed Restrictions Web page appears as its own page in the main frame of the frames page. There are five sections in the current Deed Restrictions Web page: Dwellings, Fences, Nuisances, Vehicles, and Other. The content in the original Deed Restrictions Web page has been used to create separate Web pages for each section. These Web pages have been saved as dwelling.htm, fences.htm, nuisance.htm, vehicles.htm, and other.htm. Now you need to create the frames page, replace the existing restrict.htm page in the Web site, and set the frame's properties and hyperlink targets.

a. Start FrontPage, open the village Web site from the location where your Web sites are stored, then if necessary change to Folders view. (If you did not create and change this Web site in Units A through E, contact your instructor for assistance.)

b. Import into the root folder of the village Web site the files dwelling.htm, fences.htm, nuisance.htm, other.htm, and vehicles.htm from the UnitF\IC2 folder on the drive and folder where your Data Files are stored.

c. Create a new Web page using the Banner and Contents frames page template. Save the frames page as **restrict.htm** and with the title **Deed Restrictions**. Click Yes to replace the existing restrict.htm Web page.

d. In the main frame, set the dwelling.htm page to open initially.

e. In the contents frame, create a new Web page that contains hyperlinks to each of the pages that will open in the main frame (Dwellings, Fences, Nuisances, Vehicles, and Other). Set these hyperlinks to open the correct page in the main frame. Save the new Web page as **contents.htm** and with the title **Contents**.

f. In the banner frame, create a new Web page that contains hyperlinks to the following pages in the village Web site: Home, Calendar, News, Officers, Canada Day Picnic, and Pool News. Enclose each link in square brackets ([and]). All links should appear on one single, centered line separated by one space. Set these hyperlinks to open the correct page in the full browser window. (*Hint:* You will need to create these hyperlinks manually; do not create a FrontPage link bar component for this purpose.) Save the new Web page as **banner.htm** and using the title **Banner**.

▼ INDEPENDENT CHALLENGE 2 (CONTINUED)

g. Examine the frames page and decide whether you need to resize any of the frames. If so, use the pointer to resize the frames and then save the frames page.

h. Change the properties of the contents and banner frames so they never display scroll bars.

i. Change the frame spacing value for the frames page to 4.

j. Save the frames page, preview it in a browser, and then test your hyperlinks to confirm that they are working correctly. (*Hint:* Click the Deed Restrictions hyperlink in other pages in the Web site to return to the frames page.) If necessary, return to FrontPage and make any corrections.

k. Use your browser to print the frames page as it appears in the browser window with the Nuisances page displayed in the main frame, then close your browser.

l. Close the village Web site, then exit FrontPage.

▼ INDEPENDENT CHALLENGE 3

The businesses and vendors in Tryon, North Carolina are busy gathering data for you to post on the new Web site. One of the changes that Nick Dye, city manager of Tryon, wants you to make is to change the organization of the Bed and Breakfast, Camping, and Hotels pages in the Web site so that the links for each of these lodging categories is always visible. He also wants to ensure that it is easy to identify Tryon as the location of each lodging facility. This change will bring more awareness to Tryon. Nick asks you to create a new page using the sketch he provided (see Figure F-21).

FIGURE F-21

a. Start FrontPage, then open the tryon Web site from the location where your Web sites are stored. (If you did not create and change this Web site in Units A through E, contact your instructor for assistance.)

b. Create a new frames page using the Horizontal Split frames page template. Save the frames page as **stay.htm** and with the title **Places to Stay in Tryon**.

c. Reduce the height of the top frame by approximately 50%.

d. Split the top frame to create the new frame shown in the upper-left corner of Figure F-21.

e. Import into the root folder of the Web site the files b_and_b.htm, camping.htm, hotels.htm, and lodging.htm from the UnitF\IC3 folder on the drive and folder where your Data Files are stored (*Hint:* Overwrite the existing files with the same filenames).

f. Set the b_and_b.htm page to open initially in the bottom frame.

g. Set the lodging.htm page to open initially in the upper-right frame.

h. In the lodging.htm page, create hyperlinks using the text **hotels and inns**, **bed-and-breakfast inns**, and **camping** to open the following pages in the bottom frame: hotels.htm, b_and_b.htm, and camping.htm. (*Hint:* To open a page in the bottom frame, click the correct frame in the diagram that appears in the Target Frame dialog box. FrontPage will insert "bottom" in the Target setting text box.)

i. In the upper-left frame, create a new Web page named **tyron.htm** and with the title **Tryon**. In this new page, type **We look forward to seeing you in Tryon very soon! Click here to return to the Tryon home page.** Change the word **here** to a hyperlink that opens the home page in the full browser window.

j. If necessary, resize the upper-left and upper-right frames so all of the text in the page in each frame is visible without scrolling.

k. Change to Navigation view, then delete the existing Tryon Lodging page and its child pages from the navigation structure, but not from the Web site. (*Hint:* Right-click the Tryon Lodging page icon in the navigation structure, click Delete on the shortcut menu, and then click the option to remove the page and all pages below it from the navigation structure. Do not delete these pages from the Web site.) In its place, add the stay.htm page to the navigation structure as a child page of the home page. Position the stay.htm page between the Tryon Hotspots and Photo Gallery pages.

l. Make sure that the frames page will display scroll bars in each frame when necessary.

▼ INDEPENDENT CHALLENGE 3 (CONTINUED)

m. Save the frames page, then preview it in a browser. Test the hyperlinks in the frames page to confirm that you set them correctly. With the Camping Web page displayed in the bottom frame, print the frames page as displayed by the browser. Test the hyperlink to the home page to make sure that it opens correctly, then use a hyperlink to open the frames page again.

n. Close your browser and the tryon Web site, then exit FrontPage.

▼ INDEPENDENT CHALLENGE 4

An interesting spin-off of the frames that you created in Unit F is the iframe, or inline frame. An iframe is a frame that is created in a normal Web page and not in a frames page. Because the iframe is an embedded object, it can appear anywhere in a Web page, much like a picture. Webmonkey is a Web developer's resource that provides information about creating Web pages. The Webmonkey Web site includes an internal search engine that you can use to learn more about specific Web-related topics, such as frames. Many of the documents located by Webmonkey's internal search engine are tutorials that guide you when creating your own materials. Some of the tutorials are geared for developers working with HTML and not just FrontPage. Although there are some advanced sections describing HTML in the tutorial you will locate and read, there is still a lot of informative and interesting content included to help you understand how to develop better Web pages. You'll use Webmonkey to learn more about iframes.

a. Start your Web browser and use your favorite search engine to search for the Webmonkey site using the keyword **Webmonkey**. (Read the descriptions of the results page to find the home page for the Webmonkey site.) Use the search text box on the Webmonkey home page to enter the keyword **iframes**, then click the go button. Click the **The IFrames Lowdown** link to open a Web page containing a five-page tutorial about iframes. (If the link you clicked opens a page other than page 1, click the link to page 1 on the left side of the screen.) Read the information in each Web page, clicking the next page link at the bottom of each page to open the next page. On page 3, click the example hyperlink to open a Web page in a new browser window that features an iframe. Make sure that you use this page to understand how iframes work. (After viewing the sample page, click the Close button on the browser window to close it.)

b. Use the tutorial to answer the following questions in a Word document or on a piece of paper. Make sure that you write or type your name on the page before submitting it to your instructor.

   1. Why is an iframe a floating frame?
   2. Can you align an iframe in a Web page? How would you accomplish this goal?
   3. By default, do iframes have borders? What design practice is described in the tutorial to help distinguish iframes without borders from other content in the Web page in which the iframe appears?
   4. Do all browsers support iframes? If not, which browsers don't support iframes?

c. Start FrontPage and use the Help system to determine how to insert an inline frame in a Web page. In your report, briefly describe how you would insert an inline frame in a normal Web page, identify which inline frame properties you can change, and provide some examples of when you might use an inline frame instead of a frames page.

d. When you are finished, close your browser, FrontPage, and Word.

▼ VISUAL WORKSHOP

Use the Empty Web Site template to create a new Web site named **pets** in the location where your Web sites are stored. Use a frames page template to create the frames page shown in Figure F-22. Save the frames page using the filename **products.htm** and the title **Pet Corral**. Save the page in the upper frame using the filename **banner.htm** and the title **Welcome**. (*Hint:* The links are regular text, not a FrontPage link bar component.) Save the page in the middle-left frame using the filename **canine.htm** and the title **Canine Products**. Save the page in the middle-right frame using the filename **dog_food.htm** and the title **Dog Food**. Save the page in the lower frame using the filename **location.htm** and the title **Location**. Make sure that the two active hyperlinks shown in the frames page are set to open their hyperlink targets in the correct frame. (*Hint:* Look at the content and think about how a customer will use this page. Clicking a hyperlink in the top frame should open a page in the middle-left frame, and clicking a hyperlink in the middle-left frame should open a page in the middle-right frame.) Set each frame so it displays a scroll bar when necessary. Only the two middle frames should be resizable in the browser. Print the frames page as displayed by the browser, then close your browser. Close the pets Web site, then exit FrontPage.

FIGURE F-22

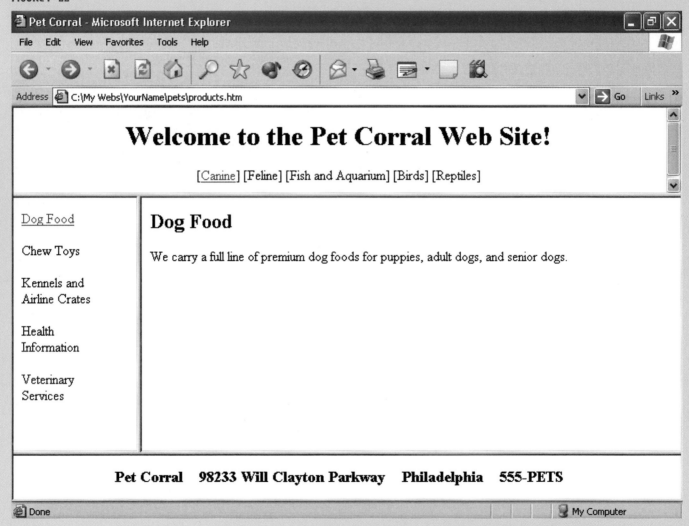

Creating a Form

OBJECTIVES

Understand forms
Open a Web page that contains a form
Add a text box and a text area
Add a drop-down box
Add an option button group
Add a check box
Set form properties
Create a search form

Within any Web site, you might need to provide a way for your site's visitors to supply information, such as their name and address, or to answer questions about the site, their needs, or a product for which they are searching. Most Web sites include a page that contains a form to collect this and other types of data from visitors. After completing the form, which has an appearance similar to a paper form, the visitor submits it. When a visitor submits a form—usually by clicking a Submit button—it is sent to a Web server, where the data is processed and stored. Usually, the Web server will send a Web page back to the browser that sent the form, to confirm that the server received the form correctly. Jason Tanaka, manager of the Vail Valley Marathon, has started designing a registration form for the marathon Web site. He asks you to finish creating the form so that Web site visitors can register for the marathon online.

Understanding Forms

As shown in Figure G-1, a **form** in a Web page is similar to a paper form that you might use to register for a class, apply for a job, or order a product. A form contains form fields that collect information. A **form field** is a data-entry field in a form, such as a text box or an option button. A user enters data by typing text into a text box or a scrolling text box, by selecting an option button or a check box, or by selecting a choice from a drop-down menu list. After completing the form, the user clicks a button that sends the form to the specified server, where a form handler processes it. A **form handler** is a program that collects and processes the data contained in a form. The collection of data entered into the form by the user and processed by a server is the **form's results** (also called a **results file**). A form handler might store a form's results in a file, in an HTML document, or in a database. Some servers can also send a form's results to an e-mail address. In addition to processing the form's results, the server usually sends a confirmation page to the user via the browser from which the form was submitted. A **confirmation page** might include a copy of the form results so the user can verify its accuracy; other times it might only send a message indicating that the server received the form. A sample confirmation page appears in Figure G-2. Jason asks you to learn more about the types of forms available in FrontPage and the different ways of processing the data they contain.

DETAILS

- You can create a form in any Web page by inserting a form component in it. A **form component** is a container that stores all of the form's fields and other form content and identifies the part of the Web page that the server will process. Except for the Submit and Reset buttons, a form component is empty when you create it. You add form fields and text to create the form in the form component.

- You can create a variety of predesigned forms using FrontPage form templates and a wizard. Some important forms and wizards that you might use in your Web sites are:
  - **Confirmation Form:** A page that acknowledges the receipt of a form by a server
  - **Feedback Form:** A page that collects data entered by a user, such as comments and personal information
  - **Form Page Wizard:** A wizard that creates a Web page containing a form with appropriate data fields to collect the desired information
  - **Guest Book:** A page that asks a Web site's guests to add comments that other site visitors can view
  - **Search Page:** A page that accepts keywords entered by a user and returns a list of hyperlinks to pages with matching entries
  - **User Registration:** A page that lets a site visitor register to use a Web site by providing a user name and a password

- FrontPage lets you specify a form handler. Depending on the type of form handler you use, the form results are saved in a text file, an HTML document, a database, or a location that you specify using a script. In addition, you can send the form results to an e-mail address if the server on which the Web site is stored is configured to send e-mail messages. In some cases, you might collect the form results in multiple formats to provide options for future data analysis.

- To test pages containing forms, the Web site must be stored on a server that has the FrontPage 2002 Server Extensions or SharePoint Services installed on it. (*Note:* There are no FrontPage 2003 Server Extensions.) In this unit, you will create forms in two Web pages in the marathon Web site. In the next unit, you will publish the marathon Web site to a server so you can test the forms in these pages.

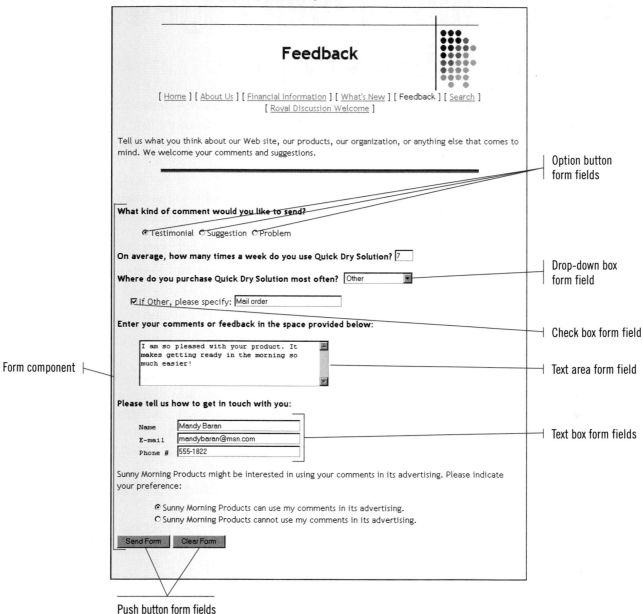

Feedback

[Home] [About Us] [Financial Information] [What's New] [Feedback] [Search]
[Royal Discussion Welcome]

Tell us what you think about our Web site, our products, our organization, or anything else that comes to mind. We welcome your comments and suggestions.

What kind of comment would you like to send?

⊙ Testimonial ○ Suggestion ○ Problem

On average, how many times a week do you use Quick Dry Solution? 7

Where do you purchase Quick Dry Solution most often? Other ▾

☑ If Other, please specify: Mail order

Enter your comments or feedback in the space provided below:

I am so pleased with your product. It makes getting ready in the morning so much easier!

Please tell us how to get in touch with you:

Name — Mandy Baran
E-mail — mandybaran@msn.com
Phone # — 555-1822

Sunny Morning Products might be interested in using your comments in its advertising. Please indicate your preference:

⊙ Sunny Morning Products can use my comments in its advertising.
○ Sunny Morning Products cannot use my comments in its advertising.

[Send Form] [Clear Form]

Option button form fields

Drop-down box form field

Check box form field

Text area form field

Text box form fields

Form component

Push button form fields

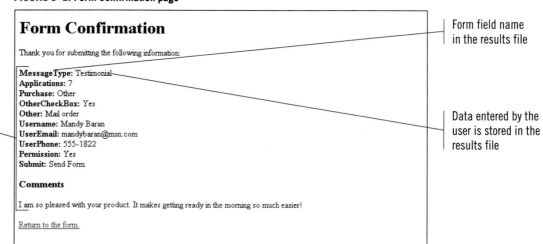

Form Confirmation

Thank you for submitting the following information:

MessageType: Testimonial
Applications: 7
Purchase: Other
OtherCheckBox: Yes
Other: Mail order
Username: Mandy Baran
UserEmail: mandybaran@msn.com
UserPhone: 555-1822
Permission: Yes
Submit: Send Form

Comments

I am so pleased with your product. It makes getting ready in the morning so much easier!

Return to the form.

Form field name in the results file

Data entered by the user is stored in the results file

Data entered by the user of the form appears as regular text; the form field names appear as bold text

Opening a Web Page That Contains a Form

If you use a template or wizard to create a form, the new page that you create will contain content and form fields that you can edit and format to match your needs. If you create the form from scratch by inserting a form component using the Form command on the Insert menu, it's up to you to enter and insert all of the form's fields and content. In either case, you must enter text that helps users enter data in the form, create the form fields that will collect the data you require, and specify a form handler to process the form results. When you created the marathon Web site, you imported Jason's partially completed Web page that contains the form component, online.htm, into the Web site. You will examine this page next.

STEPS

1. **Start** FrontPage **and open the** marathon **Web site from the location where your Web sites are stored, then if necessary change to** Folders view

2. **Double-click** online.htm **in the Contents pane**

3. **Scroll down the page until the text** Please enter your information in the form... **appears at the top of the Contents pane**

   As shown in Figure G-3, the page contains a form component and form fields. A dotted line indicates the form component in the Web page; this dotted line doesn't appear when you view the page in a browser. The Address, City, State/Province, Zip/Postal Code, Country, E-mail Address, and Home Phone labels each contain a text box to their right. To maintain the columnar format of this data, Jason stored it in a table. Jason formatted the table with invisible borders so users won't see the table's gridlines in the browser. However, you can see the dotted lines indicating the table's structure in Design view.

   > **QUICK TIP**
   >
   > You can format an option button to include an initial selection. For example, if most runners are between the ages of 19 and 35, you might set the "19-35" option button so it is selected when the page opens.

4. **Scroll down the page until the** Age (on May 31) **heading appears at the top of the Contents pane**

   Jason created the option button group shown in Figure G-4 so runners can indicate their age as of May 31. None of these option buttons is selected, thereby forcing a user to make a selection. In addition to the Age option button group, this form contains a second option button group below the heading that begins "Do you wish" and a third option button group below the "T-shirt Size" heading. These three option button groups are separate. Within any option button group, only one selection is permitted.

5. **Scroll down the page until you see the** Credit Card Number **heading**

   As shown in Figure G-5, Jason created a drop-down box form field below the "Expiration Date" heading. When you open this page in a browser and click the list arrow, a list of choices appears. Selecting a choice from the list enters that choice in the form results and closes the list. A drop-down box form field is an excellent form field type to use when you are able to provide users with predetermined choices, such as the months in the year.

   > **QUICK TIP**
   >
   > You can change the labels (text) on these buttons as necessary.

6. **If necessary, scroll down the page until you can see the** Submit **and** Reset buttons

   Every form created by FrontPage contains a button to submit the form to the server and a button to reset or clear the form fields (see Figure G-5). Usually, these buttons appear at the bottom of the form component, so they are the last items the user sees.

7. **Press** [Ctrl][Home] **to scroll to the top of the page**

FIGURE G-3: Online Registration page

Dotted outline indicates the form component

Data organized using a table with invisible borders (dotted lines indicate table cell borders)

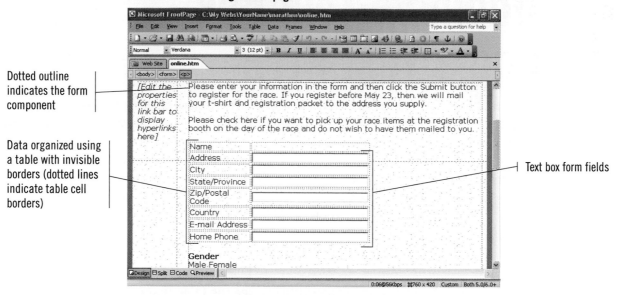

Text box form fields

FIGURE G-4: Option button groups in the form

Age option button group

SpecialCategory option button group

TShirt option button group

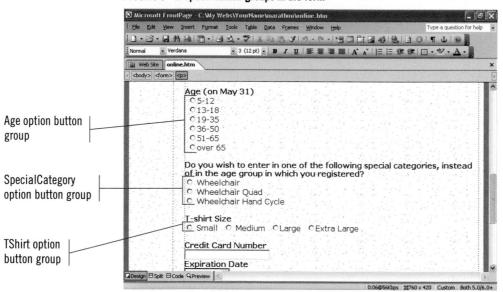

FIGURE G-5: Remaining form fields

Text box form field

Drop-down box form field

Submit button sends the form to the server

Reset button clears the form fields

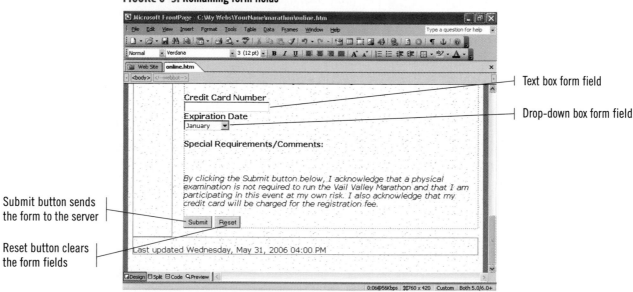

Adding a Text Box and a Text Area

A **text box** accepts a single line of typed information, such as a name or phone number. When you create a text box in a form, its initial width is 20 characters. Sometimes the initial width of a text box form field is sufficient; other times you will need to decrease or increase its size. If a user enters more data in the text box than it can display, the data will scroll to the left. A **text area**, also called a **scrolling text box**, has the same characteristics as a text box, except that it accepts multiple lines of data. When you create a text area in a form, its initial width is 20 characters and its initial height is two lines. If a user enters more data than the text area can display, the data scrolls up the page. ▧▧▧▧ You need to create the text box form field that collects the user's name and a text area in which users can input comments or special requests.

STEPS

1. **If necessary, scroll down the page until you see the table that contains the** Name **label, then click the** row 1, column 2 cell **of the table**

   The insertion point appears in the empty cell where you'll insert the text box that collects the user's name.

2. **Click** Insert **on the menu bar, then point to** Form

   Figure G-6 shows the different form fields you can insert in the form component.

3. **Click** Textbox

   A text box form field is inserted in the cell. The text box is 20 characters wide. You'll need to change the width to 35 characters to match the presentation of other text boxes in the table.

4. **Double-click the** text box form field **you inserted in Step 3**

   As shown in Figure G-7, the Text Box Properties dialog box opens. When you create a form field, FrontPage gives it a name; in this case, the initial name is "T1." This name will appear in the results file to identify each form field in the form. When you view the results file, you want each form field to have a meaningful name so it is easy to identify, so you'll change the initial name "T1" to "Name."

5. **With T1 selected in the Name text box, type** Name, **press** [Tab] **twice, type** 35 **in the Width in characters text box, then press** [Enter]

   The Text Box Properties dialog box closes, and the Name text box appears in the form with the new specifications. The form field name in the results file will be "Name."

6. **Press** [Page Down] **twice, then click the** blank line **below the** Special Requirements/Comments **heading**

7. **Click** Insert **on the menu bar, point to** Form, **then click** Text Area

   A text area form field is inserted in the page.

8. **Double-click the** text area form field **you inserted in Step 7**

   The Text Area Box Properties dialog box opens.

9. **With S1 selected in the Name text box, type** Comments, **press** [Tab] **twice, type** 50 **in the Width in characters text box, press** [Tab] **twice, type** 5 **in the Number of lines text box, then press** [Enter]

   The Text Area Box Properties dialog box closes. As shown in Figure G-8, the text area will now accommodate five lines of text with 50 characters per line.

FIGURE G-6: Form submenu

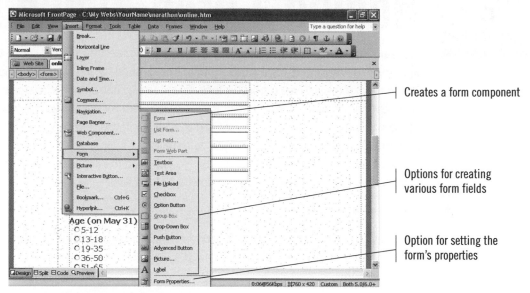

Creates a form component

Options for creating various form fields

Option for setting the form's properties

FIGURE G-7: Text Box Properties dialog box

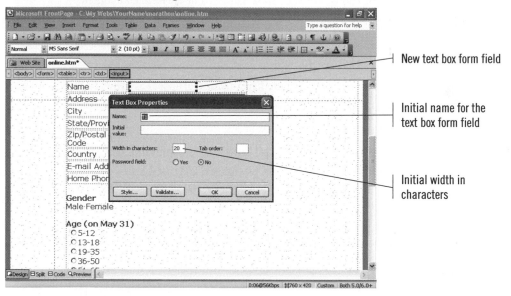

New text box form field

Initial name for the text box form field

Initial width in characters

FIGURE G-8: Text area added to form

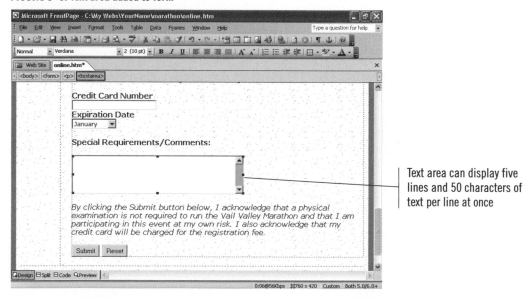

Text area can display five lines and 50 characters of text per line at once

Adding a Drop-Down Box

A **drop-down box** organizes choices in a list. A user can select the desired choice by clicking the list arrow that appears on the form field, then scrolling the choices as necessary and clicking the desired choice in the list. When the list is not displayed, you can set the form field to display one or more choices. In addition, you can set the list to accept one or more selections when the list is displayed. For most drop-down boxes, the default is to display one choice when the list is not displayed and to accept only one selection. Jason used a drop-down box form field to store the months of the year so runners can indicate the month in which the credit card they are using to pay the registration fee expires. Runners also need to indicate the year of expiration; you decide to provide this functionality by creating a drop-down box form field.

STEPS

1. **Click the** Expiration Date drop-down box form field, **then press** [End]

   The insertion point is positioned a few spaces to the right of the drop-down box form field that displays the months.

> **QUICK TIP**
>
> After you add the choices to the drop-down box form field, its width will increase.

2. **Click** Insert **on the menu bar, point to** Form, **then click** Drop-Down Box

   A drop-down box form field is inserted in the form component.

3. **Double-click the** drop-down box form field **that you inserted in Step 2**

   As shown in Figure G-9, the Drop-Down Box Properties dialog box opens.

> **QUICK TIP**
>
> In the name "D1," the "D" represents a drop-down box form field.

4. **Select** D1 **in the Name text box, then type** Year

   The drop-down box form field's name will appear as "Year" in the form results.

5. **Click** Add

   The Add Choice dialog box opens.

6. **In the Choice text box, type** 2006, **then click the** Specify Value check box **to select it**

   Each choice in the list has two names. The first name is the choice that appears in the drop-down box form field list (this choice is the one the user sees). The second name is the value that appears in the form results. These names can be the same; however, the first name can contain spaces but the second name cannot. In this case, the choice and the value can be the same because 2006 doesn't contain any spaces. See Figure G-10.

7. **In the Initial state section, click the** Selected option button

   In the Initial state section, you indicate whether the choice is selected when the form opens.

8. **Click** OK

   The 2006 choice will be the selected choice in the list.

9. **Repeat Steps 5 though 8 to create the choices** 2007, 2008, **and** 2009; **for each of these choices, make sure that the** Not selected option button **is selected**

   The completed Drop-Down Box Properties dialog box appears in Figure G-11.

10. **Click** OK **in the Drop-Down Box Properties dialog box to close it, then click the** Save **button** 📄 **on the Standard toolbar**

    The drop-down box form field now displays 2006 as the initially selected choice, and your changes to the page are saved. You can display the list of choices only in Preview view or in a browser. If you click the list arrow for a drop-down box form field in Design view, you'll select the form field.

FIGURE G-9: Drop-Down Box Properties dialog box

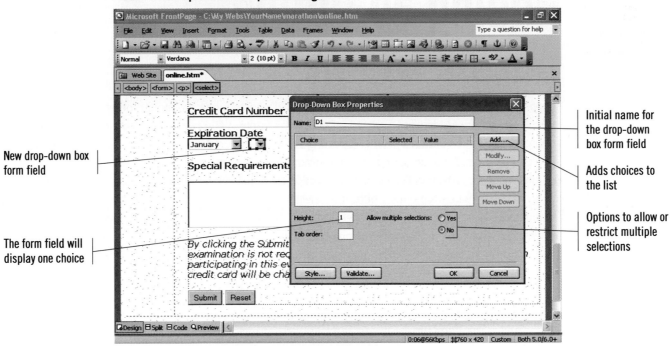

New drop-down box form field

The form field will display one choice

Initial name for the drop-down box form field

Adds choices to the list

Options to allow or restrict multiple selections

FIGURE G-10: Add Choice dialog box

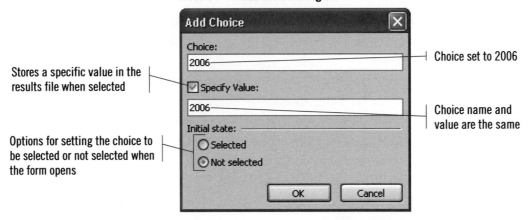

Stores a specific value in the results file when selected

Options for setting the choice to be selected or not selected when the form opens

Choice set to 2006

Choice name and value are the same

FIGURE G-11: Completed Drop-Down Box Properties dialog box

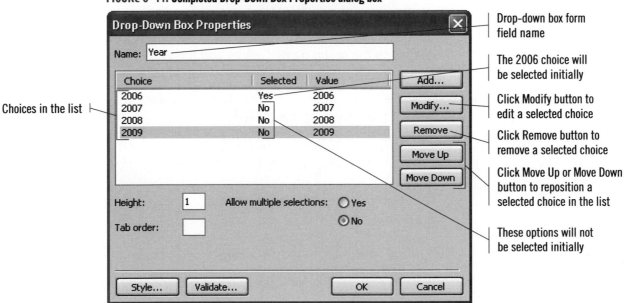

Choices in the list

Drop-down box form field name

The 2006 choice will be selected initially

Click Modify button to edit a selected choice

Click Remove button to remove a selected choice

Click Move Up or Move Down button to reposition a selected choice in the list

These options will not be selected initially

Adding an Option Button Group

An **option button**, also called a **radio button**, usually appears in a group with other option buttons in a form. **A group name** identifies a related set of option buttons. Within a group of option buttons, a user can select only one option button at a time—selecting an option button deselects another selected option button. Just like other form fields, an option button is given an initial name until you rename it. An option button is also given a value, which indicates what to store in the results file when the button is selected. The value might be "Yes" (when the option button is selected) or "No" (when the option button is not selected). Option buttons are useful when you need to limit the form's users to one of a few mutually exclusive choices, such as when identifying gender or age. ▰▰▰▰ You need to create an option button group in the form so users can indicate their gender. Jason already typed the labels "Male" and "Female," so you just need to insert the option button form fields and specify the group name "Gender."

STEPS

1. **Scroll up the page until you can see the** Gender **heading at the top of the Contents pane**
   You'll insert the option button form fields to the left of the labels "Male" and "Female."

2. **Click to the left of the word** Male

3. **Click** Insert **on the menu bar, point to** Form, **then click** Option Button
   An option button is inserted to the left of the "Male" label. By default, the first option button that you create in a group is selected.

4. **Double-click the** option button form field **that you inserted in Step 3**
   The Option Button Properties dialog box opens. FrontPage assigned the option button group name "Age" to this new option button group based on an existing option button group in the page.

5. **With** Age **selected in the Group name text box, type** Gender, **then press** [Tab]
   This option button is not part of the Age option button group; you changed the group name to "Gender." FrontPage assigned the initial value "V1" to the option button.

6. **With** V1 **selected in the Value text box, type** Male, **then click the** Not selected option button **in the Initial state section**
   As shown in Figure G-12, the value "Male" in the results file will indicate that the user selected the Male option button. This option button will not be selected when the form opens.

7. **Click** OK, **then repeat Steps 3 through 6 to create an option button to the left of the** Female **label, using the group name** Gender **and the value** Female; **the option button should not be selected**

8. **Click** OK, **click the** Save button 🖫 **on the Standard toolbar, then click anywhere in the page to deselect the Female option button**
   Figure G-13 shows the new Gender option button group.

FIGURE G-12: Option Button Properties dialog box

Selected option button form field

Group name

Value to add to the results file when this option button is selected

Option button will not be selected when the form opens

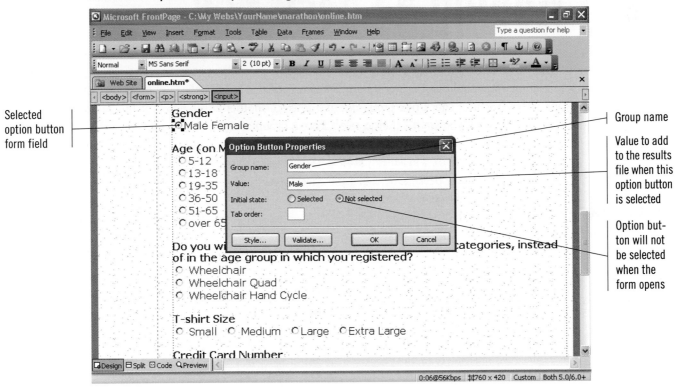

FIGURE G-13: Completed Gender option button group

Option button for Female selection

Option button group with no initial selection

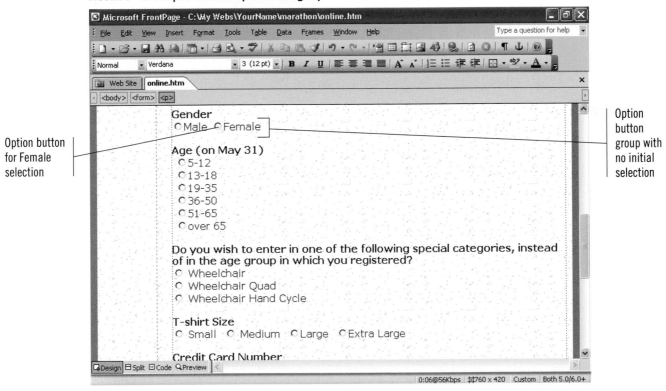

FrontPage 2003

Adding a Check Box

A **check box** lets users indicate a yes/no response to a single question or statement, such as "I would like someone to contact me." You can also use check boxes in groups so users can indicate a yes/no response to a group of related questions or statements that appear in a list. Unlike option button groups, selecting one check box in a check box group doesn't deselect another check box. For this reason, you can use check boxes when you want a user to select from a group of one or more independent and nonexclusive choices. Similar to working with option buttons, you specify a name and the value to store in the results file when creating check boxes in a form. You will use a check box to let users indicate their preference for receiving their race packets. Selecting the check box will indicate that the runner wishes to pick up the packet on the day of the race.

STEPS

1. **Scroll up the form until you can see the text that begins** Please check here if you want..., **then click to position the insertion point to the left of** Please

2. **Click** Insert **on the menu bar, point to** Form, **then click** Checkbox
   A check box form field is inserted in the form. The initial setting for a check box is "Not checked."

3. **Double-click the** check box form field **that you inserted in Step 2**
   As shown in Figure G-14, the Check Box Properties dialog box opens.

4. **With C1 selected in the Name text box, type** PickUp
   The name of the check box form field is "PickUp."

5. **Press** [Tab], **then type** Yes **in the Value text box**
   When a user selects (checks) the check box form field, the value "Yes" will appear in the results file. A value of "Yes" will more clearly indicate the user's response than the initial value "ON." The results file will show "PickUp: Yes" when a user selects the check box.

6. **Click** OK
   The check box form field is complete.

7. **Click the** Save button 🖫 **on the Standard toolbar**

FIGURE G-14: Check Box Properties dialog box

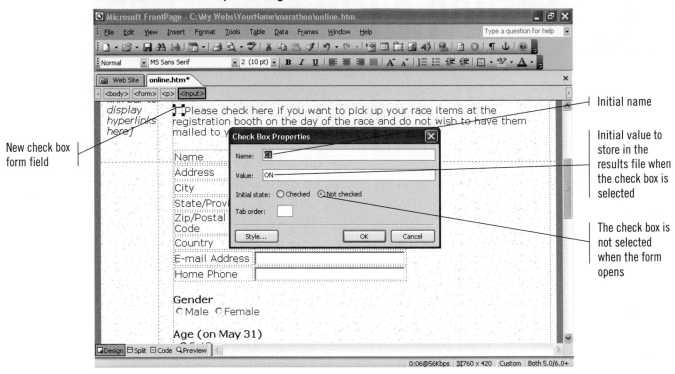

New check box form field

Initial name

Initial value to store in the results file when the check box is selected

The check box is not selected when the form opens

Clues to Use

Options for storing a form's results

After completing a form's design and content, you need to select options to store the form results in a text file, in an HTML document, in a database, or using a script that you create. In addition, if the server on which the Web site is stored is configured to send e-mail messages, you can also specify to send the form results for each form submitted to an e-mail address. When you save the form results in a text file, the first entry of the results file contains the names of the form fields. As forms are submitted to the server, the data entered by each user appears as a new line in the file, with the data for each form field separated by commas or another character. When you save the form results in an HTML document, the data for each form is included; each form field name appears on a separate line along with the data entered by the user. A line or other separating feature marks the end of each form submitted to the server. When you save a form's results in a database, the data is added to the database table that you specify. Except when using a database, the file containing the form's results is usually stored in the _private folder of the Web site so that it is protected from being accessed by Internet visitors. (Database files are protected from being accessed in a different hidden folder.) You will learn how to set a form's properties in the next lesson.

Setting Form Properties

After creating a form component in a Web page, you need to set its properties so it will store the form results in the format that you need. In some cases, you'll store the form results in more than one format, providing maximum flexibility for future data analysis. You can store the form results in a text file, in an HTML document, in a database, or using a script that you create. ▰▰▰ Jason asks you to collect the data from the form in the Online Registration page in a file and also in an HTML document.

STEPS

1. **Right-click anywhere in the form component to open the shortcut menu, then click Form Properties**

   As shown in Figure G-15, the Form Properties dialog box opens.

2. **Make sure that the Send to option button is selected, then click Options**

   The Saving Results dialog box opens. The tabs in this dialog box let you specify where to store the form results, the e-mail address to which to send the form results, the name of any custom confirmation page that you have created, and the form fields to save in the results file.

3. **In the File name text box at the top of the dialog box, type _private/results.csv**

   The form's results will be saved as results.csv in the _private folder of the Web site.

4. **Click the File format list arrow at the top of the dialog box, then click Text database using comma as a separator**

   This setting specifies that commas will separate the data from each form field in the form. This file type is also called **comma-delimited text**.

5. **Click in the File name text box in the Optional second file section, type _private/results.htm, then make sure the format in the File format list box in the Optional second file section is HTML**

   The form results will also be saved in a Web page named results.htm in the _private folder of the Web site. The completed File Results tab appears in Figure G-16.

6. **Click the E-mail Results tab**

   Because you are working in a disk-based Web site, you cannot configure the form to send results to an e-mail address at this time. After you publish the Web site to a server configured to send e-mail results, you can enter an e-mail address in the E-mail address to receive results text box. As each form is submitted to the server, its results will be stored in the results.csv and results.htm files. In addition, as each form is submitted, the individual form results can also be sent to the specified e-mail address.

7. **Click the Confirmation Page tab**

   You won't specify a confirmation page; instead, FrontPage will create one for you.

8. **Click the Saved Fields tab**

   As shown in Figure G-17, each form field that you created in the form component appears in the Form fields to save list box.

9. **Click OK to close the Saving Results dialog box, click OK to close the Form Properties dialog box, then click the Save button 🖫 on the Standard toolbar**

FIGURE G-15: Form Properties dialog box

Form handler options for storing the form results

Click to set options for the selected form handler

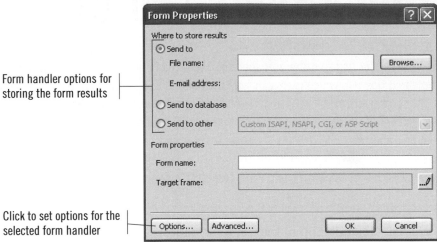

FIGURE G-16: Completed File Results tab

Results for all forms will be stored in two files in the site's _private folder

Comma-delimited file selected

HTML document selected

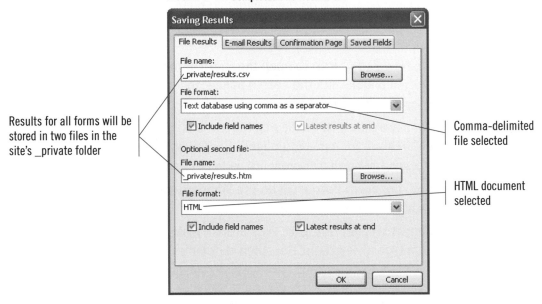

FIGURE G-17: Saved Fields tab

Form fields in the form component

Stores the computer name, user name, and/or browser type in the results file

Use list arrows to select a different date and time format or click (none) to omit these items from the results file

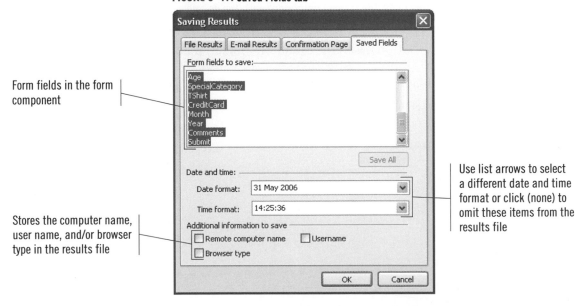

Creating a Search Form

Another type of form that you can create in your Web pages is a search form, which contains a component that searches the Web site for text that the user specifies. When you create a search form, the default settings create a single text box into which users can type their search text, along with two push buttons that let users submit the form (start the search) and clear the text box. When you submit a search form to a server, the server searches the Web site for matching entries and displays a revised page that includes the search component and a results table. The results table displays a list of hyperlinks to pages in the Web site that contain the search text. ▬▬▬ Jason wants to include a page that lets site visitors search the entire site. You accomplish this goal by adding a search component to a new Web page.

STEPS

1. **Click the** Web Site tab **at the top of the Contents pane, click the** Navigation View button **꜀Navigation at the bottom of the Contents pane, then if necessary click the** Vail Valley Marathon page icon **to select it**

TROUBLE
If necessary, click the Zoom list arrow on the Navigation pane, then click Size To Fit.

2. **Click the** New Page button 🗋 **on the Navigation pane**
   A new Web page is created to the right of the Marathon Pictures page using the initial title "New Page 1." In Navigation view, new pages are created at the level below the selected page.

3. **Right-click the** New Page 1 icon **to open the shortcut menu, click** Rename, **type** Search, **press** [Enter], **then double-click the** Search page icon
   The Search page opens in Page view. The page already uses the Web site's theme and shared borders.

4. **Type** Enter your search text in the Search for text box, then click Start Search to search the marathon Web site for matching pages., **then press** [Enter]
   The directions for using the search component that you're adding to the page are complete.

5. **Click the** Web Component button 📳 **on the Standard toolbar**
   The Insert Web Component dialog box opens.

6. **In the Component type list box, click** Web Search, **make sure that** Current Web **is selected in the Choose a type of search list box, then click** Finish
   As shown in Figure G-18, the Search Form Properties dialog box opens. You use this dialog box to change the label for the text box into which users type their search text, the width of the text box, and the labels for the buttons that let users initiate the search or clear the form.

QUICK TIP
The search component will not work in a disk-based Web site. Attempting to submit the page from a disk-based Web site will result in an error message.

7. **Click** OK
   As shown in Figure G-19, the search component with the default settings appears in the page. After you publish the marathon Web site to a server, you will test this page using a browser.

8. **Click the** Save button 🖫 **on the Standard toolbar, then close the marathon Web site and FrontPage**
   In Unit H, you will publish the marathon Web site to a server and test all of its pages, including the Online Registration and Search pages, which contain forms.

FIGURE G-18: Search Form Properties dialog box

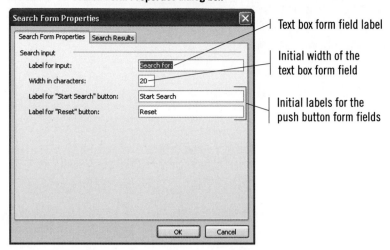

Text box form field label

Initial width of the text box form field

Initial labels for the push button form fields

FIGURE G-19: Search form added to the Search page

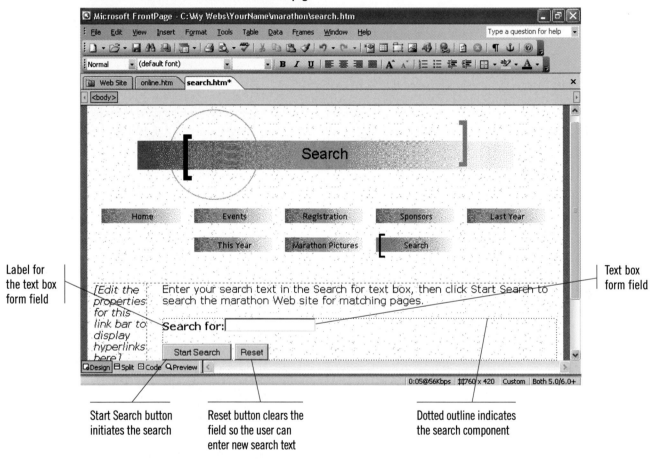

Label for the text box form field

Text box form field

Start Search button initiates the search

Reset button clears the field so the user can enter new search text

Dotted outline indicates the search component

Clues to Use

Creating a "Search the Web" component

FrontPage includes another search component that you can easily include in your Web pages. The Search the Web component lets site visitors enter keywords in a text box, similar to the one appearing in the search component. Clicking the Search button in this component opens a page at msn.com that searches the Internet for matching pages and then creates a list of hyperlinks to those Web pages.

To use this component, click the Web Component button 🔲 on the Standard toolbar, scroll down the Component type list and click MSN Components, click the Search the Web with MSN option in the Choose a MSN component list, then click Finish. After connecting to the Internet, you can use this component to search the Internet.

Practice

▼ CONCEPTS REVIEW

Label each element in the Microsoft FrontPage window shown in Figure G-20.

FIGURE G-20

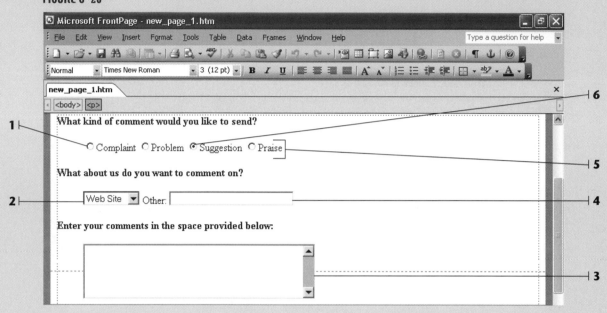

Match each of the following terms with the statement that best describes its function.

7. Check box
8. Confirmation page
9. Form
10. Form field
11. Form handler
12. Group name
13. Text area
14. Text box

a. A data-entry field in a form
b. A form field for storing a single line of text
c. A form field for storing a yes/no response
d. A form field for storing multiple lines of text
e. A program that collects and processes data contained in a form
f. A Web page that displays input entered by a form's user
g. An HTML container for fields that collect data
h. The HTML name of a set of related option buttons in a form

Select the best answer from the following list of choices.

15. **You can use FrontPage to store form results in which of the following types of files?**
    a. HTML
    b. Text
    c. Database
    d. All of the above

16. **Which form field should you use when you need to determine whether a person smokes?**
    a. Check box
    b. Drop-down box
    c. Text area
    d. Text box

17. **Which form field should you use when you want to ask a user for a detailed response?**
    a. Drop-down box
    b. Option button group
    c. Text area
    d. Text box

18. **When assigning properties to a text area form field, you must identify which of the following?**
    a. The width in characters
    b. The number of lines
    c. The name to store in the results file
    d. All of the above

19. **Which of the following statements about a drop-down box form field is FALSE?**
    a. You can permit multiple selections.
    b. You can use a choice as a password field.
    c. You can create an initial selection.
    d. You can rearrange the choices in a list.

20. **A _____ form lets users search the pages in a Web site to find matching entries.**
    a. feedback
    b. confirmation
    c. search
    d. None of the above

▼ SKILLS REVIEW

1. **Open a Web page that contains a form.**
   a. Start FrontPage, then use the Empty Web Site template to create a new Web site named **dentist** in the location where your Web sites are stored.
   b. Import into the root folder of the dentist Web site the index.htm file from the UnitG\SR folder on the drive and folder where your Data Files are stored.
   c. Open the home page in Design view.
   d. Examine the form component in the page, reviewing its content. As you read the page's content, consider the type of form fields you might use in the page.

2. **Add a text box and a text area.**
   a. Scroll to the bottom of the page, then click the row 1, column 2 cell in the table below the heading that begins **If you would like someone**. Insert a text box form field in this cell with the name **Name** and a width of **40** characters.
   b. In the cell to the right of the Phone label, insert a text box form field with the name **Phone** and a width of **40** characters. In the cell to the right of the E-mail label, insert a text box form field with the name **Email** and a width of **40** characters.
   c. Click the blank line below the **If no, why not?** text. Insert a text area form field on this line with these properties: name **WhyNot**, width of **55** characters, and number of lines **3**.
   d. Save the page.

3. **Add a drop-down box.**
   a. Click the blank line below the heading that begins **When visiting a dentist's office**. Insert a drop-down box form field on this blank line.
   b. Change the name for the drop-down box form field to **Services**. Add the following choices to the drop-down box form field: **Dentist, Hygienist, Orthodontics,** and **Office Staff**. For each choice, the value is the same, except for the Office Staff choice, which should store the value **OfficeStaff** in the results file. (*Hint:* Use the Specify Value check box and text box to change the value to be stored.) The Dentist choice should be selected when the form opens. The drop-down box form field should not permit multiple selections, and it should use the initial height (1).

4. Add an option button group.

a. Click to the left of the word **Yes** below the heading that begins **Was this your first visit**. Insert a selected option button form field in this location. Use the group name **FirstVisit** and the value **Yes**.

b. Click to the left of the word **No** appearing on the same line, then add a second option button to the FirstVisit group. The value is **No**, and the option button should not be selected when the form opens.

c. Click to the left of the word **Yes** below the heading that begins **Would you refer a friend**. Insert a selected option button form field in this location. Use the group name **Refer** and the value **Yes**.

d. Click to the left of the word **No** appearing on the same line, then add a second option button form field to the Refer group. The value is **No**, and the option button should not be selected when the form opens.

5. Add a check box.

a. Click to the left of the **Cleaning/Checkup** text that appears below the heading that begins **What was the purpose**. Insert a check box form field that is not selected in this location. Use the name **Cleaning** and the value **Yes**.

b. Create an unselected check box for each item in the list using the following names and the value **Yes** for each one: **Xrays**, **Restorative**, **TeethWhite**, **Ortho**, **Dentures**, and **MajorDental**.

c. Save the page.

6. Set form properties.

a. Set the form to send its results to a file named **dentist.csv** in the Web site's _private folder. If necessary, change the file format to text database using a comma as a separator. Set the form to send its results to a second file named **dentist.htm** using the HTML file format. Store this file in the Web site's _private folder.

b. Change the form so that it stores only the date the form was submitted to the server. (*Hint:* Change the Time format to (none) on the Saved Fields tab.)

c. Set the form to save each form field in the form component, plus the remote computer name. Do not save the user name or browser type.

d. Save the Web page, then preview it in a browser. Close the message box that opens, scroll down the page and type your name in the Name text box, use your browser to print the page, then close your browser.

e. In FrontPage, change to Code view for the index.htm page, scroll to the top and type your name below the <html> tag, then print the HTML document. Close the index.htm page without saving changes.

7. Create a search form.

a. Use the New task pane to create a new blank page.

b. Change the first line to center alignment and the Heading 1 style, then type **Search**.

c. Change the next line in the document to left alignment, then type **Please enter your search text in the text box, then click Search.**

d. On the next line, insert a search form using the Web Component button on the Standard toolbar.

e. Change the label for the text box to **Search the Web site for:** and change its width to **30** characters.

f. Change the label for the Start Search button to **Search**, then change the label for the Reset button to **Clear Form**.

g. Save the page using the filename **search.htm** and the title **Search**.

h. Preview the page in a browser, close the message box, type your name in the Search the Web site for text box (but do not click the Search button), then print the page.

i. Close your browser and the dentist Web site, then exit FrontPage.

▼ INDEPENDENT CHALLENGE 1

Grace Baxter is president of Baxter Air, Inc., a manufacturer of all types of fans and air purifiers. The company is conducting an online survey of the effectiveness of its new M-540 air purifier. Grace plans to send an e-mail message to all customers who purchased this product. The e-mail message will contain a link to the Web page that contains the survey. Grace has asked you to create the survey using FrontPage.

a. Start FrontPage, then use the One Page Web Site template to create a new Web site named **baxter** in the location where your Web sites are stored.

b. Change the title of the index.htm page to **M-540 Owner's Survey**, then open it in Design view.

c. On the first line of the page, type **M-540 Owner's Survey**. Format this text using the Heading 1 style and center alignment.

d. On a new left-aligned line below the heading, insert a form component. After creating the form component, press [Enter], then click the blank line that you just created.

e. Create a table with eight rows, two columns, and invisible borders. In the first column, enter appropriate labels to collect the following information about each owner: **First Name**, **Last Name**, **Address**, **City**, **State/Province**, **Postal Code**, **Country**, and **E-mail Address**. In the second column, insert text box form fields to collect the information. You pick the design, form field names, and dimensions for these form fields.

f. On a new line below the table, ask the owner who uses the M-540 model. Display the following choices as unselected check boxes: **Self**, **Spouse**, **Child**, and **Other**. The values stored in the results file should be **Yes** for each check box.

g. On a new line below the check boxes, insert an option button group named **Rating** to ask the owner for his or her rating of the operation of the M-540: **Excellent**, **Very Good**, **Fair**, **Poor**. The initial selection is Excellent; the value to store in the results file for each option button is the same as the label, with spaces omitted.

h. On a new line below the option button group, create a drop-down box form field named **Improvement** to ask the owner for his or her rating of the perceived health improvement after using the M-540. Display the following choices in the list: **Significant Improvement**, **Slight Improvement**, **No Noticeable Improvement**. The choice and value names are the same, with spaces omitted for the values. The initial selection is Significant Improvement.

i. On a new line below the drop-down box form field, create a text area named **Comments**. Provide directions above the text area, asking owners to enter their comments. You choose the text area's width in characters and number of lines.

j. Set the form to send its results to a comma-delimited file named **survey.csv** in the Web site's _private folder. (*Hint:* Select and replace any existing text in the File name text box, if necessary, and then type **_private/survey.csv**.) Do not collect any additional information or any date/time information.

k. Save the page, preview it in your browser, then close the message box. Simulate the way that a site visitor would use the page by entering your name and other information into the form. Do not click the Submit button; use the browser to print the page. Close your browser.

l. Change to Code view for the index.htm page, scroll to the top of the page, type your name on the blank line below the <html> tag, print the page, then close the page without saving changes.

m. Close the baxter Web site, then exit FrontPage.

▼ INDEPENDENT CHALLENGE 2

When the village Web site is published to a server, many residents of the Villages at Kensington Neighbourhood Association will register online for their swim bands. Your task today is to create a form in the Registration Form page to collect the appropriate data.

a. Start FrontPage, then open the village Web site from the location where your Web sites are stored. (If you did not create and change this Web site in Units A through F, contact your instructor for assistance.)

b. Open the Registration Form Web page (register.htm) in Design view. On a new line below the existing text, insert a form component, insert a new paragraph above the push buttons, then click the paragraph you just created.

FrontPage 2003

c. Create the form with the following minimum requirements. You decide the appropriate form fields to create, their names, and initial values and sizes.

- Create form fields to collect the resident's last name, address, and phone number. (*Hint:* Create a table with invisible borders, insert labels in the first column, and insert form fields to collect the data in the second column. Resize the columns until you are satisfied with the arrangement.)
- Create a form field to request the number of swim bands needed by the resident. Create choices in the list so residents can request 1 to 10 swim bands. The initial selection is 1.
- Create a form field that asks the resident if anyone in the household is interested in registering for the swim team and indicate that information will be mailed to them later. Do not provide an initial selection.
- Create a form field that asks residents how they intend to pay the fees associated with using the pool. The choices are credit card, cash, and check. The initial selection is credit card.
- Create a form field that residents can use to enter open-ended comments related to the pool.

d. Set the form to send its results to a comma-delimited file named **reg_info.csv** in the Web site's _private folder. (*Hint:* Select and then replace any existing text in the File name text box, if necessary, and then type **_private/reg_info.csv**.) Do not collect any additional information or any date/time information.

e. Save the Registration Form page, preview it in your browser, then close the message box. Simulate the way that a site visitor would use the page by entering your name and other information into the page. Do not click the Submit button, use the browser to print the page, then close your browser.

f. Change to Code view for the register.htm page, scroll to the top of the page, type your name on the blank line below the <html> tag, print the page, then close the page without saving changes.

g. Close the village Web site, then exit FrontPage.

INDEPENDENT CHALLENGE 3

Nick Dye, city manager of Tryon, North Carolina, wants to create an online form to provide an easy way for potential visitors to request information about businesses, lodging, and recreational activities in the area. Nick asks you to change the Request Information page by creating the form shown in Figure G-21.

a. Start FrontPage, then open the tryon Web site from the location where your Web sites are stored. (If you did not create and change this Web site in Units A through F, contact your instructor for assistance.)

b. Open the Request Information Web page (request.htm) in Design view.

c. On a new line below the existing text in this page, insert a form component. Insert a new paragraph, then move the insertion point to paragraph you just created in the form component.

FIGURE G-21

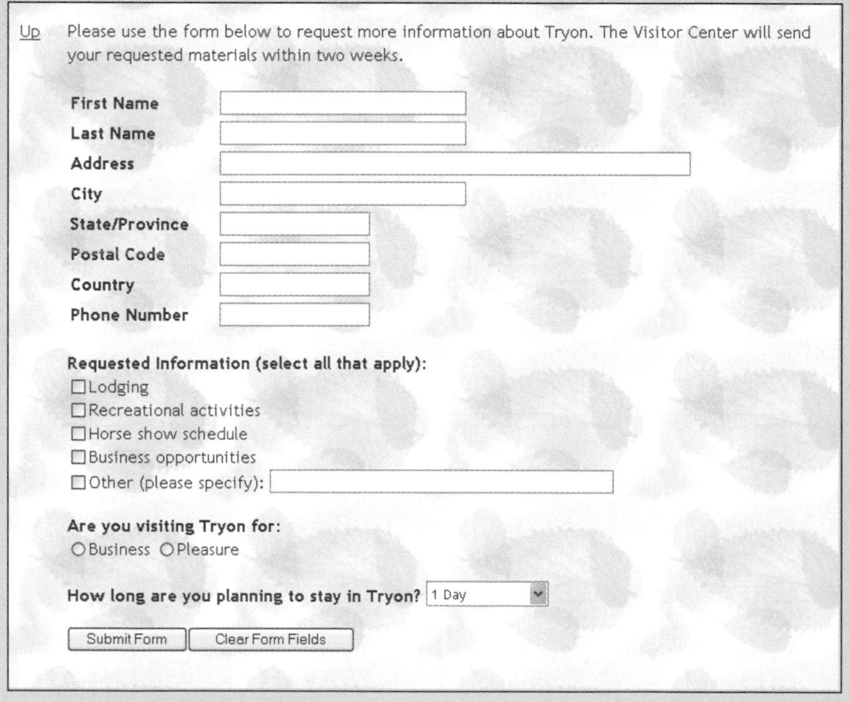

Up Please use the form below to request more information about Tryon. The Visitor Center will send your requested materials within two weeks.

First Name
Last Name
Address
City
State/Province
Postal Code
Country
Phone Number

Requested Information (select all that apply):
☐ Lodging
☐ Recreational activities
☐ Horse show schedule
☐ Business opportunities
☐ Other (please specify):

Are you visiting Tryon for:
○ Business ○ Pleasure

How long are you planning to stay in Tryon? 1 Day

Submit Form   Clear Form Fields

d. Create the form shown in Figure G-21 using the following guidelines. (*Hint:* To create new lines in the page without adding space between lines, press [Shift][Enter].)

- Insert a table with eight rows, two columns, and invisible borders in the form component.
- Add the labels to cells in the first column of the table, using Figure G-21 for their content and placement.
- Add text box form fields to the cells in the second column of the table as follows: **FirstName** (**35** characters), **LastName** (**35** characters), **Address** (**70** characters), **City** (**35** characters), **StateProv** (**20** characters), **PostalCode** (**20** characters), **Country** (**20** characters), and **Phone** (**20** characters).
- Create the unselected check boxes and their associated text as follows: **Lodging**, **Recreation**, **HorseShow**, **Business**, and **Other**. The value for each check box is **Yes** when it is selected. The form field name of the text box on the same line as the Other check box is **Other1**, and its width is **50** characters.
- Add the two unselected option buttons using the group name **VisitPurpose** and the values **Business** and **Pleasure**.
- Add the drop-down box form field with the name **HowLong** and the choices **1 Day**, **2 to 4 Days**, and **5 or More Days**. The choices and values are the same, except to remove any spaces from the values. The initial selection is 1 Day.
- Change the label for the Submit button to **Submit Form**, then change the label for the Reset button to **Clear Form Fields**. (*Hint:* Double-click a push button to change its label.)
- Set the form to send its results to a comma-delimited file named **reqinfo.csv** in the Web site's _private folder. Do not collect any additional information or any date/time information.

e. Save the Request Information page, preview it in your browser, then close the message box. Simulate the way that a site visitor would use the page by entering your name and other information into the page. Do not click the Submit Form button, use the browser to print the page, then close your browser.

f. Change to Code view for the request.htm page, scroll to the top of the page, type your name on the blank line below the <html> tag, print the page, then close the page without saving changes.

g. Close the tryon Web site, then exit FrontPage.

▼ INDEPENDENT CHALLENGE 4

If you have used the Internet to purchase goods and services, you are already familiar with the many types of forms that Web sites use to collect information about the items a customer wants to buy from the site, the customer's name and mailing address, and payment information, such as a credit card number or other electronic account data. Most sites use an Internet protocol called Secure Sockets Layer (SSL) to protect data being transmitted between a browser and a Web server so it is safe from being intercepted, invalidated, or stolen during its transmission. SSL works only while data is being transmitted. After data is stored on the Web server, it's up to the site that collected it to protect it from being stolen or misused. As a consumer, you need to know more about how data that a site collects about you is going to be secured. In this Independent Challenge, you'll learn more about programs that work to ensure the safety of information collected about individuals.

a. Start your browser, then use your favorite search engine to open the home page for TRUSTe, a not-for-profit Web site dedicated to online privacy issues.

b. Review the content of the TRUSTe home page to become familiar with the services offered by this site. Locate a link that describes the TRUSTe privacy seal (trustmark) and read the information.

c. Use your search engine to locate and open the home page for WebTrust.org, a site that examines and certifies sites to ensure compliance with current WebTrust principles, including online privacy and security. Use the Consumers link on the home page to learn more about the WebTrust seal and the WebTrust Online Privacy Program.

d. Use your search engine to locate and open the home page for BBBOnline.org. Search for information about the BBBOnline Privacy Seal and learn about the BBBOnline Privacy Seal.

e. On a sheet of paper with your name on it, describe one of the trustmark and privacy seal programs that you explored. Answer the following questions about the program:
- Is a Web site's pursuit of the program voluntary or compelled by some federal, state, or local law?
- How do members obtain the trustmark or privacy seal offered by the program?
- As a consumer, would you feel safe doing business with a Web site that includes this seal? Why or why not?

f. Close your browser.

▼ VISUAL WORKSHOP

Start FrontPage, then use the One Page Web Site template to create a new Web site named **games** in the location where your Web sites are stored. Insert text, a form component, and form fields in the home page to create the form shown in Figure G-22. Configure the form to send its results to a comma-delimited file named **video.csv** in the Web site's _private folder. In addition, use the Saved Fields tab to collect the date and time that the form was submitted (select a date and time format of your choice). Do not collect any additional information. When you are finished, preview the page in your browser, close the message box, enter your name in the text box, do not click the Submit Survey button, print the page, then close your browser. Change to Code view for the home page, scroll to the top of the page, type your name on the blank line below the <html> tag, print the page, then close the page without saving your changes. Close the games Web site, then exit FrontPage.

FIGURE G-22

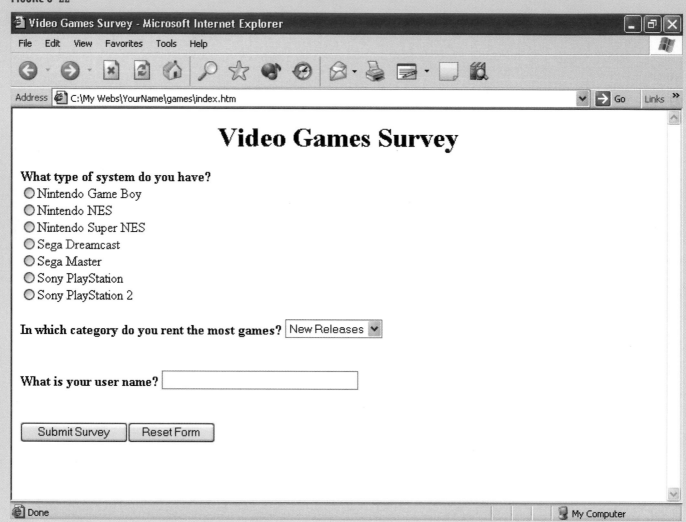

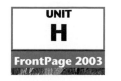

Working in a Published Web Site

OBJECTIVES

Publish a Web site
Open a Web site from a server
Recalculate and verify hyperlinks
Test a page that contains a form component
Test a page that contains a search component
Set permissions in a Web site
Create a hit counter
Maintain a published Web site

Until now, you have been working in a disk-based Web site. Some of the components that you have created, such as the pages containing form and search components, require a server for processing. This server might be an intranet, a local Web server that you install on your computer, or the Internet Web server on which you publish your Web site. Windows 2000/XP Professional lets you install a Web server on your computer so you can test a Web site before publishing it on an Internet Web server. You can also use this Web server to make your desktop computer function as an Internet Web server when it is properly connected to the Internet. Most developers use a local Web server to test pages and make other changes to ensure that a site is operating as expected before publishing it on an Internet Web server. Jason Tanaka, manager of the Vail Valley Marathon, asks you to publish the marathon Web site on your computer's server and to test its pages.

Publishing a Web Site

When you create a disk-based Web site, the folders and files in the Web site are stored on a disk, such as your computer's hard drive or a Zip disk. After you finish working in your disk-based Web site, you'll need to publish it to a Web server. **Internet Information Services (IIS)** is a Web server that you can install on your computer using your Windows 2000/XP Professional CD. IIS provides the services necessary to make your desktop computer function as a Web server. You can use IIS to publish your FrontPage Web site on your computer, without needing a network connection to an Internet Web server. Many Web site developers test their Web sites using IIS to ensure that the Web sites function correctly before publishing them on an Internet Web server. The default configuration for IIS is for it to start when you start Windows; IIS is just like any other program and runs in the background. If you are unsure about whether IIS is installed on your computer, ask your instructor or technical support person for help. ▰▰▰ Now that you have created all of the pages in the marathon Web site, you are ready to publish it.

STEPS

TROUBLE
The steps in this lesson assume that you can publish Web sites to IIS or a compatible server. If you are unsure about where to publish your Web sites, ask your instructor or technical support person for help.

1. **Start** FrontPage, **then open the** marathon **Web site from the location where your Web sites are stored**

2. **Click the** Remote Web Site View **button** ⊞Remote Web site **at the bottom of the Contents pane**
   Remote Web Site view displays a message indicating that you need to set up a remote Web site. The steps in this lesson assume that IIS 5.0 or higher and the FrontPage 2002 Server Extensions or SharePoint Services have been installed on the server to which you have access.

3. **Click the** Remote Web Site Properties **button** 🖳 Remote Web Site Properties... **on the Contents pane**
   The Remote Web Site Properties dialog box opens, as shown in Figure H-1.

TROUBLE
If you have problems publishing your Web site, ask your instructor or technical support person for help.

4. **Make sure that the** FrontPage or SharePoint Services option button **is selected, delete any text in the Remote Web site location text box, then type**
   http://localhost/marathon[YourName]
   The default name of the computer when you install IIS is **localhost**. Your instructor or technical support person might provide you with a different computer name or path, in which case you will use that information in the steps.

5. **Click** OK
   A dialog box opens to tell you that a Web site doesn't exist at the location you specified.

6. **Click** Yes
   As shown in Figure H-2, Remote Web Site view shows your disk-based Web site in the Local Web site pane. The Remote Web site pane shows the Web site you just created on the server. The remote Web site is empty, except for the _private and images folders that FrontPage created.

7. **Make sure that the** Local to remote option button **is selected, then click** Publish Web site
   The Status section indicates the publish status of the site. Depending on your computer, it might take just a few seconds or a couple of minutes to publish the site. When the site has been published, the Last publish status option changes to "successful" in the Status section, and folders and files appear in the Remote Web site pane.

8. **Click the** View your Remote Web site link **in the Status section**
   The home page for the remote Web site opens in a browser. Notice that the page's URL is http://localhost/marathon[YourName], which is the address of the remote Web site. You'll test the Web pages in another lesson.

9. **Close your browser, click** File **on the menu bar, then click** Close Site
   The disk-based marathon Web site closes, but FrontPage remains open.

FIGURE H-1: Remote Web Site Properties dialog box

Use to optimize the HTML of published pages

Options for publishing a Web site using different transfer methods

Location of remote Web site (your initial text might differ)

Link to find ISPs that support FrontPage Web sites

Use to change the way pages are published, how changed pages are detected, and to enable or disable the creation of a log file

Use to locate an existing Web site

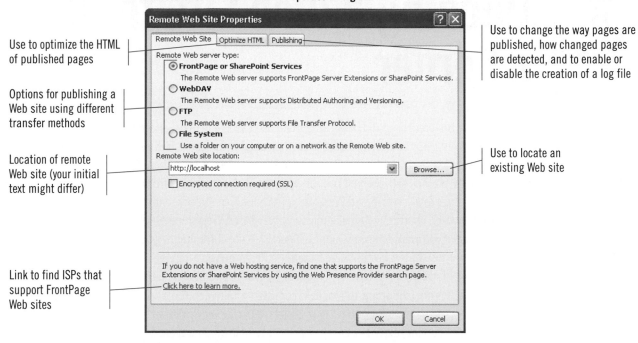

FIGURE H-2: Remote Web Site view

Local Web site pane

Status, date, and time the local Web site was last published

Remote Web site pane

Options for publishing the local Web site to the remote server, publishing the remote Web site to the local drive, or synchronizing both Web sites

Publish Web site button

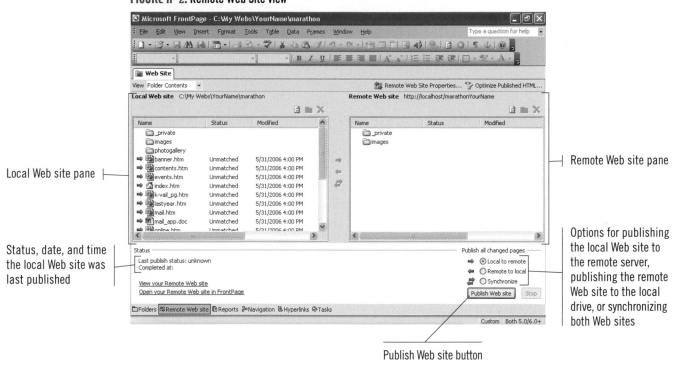

Clues to Use

Publishing a Web site to an Internet Web server

You can publish a Web site from IIS to an Internet Web server. For example, after you thoroughly test your Web site using IIS and are satisfied with its content, you can use the Publish Site command on the File menu to enter the address of the Internet Web server that you selected to host your site. This Web server might be your company's Web server or intranet, or an Internet service provider (ISP) on which you have purchased space to host your Web site. In either case, the Web server must support the FrontPage 2002 Server Extensions or SharePoint Services for your Web site to function correctly when accessed by Internet visitors. (*Note:* There are no FrontPage 2003 Server Extensions.) If the Web server does not support these services, you can work with the ISP to develop scripts to take the place of them.

FrontPage 2003

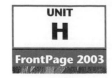

Opening a Web Site from a Server

After you publish a Web site to your computer's server (or another server), you have two copies of the Web site—one that is stored on a disk drive (the disk-based Web site) and another that is stored on a server (the server-based Web site). The server-based Web site contains the same files as the disk-based Web site, but it is stored in a location that has the FrontPage 2002 Server Extensions or SharePoint Services installed; these programs run the Web site on the server. You can open the Web site directly from the server using FrontPage. When you make changes to a server-based Web site, your changes are updated immediately in the Web site stored on the server. However, changes you make to your server-based Web site are not automatically saved to your disk-based Web site. If you want to keep your disk-based Web site current after publishing a Web site, you must make changes to your disk-based Web site, and then use Remote Web Site view either to publish your remote Web site back to your local Web site or to synchronize the two copies of the Web sites. In most cases, once you publish a Web site, it is not important to maintain consistency between the original disk-based and the new server-based Web sites. However, it is good practice to keep a backup copy of the "live" Web site on your hard drive in case your ISP goes offline, experiences server problems, or loses your files. ▰▰▰▰ You need to open the server-based marathon Web site from IIS so you can test its pages.

STEPS

1. **Click File on the menu bar, then click Open Site**
    The Open Site dialog box opens.

2. **Click the My Network Places button** 🖧
    The Open Site dialog box lists the network shortcuts for your computer, as shown in Figure H-3. The name of your Web server (the default is localhost) appears either in the Look in list box or in the dialog box. Your Web server might have a different name.

TROUBLE
If you see a marathon[YourName] on localhost folder in the list box, click it to select it, then continue with Step 4.

3. **Double-click the localhost folder in the window, then click the marathon[YourName] folder**
    The remote marathon Web site is selected.

4. **Click Open, then if necessary change to Folders view**
    The marathon Web site opens from the server. See Figure H-4.

5. **Double-click index.htm in the Contents pane**

6. **Select the text May 31 in the first sentence below the Welcome heading, click the Bold button ⓑ on the Formatting toolbar, then click the Save button 🖫 on the Standard toolbar**
    The page stored on the server is updated. Your disk-based Web site remains the same.

7. **Click the Preview button 🔍 on the Standard toolbar**
    The home page opens in a browser and shows the revision that you just made.

8. **Close your browser**

FIGURE H-3: Open Site dialog box

Server name
(yours might differ)

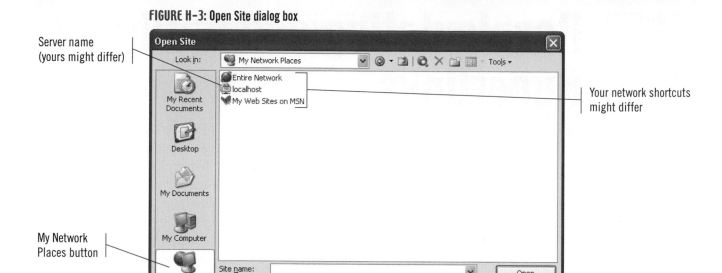

Your network shortcuts
might differ

My Network
Places button

FIGURE H-4: Remote marathon Web site in Folders view

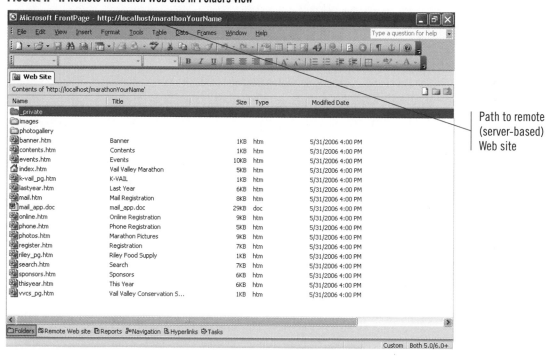

Path to remote
(server-based)
Web site

Clues to Use

Selecting an ISP to host your Web site

When you are ready to publish your server-based Web site from your computer's server to an Internet Web server, you need to make sure that the Internet Web server supports Web sites that use the FrontPage 2002 Server Extensions or SharePoint Services. If it does not, you can click Tools on the menu bar, click Page Options, click the Authoring tab in the Page Options dialog box, click the FrontPage and SharePoint technologies list arrow, then click None to disable features in your Web site that use the FrontPage 2002 Server Extensions or SharePoint Services. Another option is to locate

a different ISP that will accept FrontPage Web sites. Some sites, such as Tripod (www.tripod.lycos.com) and Yahoo! GeoCities (http://geocities.yahoo.com/home), provide free Web space and support for FrontPage Web sites. (In some cases, you must enable your Web site to use the FrontPage Server Extensions or SharePoint Services; check with your ISP for more information.) In exchange for free Web space, the ISP displays advertisements that your Web site's visitors will see when they visit your site.

FrontPage 2003

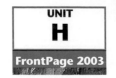
Recalculating and Verifying Hyperlinks

After publishing your Web site, it is good practice to repair any broken hyperlinks, update the shared border and link bar files, update all FrontPage components, update data on the server, and delete any unused theme files. This process is known as **recalculating hyperlinks** in a Web site. You can also **verify hyperlinks** in a Web site, which causes FrontPage to check the validity of each hyperlink in a Web site to look for broken links. Testing the hyperlinks in a Web site involves both recalculating and verifying them. Recalculating hyperlinks ensures that the Web site's links *exist;* verifying hyperlinks ensures that the Web site's links are *valid.* The Broken Hyperlinks report in Reports view identifies each link that is broken or that cannot be verified. Other reports in Reports view list detailed information about a Web site's files (recently added, recently changed, older files), problems (unlinked files, pages that are slow to download, component errors), workflow reports (review status, pages assigned to individuals, publish status for pages), and usage reports (daily, weekly, and monthly usage for the site; daily, weekly, and monthly hit reports; and information about site visitors). You recalculate and verify the hyperlinks in the marathon Web site.

STEPS

QUICK TIP

Depending on the size of a Web site, the recalculation process can take several minutes. You can recalculate hyperlinks from any FrontPage view.

1. **With the home page open in Design view, click** Tools **on the menu bar, then click** Recalculate Hyperlinks

   The Recalculate Hyperlinks dialog box opens, as shown in Figure H-5.

2. **Read the information in the dialog box, then click** Yes

   The Recalculate Hyperlinks dialog box closes and FrontPage recalculates the hyperlinks in the Web site. After a moment, the Web site is refreshed. You will know that the recalculation process is complete when the status bar does not contain any messages. You won't see any changes in your Web site; the recalculation process is transparent.

3. **Click the** Web Site tab **at the top of the Contents pane, then click the** Reports View button 🗎 Reports **at the bottom of the Contents pane**

   A Site Summary report opens in Reports view. Table H-1 describes reports available in a Site Summary report.

4. **Click the** Verifies hyperlinks in the current web button 🗹 **in the upper-right corner of the Contents pane**

   The Verify Hyperlinks dialog box opens, as shown in Figure H-6.

QUICK TIP

Use the Help system to learn more about identifying and fixing broken links.

5. **Make sure that the** Verify all hyperlinks option button **is selected, then click** Start

   Broken hyperlinks in the Web site are displayed with a broken link icon; verified hyperlinks are displayed with a green check mark. Other messages, such as "Unknown" or "Edited," might also appear in the Status column. As you gain experience working with FrontPage, you will find that you won't need to fix every broken link identified by FrontPage. However, you must fix broken hyperlinks to missing pages in the Web site or to pages that have had filename changes.

6. **Click the** Hyperlinks button list arrow **at the top of the Contents pane, then click** Site Summary

   The Site Summary report appears again in Reports view.

FIGURE H-5: Recalculate Hyperlinks dialog box

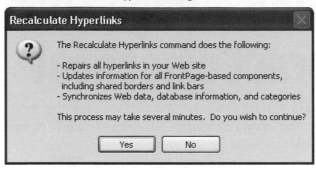

FIGURE H-6: Verify Hyperlinks dialog box

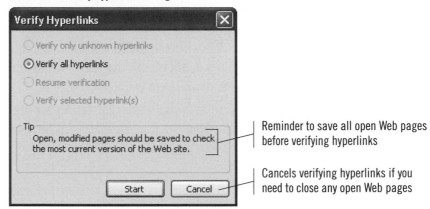

Reminder to save all open Web pages before verifying hyperlinks

Cancels verifying hyperlinks if you need to close any open Web pages

TABLE H-1: Reports available in a Site Summary report

report name	description
All Files	The total number of files in a Web site and their cumulative file size in kilobytes
Pictures	The total number of pictures in a Web site and their cumulative file size in kilobytes
Unlinked Files	The number of files in a Web site that are *not* linked to the home page and their cumulative file size
Linked Files	The number of files in a Web site that are linked to the home page and their cumulative file size
Slow Pages	The number of files in a Web site that exceed a specific download time at a specified connection rate and their cumulative file size
Older Files	The number of files in a Web site that have not been updated in a specific number of days and their cumulative file size
Recently Added Files	The number of files in a Web site that were created within a specific number of days and their cumulative file size
Hyperlinks	The number of internal and external hyperlinks in a Web site
Unverified Hyperlinks	The number of hyperlinks in a Web site that have not been verified
Broken Hyperlinks	The number of broken hyperlinks in a Web site
External Hyperlinks	The number of hyperlinks in a Web site that connect to files or locations outside the Web site
Internal Hyperlinks	The number of hyperlinks in a Web site that connect to files or locations within the Web site
Component Errors	The number of files in a Web site that have component errors, such as errors in shared borders or link bars
Uncompleted Tasks	The number of uncompleted tasks in Tasks view
Unused Themes	The number of unused theme files in the Web site
Style Sheet Links	The number of pages that link to a style sheet in the Web site
Dynamic Web Templates	The number of files associated with a Dynamic Web Template

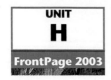

Testing a Page That Contains a Form Component

After publishing a Web site to a server, you must test pages that contain components to ensure that they work correctly. When testing a Web page that contains a form component, you need to verify that the form collects and stores data in the correct format. In addition, you can view the results file on the server to confirm that the data is being stored in the correct format. ▰▰▰ In Unit G, you finished your work on the Online Registration page, which contains a form component. Jason asks you to test the Online Registration page using a browser to ensure that it is correctly storing the form's results on the server.

STEPS

1. **Click the Folders View button** 📁Folders **at the bottom of the Contents pane, click online.htm to select it, then click the Preview button** 🔍 **on the Standard toolbar**
   The Online Registration page opens in a browser.

2. **Complete the form as if you were registering for the race**
   When completing the form, click an option button or check box to select it, click in a text box or text area to type text into it, and click the list arrow for a drop-down box to select a choice from the list.

3. **Click Submit**
   The default Form Confirmation page opens, as shown in Figure H-7, and shows the form field names in the form component and the data you entered into them.

4. **Scroll down the Form Confirmation page, then click the Return to the form link**
   The Online Registration page opens in the browser. Notice that the browser cleared the form fields. The form is ready to accept another submission.

5. **Click the Home link in the top shared border**
   The home page opens in the browser.

FIGURE H-7: Form Confirmation page

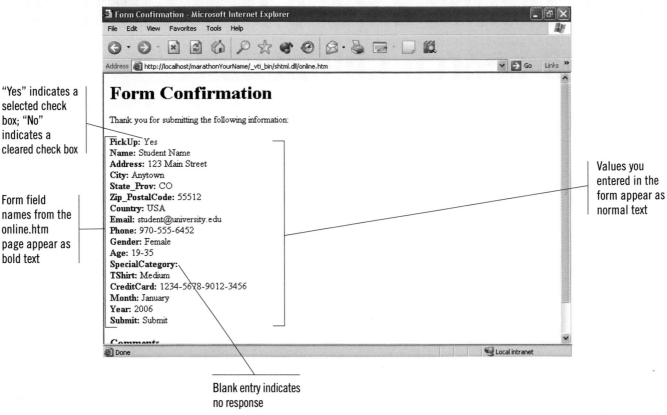

"Yes" indicates a selected check box; "No" indicates a cleared check box

Form field names from the online.htm page appear as bold text

Values you entered in the form appear as normal text

Blank entry indicates no response

Clues to Use

Viewing a results file

When a Web page contains a form, you must use the Form Properties dialog box to specify the way to store the data collected by the form. You can store the data in multiple file formats, including as a text file with comma-separated values, as an HTML document, or in a database table. With the exception of storing form results in a database, the general practice is to store the form results in the Web site's _private folder, thereby protecting the data from being accessed by an Internet visitor. You can view the contents of a results file by opening the _private folder in FrontPage. Usually you can double-click the results file to start a program and open the file at the same time. If you have stored the results as a text file (with a .txt filename extension), then WordPad or Notepad will open; Excel usually opens files with comma-separated values (and the .csv filename extension), and a Web browser or FrontPage opens files with .htm filename extensions. In most cases, each form submitted to the server appears as a single line or section in the file, and new form results are appended to the end of the file. Figure H-8 shows the HTML results file from the form submitted to the server in this lesson.

FIGURE H-8: Form results collected by the online.htm page

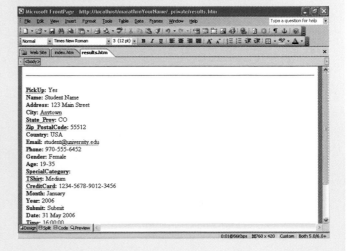

Testing a Page That Contains a Search Component

In Unit G, you created the Search Web page, which contains a search component that searches every page in the marathon Web site for matches to keywords entered by the user. After clicking Start Search, every page in the current Web site is searched for the text in the Search for text box. The search results appear in a table, with each page containing the search keywords appearing as a hyperlink using the page's title.  You decide to test the Search Web page to make sure that the component works correctly.

STEPS

1. **Click the Search link in the left shared border**

   The Search Web page opens in a browser.

2. **Click in the Search for text box**

   The insertion point appears in the text box.

3. **Type t-shirt**

   The search component searches all pages in the marathon Web site for the text "t-shirt." The search ignores the case of the letters typed; the component will search for T-SHIRT, t-shirt, T-shirt, etc. in every page in the marathon Web site.

TROUBLE

If you see the message "Service is not running" instead of the search results, or if the search doesn't find any matching documents, read the Clues to Use in this lesson or ask your instructor or technical support person for help.

4. **Click Start Search**

   Notice that the URL for the page has changed to one returned by the server.

5. **If necessary, press [Page Down]**

   The page now contains a Search Results section. See Figure H-9. By default, the search component returns a list of page titles formatted as hyperlinks. Each page in the Search Results list contains at least one occurrence of the search text "t-shirt."

6. **Click the Registration link in the Search Results table**

   The Registration page opens in the browser. The first paragraph contains the "t-shirt" text, as shown in Figure H-10.

7. **Click the Back button ⊙ on the browser's toolbar**

   You return to the Search Web page. The Registration hyperlink's color has changed, indicating that you've already followed this link.

8. **Close your browser**

FIGURE H-9: Search page with search results

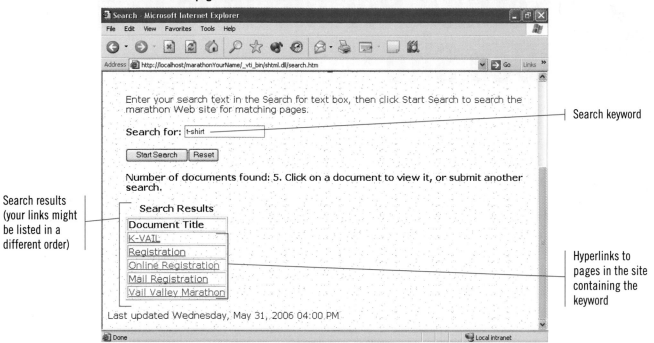

Search keyword

Search results
(your links might
be listed in a
different order)

Hyperlinks to
pages in the site
containing the
keyword

FIGURE H-10: Page containing the search text

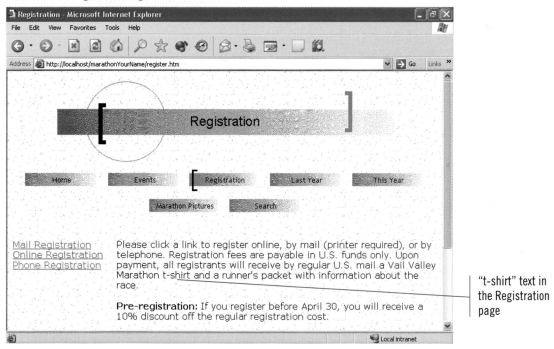

"t-shirt" text in
the Registration
page

Clues to Use

Starting the Indexing Service for IIS

After clicking Start Search, you might see a page with the message "Service is not running." If you published the marathon Web site to IIS, this message indicates that you need to start the server's Indexing Service. To do so, click the Start button on the taskbar, then click Control Panel. Double-click the Administrative Tools icon, double-click the Component Services icon, then click Services (Local) in the pane on the left. Scroll down the list of services on the right and double-click Indexing Service. In the Indexing Service Properties dialog box, click Start, click OK to close the dialog box, then close the remaining windows. It might take several minutes for IIS to index your site and provide the search results. If you see the message "No documents found. Please try again.", you will need to try your search again later.

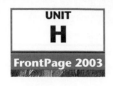
Setting Permissions in a Web Site

You can use FrontPage to secure a published Web site based on the level of access you want to provide other users. A Web site's **administrator** assigns different types of permission to users who access a Web site. (A "user" is a person with access to open a Web site stored on a server using FrontPage, and not a site visitor.) **Browsing permission** lets a user open a Web site in FrontPage and view it after it has been published. This permission is basically the same as what a user would see if he or she opened the Web site in a Web browser using the Web's URL, except the user does the browsing from FrontPage and has access to Reports view and the Web site's hidden folders. **Authoring permission** lets a user create and edit pages in the Web site. **Administering permission** lets a user create new Web sites and set permissions for other users. Usually, only the Web site's administrator has administering permission. ▓▓▓▓ Jason asks you to set the permissions for Mary Hall, who will have authoring permission. Jason verifies that all other users will have browsing permission. *Note*: Check with your instructor before completing the following steps. If you cannot change the permissions in your published marathon Web site, read the following steps without completing them at the computer.

STEPS

1. **In Folders view, click Tools on the menu bar, point to Server, then click Administration Home**
   Your browser starts and opens the Administration page. The Web site's administrator uses this page to add users to a Web site and change existing users' permissions.

2. **Click the Change subweb permissions link**
   The Edit Permissions page opens, as shown in Figure H-11. You use this page to indicate whether the current Web site should use the same permissions as the parent Web site. For IIS, localhost is the parent Web site, and all Web sites created on localhost are subwebs of localhost.

3. **Click the Use unique permissions for this Web site option button, then click Submit**
   The Operation Results page opens, then the Edit Permissions page opens again.

4. **Click the Administration link at the top of the page**
   The Administration page opens, as shown in Figure H-12.

5. **In the Users and Roles section, click the Manage users link**
   The User Management page opens, showing the users for the marathon Web site.

6. **Click the Add a user link, type Mary Hall in the User name text box, press [Tab], type pass1, press [Tab], type pass1, then scroll to the bottom of the page**
   You created the user name "Mary Hall" and a password, "pass1." When Mary needs to edit a Web page, she will use this user name and password and FrontPage to open the Web site on the server. Password data appears with asterisks or dots instead of the actual password, thereby preventing other users from viewing sensitive data.

7. **In the User Role section, click the Author check box, then click Add User**
   The Operation Results page opens as Mary is added with authoring permission for the marathon Web site, then the User Management page opens again. Now Mary's name appears in the Manage Users list and shows her role as an Author. See Figure H-13.

8. **Click the Administration link at the top of the page, then in the Users and Roles section click the Change anonymous access settings link**
   The Anonymous Access page opens, as shown in Figure H-14. The default setting for a Web site allows all Internet visitors to browse the published Web site. You could change this setting so all Internet visitors have authoring or administrating permission for the Web site, although it would be unusual to do so.

9. **Close your browser**

FIGURE H-11: Edit Permissions page

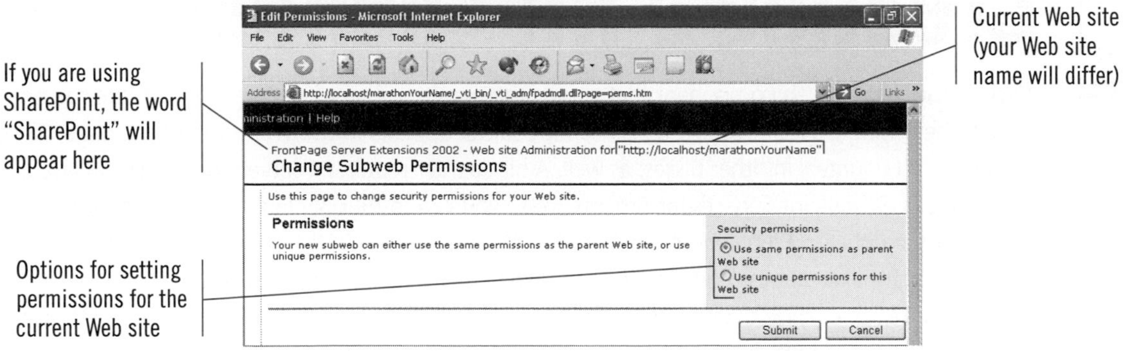

If you are using SharePoint, the word "SharePoint" will appear here

Current Web site (your Web site name will differ)

Options for setting permissions for the current Web site

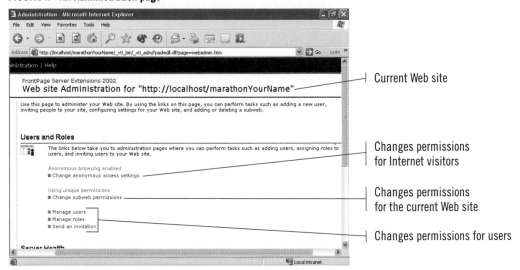

FIGURE H-12: Administration page

Current Web site

Changes permissions for Internet visitors

Changes permissions for the current Web site

Changes permissions for users

FIGURE H-13: User Management page

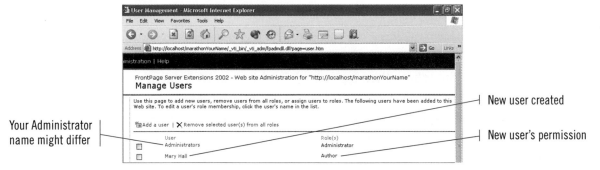

New user created

Your Administrator name might differ

New user's permission

FIGURE H-14: Anonymous Access page

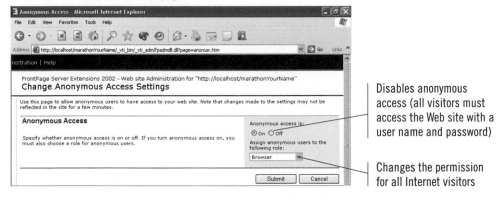

Disables anonymous access (all visitors must access the Web site with a user name and password)

Changes the permission for all Internet visitors

Creating a Hit Counter

A **hit counter** is a Web component that counts the number of times a page in a Web site has been opened or refreshed using a Web browser. Usually a hit counter appears in the Web site's home page, although you can create hit counters in other pages, as well. A hit counter requires a server and the FrontPage 2002 Server Extensions or SharePoint Services for processing, so you can test it only in a server-based Web site. Because a hit counter is a built-in Web component, you just need to insert it in the appropriate location in a Web page, and FrontPage will create the code to display and increment its counter. You can accept the default settings for the hit counter, or change the counter style and other properties if desired. The counter style is implemented using a default or custom-designed GIF picture that displays the digits zero through nine. ▓▓▓▓ Jason wants you to use a hit counter to track the number of times that Internet visitors open the Registration Web page. He can compare this number to the actual number of applications received as a way of tracking the effectiveness of the Web site.

STEPS

1. **In Folders view, double-click register.htm in the Contents pane**

   The Registration Web page opens in Design view. This page contains links to three child pages, which let runners register by mail, by using the online registration form, and by phone.

2. **Press [Ctrl][End], press [Enter], type You are visitor number, then press [Spacebar]**

   You'll include the hit counter in the sentence you began typing.

3. **Click the Web Component button 🖾 on the Standard toolbar, click Hit Counter in the Component type list, click the third counter style in the Choose a counter style list, then click Finish**

   The Hit Counter Properties dialog box opens, as shown in Figure H-15. The counter style you chose is selected.

4. **Click the Reset counter to check box, press [Tab], then type 1000**

   This setting starts the counter value at 1000.

QUICK TIP

Most Web sites begin the counter value at a number other than zero.

5. **Click OK**

   A hit counter is inserted in the page. When the page is viewed in a browser, the hit counter will show the current visitor number.

6. **Press [Spacebar], then type to the Registration Web page.**

   The hit counter and the sentence that contains it are complete.

7. **Click the Save button 🖫 on the Standard toolbar, click the Preview button 🖾 on the Standard toolbar, then scroll to the bottom of the page**

   The Registration page opens in a browser. The hit counter shows that you are visitor number 1001 to the page.

8. **Click the Refresh button 🖾 on the browser's toolbar**

   Because you refreshed the page, the hit counter value changes to 1002, as shown in Figure H-16.

9. **Close your browser, close the marathon Web site, then exit FrontPage**

FIGURE H-15: Hit Counter Properties dialog box

Selected counter style

Available counter styles

Starts the counter at a specific value

Specifies the counter's size

Hit counter will appear here

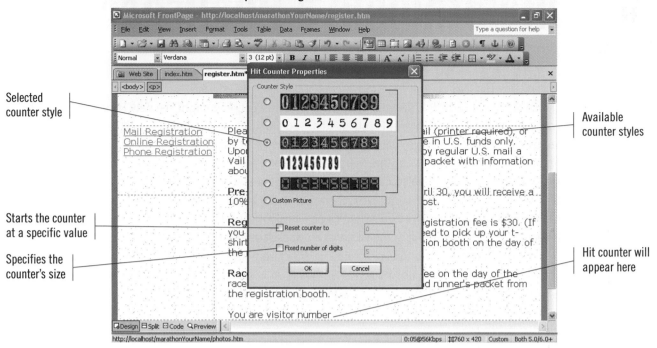

FIGURE H-16: Hit counter in the Registration page

This page has been accessed twice

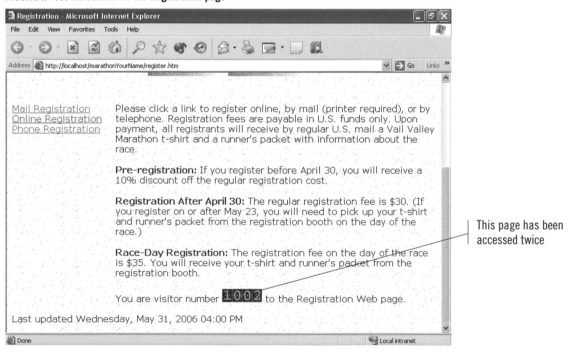

FrontPage 2003

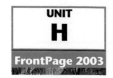

Maintaining a Published Web Site

Depending on which ISP hosts your Web site on the Internet, you might see new folders in the Folder List when you open your Web site in FrontPage that you did not see when you opened your Web site from IIS. Some ISPs create a stats, logs, data, or similarly named folder that stores Web pages created by the server. This folder contains data about the Web site's usage and files. For example, an ISP might create a **usage log**, which is a page containing information about the number of times your home page has been opened, the number of times various pages were opened each day or each hour during the day, or the total number of times a Web page was refreshed during a single session. The information provided about a Web site varies based on the ISP that hosts it. Some ISPs only provide usage information if you purchase additional services. Depending on your ISP, you can open your logs either from Reports view or by using a browser. Check with your ISP to locate its usage logs for your site. ▓▓▓▓ After publishing the marathon Web site to an ISP, you will examine some of the pages that provide usage data.

DETAILS

- **Traffic reports**

  Traffic reports provide data about the number of visitors to your Web site, page views, hits, and the total number of bytes transferred from the server to a browser. This information might be summarized in an hourly, daily, or monthly report. Figure H-17 shows a traffic report for one year that provides data on such categories as the number of visitors, page views, or hits for a Web site.

- **Page reports**

  Page reports provide data about the number of page views for each page in the Web site. One page report might show the number of hits based on the different types of files included in the Web site. Another page report might show the status of pages that were opened based on an HTTP code that represents a normal page view, a partial page view, a page forbidden error, or a page not found error. This information can help you to determine if your site's pages are opening correctly and if visitors have attempted to open pages that they did not have permission to view.

- **Domain reports**

  Domain reports provide data about the number of visitors from each domain name (such as aol.com) that used a browser to access the site. This report might also list domains from countries outside the United States separately to help you assess your site's international traffic.

- **Browser reports**

  Browser reports identify the different browsers used to access your site and the number of visitors using each browser. This report also might show the different operating systems on which the browser is used, such as Windows XP or Macintosh. Figure H-18 shows a browser report that lists the different browsers used to access a site.

FIGURE H-17: Sample usage report about Web site traffic

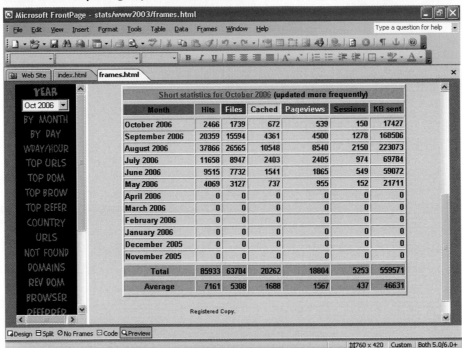

FIGURE H-18: Sample report about the browsers used to access a Web site

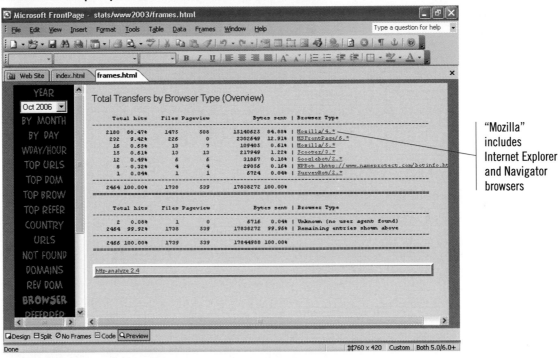

"Mozilla" includes Internet Explorer and Navigator browsers

FrontPage 2003

Clues to Use

Submitting your Web site to search engines

Normally, people don't just stumble into your Internet Web site after you publish it. A few days or weeks after you publish your Web site, a search engine will index your site's URL and keywords in its database. When users run a search using keywords that are included in your Web site, a link to your URL appears in their search results. For example, the marathon Web site's keywords might be "marathon," "Vail Valley Marathon," "mountain races," and "running." Instead of waiting for the various Web search engines—such as Yahoo!, AltaVista, HotBot, and Excite—to find your site, you can submit your site's URL to the search engines individually by following the instructions listed at their Web sites. If you don't have time to submit your URL to individual search engines, you can use a specialized Web site, such as Submit It!, to submit your site's URL to multiple search engines simultaneously.

Practice

▼ CONCEPTS REVIEW

Label each element in the Microsoft FrontPage window shown in Figure H-19.

FIGURE H-19

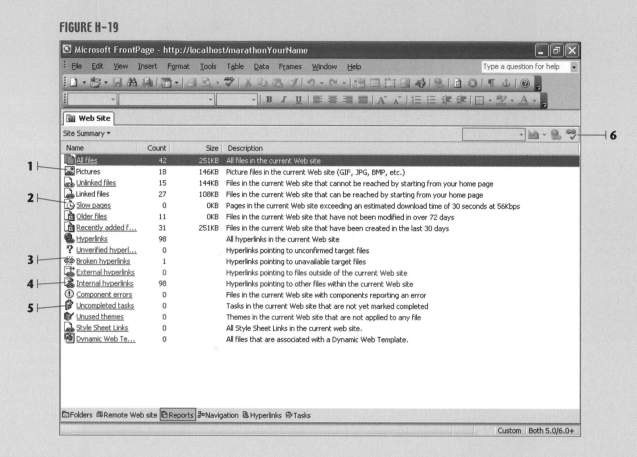

Match each of the following terms with the statement that best describes its function.

7. **Administrator**

8. **Authoring permission**

9. **Recalculate hyperlinks**

10. **Site Summary report**

11. **Slow Pages report**

12. **Verify hyperlinks**

a. A process that checks each hyperlink in a Web site to ensure its validity

b. A process that repairs any broken hyperlinks, updates shared borders and link bar files, and deletes any unused theme files in a Web site

c. Lists information about a Web site's size, features, and potential problems

d. Lists all pages that download slowly based on a specific time and download speed

e. The person who is responsible for assigning users different levels of permission for accessing a Web site

f. The specified user can create and edit pages in the Web site

Select the best answer from the following list of choices.

13. **Reports view provides information about the current Web site's:**
    a. Recently added files.
    b. Pages that are slow to download.
    c. Monthly usage.
    d. All of the above

14. **Detailed information about the broken hyperlinks in a Web site appears in the:**
    a. Recalculate Hyperlinks dialog box.
    b. Verify Hyperlinks dialog box.
    c. Broken Hyperlinks report.
    d. Site Summary report.

15. **Unused theme files are deleted when you:**
    a. Run a Site Summary report.
    b. Verify a Web site's hyperlinks.
    c. Delete them from the Theme task pane.
    d. Recalculate a Web site's hyperlinks.

16. **Which report lists both the number of files in a Web site that are not linked to the home page and their cumulative file size?**
    a. Unlinked Files report
    b. Linked Files report
    c. Unverified Hyperlinks report
    d. Component Errors report

17. **Which report lists the number of hyperlinks in a Web site?**
    a. Linked Files report
    b. Unlinked Files report
    c. Hyperlinks report
    d. Internal Hyperlinks report

18. **If you try to search a Web site and receive a "Service is not running" message, you need to start the:**
    a. Server.
    b. Browser.
    c. Indexing Service.
    d. All of the above

19. **Which of the following permission levels lets a user view a Web site using FrontPage after it has been published?**
    a. Browsing
    b. Anonymous access
    c. Authoring
    d. Administering

20. **Which of the following reports available from an ISP describes the number of visitors to a site, the number of page views, and the total number of bytes transferred?**
    a. Browser report
    b. Traffic report
    c. Page report
    d. Domain report

▼ SKILLS REVIEW

1. **Publish a Web site.**
   a. Start FrontPage, then use the Empty Web Site template to create a new Web site named **homeloan** in the location where your Web sites are stored.
   b. Import all eight files from the UnitH\SR folder on the drive and folder where your Data Files are stored into the root folder of the homeloan Web site.
   c. Publish the homeloan Web site to your server, using the publish destination **http://localhost/homeloan[YourName]**. Click Yes to create a new Web site at the specified location, then publish the local Web site to the remote Web site location.
   d. After the homeloan[YourName] Web site has been published, view the home page of your published Web site in a browser, noting that there are no navigation options. Close your browser.
   e. In FrontPage, close the disk-based Web site.

2. **Open a Web site from a server.**
   a. Open the Open Site dialog box, then navigate to My Network Places.
   b. Double-click the folder for your server, then open the homeloan[YourName] Web site. (*Note*: If the folder for your server doesn't appear in the list of network shortcuts, click the homeloan[YourName] on localhost folder, then click Open.)
   c. In Navigation view, add the convtl.htm, arms.htm, payment.htm, req_info.htm, and search.htm pages to the Web site's navigation structure as child pages of the home page, then add the 15yr.htm and 30yr.htm pages as child pages of the convtl.htm page.
   d. For all pages in the Web site, create top and left shared borders. The top shared border should include a page banner and a link bar with links to same-level pages and to the home page. Format the links using an HTML style where each link is enclosed in brackets. The left shared border should include a link bar with links to child-level pages. Format the links using the same style you used for the link bar in the top shared border.
   e. Apply the Global Marketing theme to all pages in the Web site. Select the options to use vivid colors, active graphics, and a background picture. (If you do not have this theme, select another one.)
   f. Use Design view to examine the contents of each Web page in the Web site.

3. **Recalculate and verify hyperlinks.**
   a. Close and save any open Web pages in Design view.
   b. Recalculate the site's hyperlinks.
   c. Change to Reports view, then verify all hyperlinks in the Web site.
   d. Use [Print Screen] and WordPad to print the Broken Hyperlinks report in landscape orientation. Close WordPad without saving changes.

4. **Test a page that contains a form component.**
   a. Open the req_info.htm page in Design view.
   b. Open the Form Properties dialog box for the form in this page, click Options, then set the form to send its results to a file named **_private/results.htm**. If necessary, select the HTML file format. (*Note*: Do not complete the optional second file information.)
   c. Save the Request Information page, then preview it in a browser.
   d. Complete the form using your first and last names and real or fictitious data. Before clicking Submit, print the page.
   e. Submit the form to the server, then print the confirmation page that opens.
   f. Click the link to return to the form.

5. **Test a page that contains a search component.**
   a. Click the Search link in the top shared border to open the Search page.
   b. Enter the keyword **ARM** in the Search for text box.
   c. Start the search, then print the page that opens.
   d. Click the first hyperlink in the search results.
   e. Close your browser.

6. **Set permissions in a Web site.**

   Note: Complete the following steps only if you can set permissions for your published Web site.

   a. In FrontPage, open the Administration page.

   b. Click the Change subweb permissions link, then change the current Web site to use unique permissions.

   c. Click the Administration link at the top of the page, click the Manage users link, then click the Add a user link.

   d. Add yourself as a new user by entering your user name and password (twice).

   e. Select the option to give yourself Advanced author permission, then add yourself as a user.

   f. Close your browser.

7. **Create a hit counter.**

   a. Open the home page in Design view, then on a new line at the bottom of the page, type **You are visitor number to our Web site.**

   b. Position the insertion point to the left of the word **to** in the sentence you just typed.

   c. Insert a hit counter at the location of the insertion point. Select the first style in the list and set the counter to start at 1000.

   d. Press [Spacebar], then save the home page.

   e. Preview the home page in a browser, refresh the home page, print the page, then close your browser.

   f. Close the homeloan[YourName] Web site, then exit FrontPage.

▼ INDEPENDENT CHALLENGE 1

While completing the units in this book, you have learned many new skills. Use your knowledge of FrontPage to create a Web site that features content related to a subject that you enjoy, such as a sport, hobby, or other interest, or about yourself or a business (real or fictitious).

a. Start FrontPage, then use the One Page Web Site template to create a new Web site named **myweb** in the location where your Web sites are stored.

b. Create at least five Web pages related to your topic. Your Web site must include pages containing a form component, a search component, and a hit counter. Save the pages with appropriate filenames and titles.

c. In at least two of the pages, include pictures that you have available (such as digital or scanned picture files) or from the Clip Art task pane. Resize and resample the pictures as necessary to size them appropriately, then save them with the default filenames in the Web site's images folder.

d. Add your site's pages to the Web site's navigation structure.

e. Use one or more shared borders to add navigation options to the Web site as appropriate.

f. Recalculate and then verify the hyperlinks in your site. If necessary, fix any broken hyperlinks. If you cannot fix a broken hyperlink, add it as a task for completion in Tasks view.

g. Use the information contained in the Site Summary report to identify any potential problems in your Web site, then fix them. Use WordPad to print the Site Summary report, then close WordPad without saving changes.

h. Save and close all pages in the Web site, then publish it to a remote server using the publish destination **http://localhost/myweb[YourName]**. After publishing the site, close your disk-based Web site.

i. Open your published Web site from the server and then change to Reports view. If necessary, make any changes as indicated by the report. Save your changes.

j. Set the Web site's permissions to add one user who has authoring permission and one user who has browsing permission. (*Note*: If you cannot set permissions for your published Web site, skip this step.)

k. Thoroughly test your published Web site in a browser, then close your browser.

l. Close the myweb[YourName] Web site, then exit FrontPage.

▼ INDEPENDENT CHALLENGE 2

Before publishing the Villages at Kensington Neighbourhood Association Web site on the Internet Web server that will host it, you will publish it to your computer's server so you can test pages that require the processing power of a server. In addition, you will add a Web page that searches the entire site, making it easier for residents to locate information quickly.

a. Start FrontPage, open the village Web site from the location where your Web sites are stored, then if necessary change to Folders view. (If you did not create and change this Web site in Units A through G, contact your instructor for assistance.)

b. Publish the Web site to your server using the publish destination **http://localhost/village[YourName]**.

c. After the village[YourName] Web site has been published, view your remote Web site in a browser, then use the links to navigate the site.

d. Open the Registration Form page, then complete the form. Enter your first and last names in the Last Name text box, then complete the rest of the form using fictitious or real data. Before clicking Submit, print the page.

e. Submit the form to the server, then print the confirmation page that opens.

f. Click the link to return to the form, then close your browser.

g. Close your disk-based Web site in FrontPage, then open the server-based Web site that you just published. Use the New task pane and the Search Page template to create a new page in the Web site. Save the new page using the filename **search.htm** and the title **Search**. Add the search.htm page to the Web site's navigation structure, positioning it to the right of the Deed Restrictions page.

h. Preview the Search page in a browser, then use it to identify all pages containing the keyword **fence**. Print the page containing the search results, then close your browser.

i. Recalculate and verify all hyperlinks in the village[YourName] Web site, then use WordPad to print the Broken Hyperlinks report in landscape orientation. Close WordPad without saving changes.

j. Open the Registration Form Web page (register.htm) in Design view. On a new line below the first sentence in the page (which begins **Use this page to register...**), create a hit counter and appropriate text. Use your choice of hit counter style and start the counter at 100. Save the page, preview it in a browser, refresh the page, print the page, then close your browser.

k. Close the remote Web site in FrontPage, then open the local (disk-based) Web Site. In Remote Web Site view, choose the option to synchronize the Web sites, then click Publish Web site. If necessary, choose the option to overwrite local files. Open the Registration Form page in Design view, and confirm that the hit counter appears in the disk-based Web site.

l. Close the village[YourName] Web site, then exit FrontPage.

▼ INDEPENDENT CHALLENGE 3

Before publishing the Web site commissioned by the city of Tryon, North Carolina on the Internet Web server that will host it, you will publish it to your computer's server so you can test pages that require the processing power of a server. In addition, you will add a Web page that searches the entire site, making it easier for potential visitors to the city of Tryon to locate information quickly.

a. Start FrontPage, open the tryon Web site from the location where your Web sites are stored, then if necessary change to Folders view. (If you did not create and change this Web site in Units A through G, contact your instructor for assistance.)

b. Publish the Web site to your server using the publish destination **http://localhost/tryon[YourName]**.

c. After the tryon[YourName] Web site has been published, view your remote Web site in a browser, then use the links to navigate the site.

d. Open the Request Information page in your browser, then complete the form. Enter your first and last names in the appropriate text boxes, then complete the rest of the form using fictitious or real data. Before clicking Submit Form, print the page.

e. Submit the form to the server, then print the confirmation page that opens.

f. Click the link to return to the form, then close your browser.

▼ INDEPENDENT CHALLENGE 3 (CONTINUED)

g. Close your disk-based Web site in FrontPage, then open the server-based Web site that you just published. Use the New task pane and the Search Page template to create a new page in the Web site. Save the new page using the filename **search.htm** and the title **Search**. Add the search.htm page to the Web site's navigation structure, positioning it to the right of the Request Information page.

h. Preview the Search page in a browser, then use it to identify all pages containing the keyword **bed-and-breakfast**. Print the page containing the search results, then close your browser.

i. Recalculate and verify all hyperlinks in the tryon[YourName] Web site, then use WordPad to print the Broken Hyperlinks report in landscape orientation. Close WordPad without saving changes.

j. Open the home page in Design view, then select the heading at the top of the page (**Thank you for visiting the Tryon Web site!**). Replace the selected heading with the following text: **You are visitor number [hit counter] to our Web site!** Replace the **[hit counter]** text with a hit counter. Select a style of your choice and set the starting number to 100. Save the page, preview it in a browser, refresh the page, print the page, then close your browser.

k. Close the remote Web site in FrontPage, then open the local (disk-based) Web site. In Remote Web Site view, choose the option to synchronize the Web sites, then click Publish Web site. If necessary, choose the option to overwrite local files. Open the home page in Design view, and confirm that the hit counter appears in the disk-based Web site.

l. Close the tryon[YourName] Web site, then exit FrontPage.

▼ INDEPENDENT CHALLENGE 4

Katy Ricke has just finished creating and thoroughly testing a Web site for her cosmetics business. She wants to learn more about using Remote Web Site view to publish her site.

a. If necessary, connect to the Internet.

b. Start FrontPage, type **publishing a Web site** in the Type a question for help text box, then press [Enter].

c. Locate the **Publish files and folders to a file system** link in the Search Results task pane, and then click it.

d. Examine the hyperlinks in the Microsoft Office FrontPage Help window that opens, and read the content they provide about publishing to a file system. Close the Microsoft Office FrontPage Help window.

e. Click Help on the menu bar, then click Microsoft Office Online. Click the link to FrontPage, click the 2003 assistance link, then type **About publishing files and folders** in the search text box and click the button to initiate the search. (*Note:* Microsoft might redesign its site. If you cannot find the 2003 assistance link, search the page for a link with a similar name that lets you search for help in FrontPage 2003.) Examine the links that appear in the results and then click the link with the same title as your search text. Read the information provided in the search to learn more about publishing files and folders.

f. On a sheet of paper with your name on it, answer the following questions:

1. What is an extended Web server?

2. What is File Transfer Protocol?

3. What is Web-based Distributed Authoring and Versioning?

g. Close your browser, then exit FrontPage.

▼ VISUAL WORKSHOP

Examine the Site Summary report shown in Figure H-20. What problems do you expect this Web site to have? How would you fix these problems? After you analyze the Site Summary report, write a report identifying the problems you would expect to find if you were asked to test this Web site.

FIGURE H-20

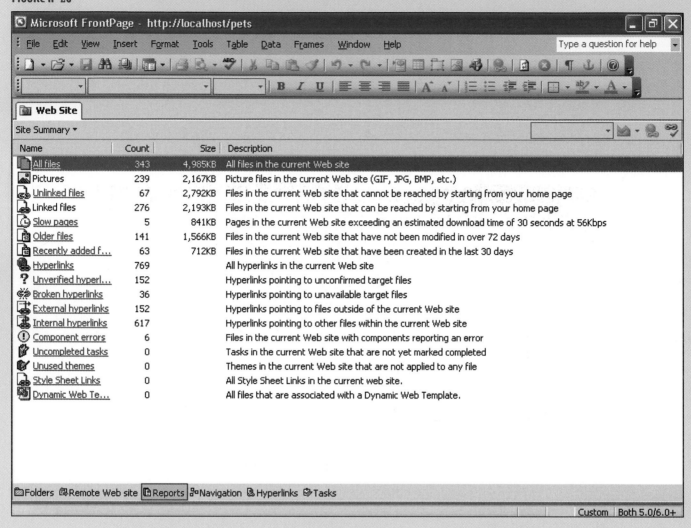

Glossary

Absolutely positioned picture A picture placed precisely in a page using coordinates.

Active graphics Theme elements that become animated in a page, such as a hyperlink button changing color when the pointer moves over it.

Administering permission A level of Web site permission that lets a user create and edit pages in a Web site.

Administrator A person who manages and assigns different types of permission to users who access a Web site.

Attributes Optional features (active graphics, vivid colors, and background picture) that you can enable to enhance a theme.

Authoring permission A level of Web site permission that lets a user create Web sites and set permissions for other users.

Background picture A picture that is used as a Web page background; the content of the Web page appears on top of the picture.

Browser reports Reports that identify the different browsers used to access a site and the number of visitors using different browsers.

Browsing permission A level of Web site permission that lets a user open a Web site and view it after it has been published.

Caption An optional title that appears above or below a table.

Cell The smallest component of a table, created by the intersection of a row and a column.

Cell border The border around each individual cell in a table.

Cell padding The distance in pixels between the content of a cell and the inside edge of a cell.

Cell spacing The distance in pixels between table cells.

Check box A form field that lets a user indicate a yes/no response to a single question.

Child page A Web page at a lower level than other pages in the navigation structure in Navigation view.

Client In a client/server network, a computer that is connected to the server.

Client/server network A network of client computers that are connected to a single server to share resources.

Code view The Page view of a Web page that shows the HTML document that creates the Web page.

Comma-delimited text A file format that separates with commas the data entered into a form's fields.

Confirmation page A Web page that the server sends to the form's user for verification after the user submits the form to the server; the confirmation page can include a copy of a form's results or simply acknowledge that the form was submitted.

Design view The default Page view of a Web page that shows the formatted Web page.

Disk-based Web site A Web site stored on a disk, such as a hard drive, a network drive, or an external drive.

Domain name The unique address for a specific Web site on the Internet.

Domain reports Reports that provide data about the number of visitors from each domain name (such as aol.com) that used a browser to access a site.

Drop-down box A form field that organizes choices in a scrollable list that a user can display by clicking a list arrow.

Embed The method used to save a picture file with a Web page, where the picture is saved in the Web site's images folder and a reference to the picture file is saved in the Web page that uses it.

External link A hyperlink that opens a location in another Web page or Web site.

Folders view A Web site view in which you examine, create, delete, copy, and move the files and folders in a Web site.

Form (Web page) An object in a Web page that contains form fields that collect information.

Form component A container that stores a form's fields and other form content and identifies the part of the Web page that the server will process.

Form field A data-entry field in a form, such as a text box or an option button.

Form handler A program that collects and processes the data contained in a form.

Form results The collection of data entered into a form by the user and processed by a server.

Form templates Predesigned Web pages with form components that you can adapt and use.

Format Painter A feature that lets you copy the formatting and style of existing text so that you can paste it to other text that you click or select.

Frame margin The amount of space between the inside border of a frame and the text or picture(s) in the frame.

Frame spacing The thickness of a frame's borders when they appear in a frames page.

Frames page A single Web page that divides the browser window into two or more windows, each containing a separate, scrollable page.

Frames page template A Web page that contains the specifications for the individual locations and sizes of the frames in a frames page.

Frameset *See* frames page.

FrontPage 2003 A program that lets you create, manage, publish, and maintain a Web site.

GIF A popular format for storing picture files used in Web pages that displays up to 256 colors in a compressed format that supports animation.

Grayscale An effect that you can apply to a picture to change its colors to shades of gray.

Group name The name assigned to identify a related set of option button or check box form fields in a form.

Hidden folder A folder in a FrontPage Web site that is not accessible to site visitors after a Web site has been published to a Web server.

Hit counter A Web component that counts the number of times a page in a Web site has been opened or refreshed using a Web browser.

Home page The main page in a Web site, around which all other Web pages are organized.

Hotspot An area in a picture that contains a hyperlink.

HTML (Hypertext Markup Language) A programming language used to create Web pages.

HTTP (Hypertext Transfer Protocol) The set of rules that a browser uses to retrieve and display a Web page requested by a client.

Hyperlink Text or an object that, when clicked, opens a location in the same Web page, a different Web page, or a different Web site.

Hyperlinks view A Web site view in which you view the hyperlinks leading to and from a selected Web page.

Iframe A frame that is created and embedded in a normal Web page and not in a frames page.

Image map A picture that contains one or more hotspots.

images folder A folder in a FrontPage Web site in which you store picture and other multimedia files used in the Web site's pages.

Internal link A hyperlink that opens a location in the same Web page.

Internet A worldwide collection of computer networks that are connected to one another using cables, phone lines, and other resources.

Internet Information Services (IIS) A Microsoft Windows application that you can install on your computer to make it function as a Web server.

JPEG (JPG) A popular format for storing picture files of photographs and other high-quality digital images used in Web pages.

Link bar A component in a Web page that contains hyperlinks to other Web pages based on the position of the Web site's pages in the navigation structure in Navigation view.

localhost The default name of the IIS Web server.

Merging cells The process of combining two or more cells in a column or row into a single cell.

Navigation buttons The hyperlinks appearing in a link bar; they can appear as buttons or as regular text.

Navigation view A Web site view in which you create or display a Web site's navigation structure, which identifies the relationships between pages in a Web site.

Nested table A table that appears in one cell of another table.

Network Two or more computers that are connected to each other to share information about resources.

No Frames page A page that contains a default message that says "This page uses frames, but your browser doesn't support them."

Nonprinting characters Characters in a Web page that are not printed but are visible on the screen when this feature is enabled.

Office Assistant An animated character that offers tips, answers questions, and provides access to the FrontPage Help system.

Option button A form field that lets a user select one choice in a group of mutually exclusive choices.

Page banner A picture or text object in a Web page that includes a page's title as shown in Navigation view.

Page reports Reports that provide data about the number of page views for each page in a Web site.

Page view A Web site view in which you create, edit, and format the content of a Web page.

Paragraph style The properties associated with paragraphs, such as line spacing, indentation, and alignment.

Parent page A Web page at a higher level than other pages in the navigation structure in Navigation view.

Photo gallery A component that displays pictures, thumbnail pictures, photo captions, and photo descriptions in a Web page.

Picture Any file that contains a graphic image.

PNG A popular format for storing picture files used in Web pages that displays pictures with up to 16 million colors in a compressed format.

Preview view The Page view of a Web page that lets you see a Web page as it will appear in a browser, without needing to start a browser.

Publish The process of transferring a Web site's files and folders to a Web server.

Radio button *See* option button.

Recalculating hyperlinks A process that repairs any broken hyperlinks, updates shared border and link bar files, updates FrontPage components, updates data on the server, and deletes any unused theme files in a Web site.

Relatively positioned picture A picture placed precisely using text in the page to specify its location.

Remote Web Site view A Web site view that lets you transfer or synchronize files between a local computer or network and a Web server or other location using different methods, including Web Distributed Authoring and Versioning (WebDAV), File Transfer Protocol (FTP), and HTTP.

Reports view A Web site view in which you analyze, summarize, and produce various types of reports about a Web site's files, folders, usage, and problems.

Resampling An action you can execute on a picture that you resized in FrontPage that removes extra pixels so it will download more quickly from the Web server on which it is stored. Resampling also improves the clarity of the picture.

Results file *See* form results.

Root Web The parent Web site in which other Web sites (subsites) are stored.

Scrolling text box *See* text area.

Server-based Web site A Web site stored on a server.

Shared border An area at the top, left, right, or bottom of every Web page in a Web site that contains the same content.

Site Summary report A report available in Reports view that includes subreports providing detailed information about a Web site.

Split (a frame) The process of creating two frames from an existing frame in a frames page.

Split view The Page view of a Web page that splits the Page view window into two panes, with the Web page in Design view on the top and the HTML document in Code view on the bottom.

Splitting cells The process of dividing a single cell into two or more columns or rows.

Subsite (subweb) A Web site stored in another Web site.

Table (Web page) An object consisting of one or more rows of cells that organize and arrange data.

Table AutoFormat A predefined combination of colors, colored borders, and special effects that you can apply to a table.

Target frame The frame in which to open a new Web page when a user clicks a hyperlink.

Tasks view A Web site view in which you maintain a list of the tasks required to complete a Web site.

Text area A form field that accepts multiple lines of typed text.

Text box A form field that accepts a single line of typed information, such as a name or phone number.

Theme A collection of coordinated graphics, colors, and fonts applied to individual pages or all pages in a Web site.

Thumbnail picture A small version of a larger picture that, when clicked, activates a hyperlink and opens the original, larger picture.

Traffic reports Reports that provide data about the number of visitors to a site, page views, hits, and the total number of bytes transferred from the server to the browsers that make connections to it.

URL (Uniform Resource Locator) The unique address for a particular Web site on the Internet.

Usage log A Web page containing information about the usage statistics for a published Web site.

Verifying hyperlinks A process that checks each hyperlink in a Web site to ensure its validity.

Vivid colors A theme's enhanced color set, which produces brighter, deeper colors.

Wash out An effect that you can apply to a picture to make its colors appear with less intensity and brightness.

Web browser Software that lets a computer interact with the Internet or other network.

Web page template A Web page containing sample content related to a specific topic on which you can create a new Web page.

Web safe color One of 216 colors that are displayed correctly and consistently on computers running different operating systems.

Web server A computer connected to the Internet and on which Web sites are stored.

Web site A collection of Web pages that are organized around a specific organization or topic and connected to one another using hyperlinks.

Web site template A Web site containing sample pages related to a specific topic and other structural information that you can use to create a new Web site.

WordArt An object in a Web page that uses text and special effects to create a picture.

Index

SPECIAL CHARACTERS
* (asterisk), B-6, B-7
\ (backslash), B-2
... (ellipsis), A-14
[ ] (square brackets), B-2

►A

absolute positioning, D-4
active graphics, C-14. *See also* graphics
ActiveX controls (Microsoft), B-5
Add File to Import List dialog box, B-12
administrators
    described, H-12
    permissions and, H-12–13
Align Left button, B-8
Align Right button, B-8
All Files report, H-7
All Programs menu, A-6
AltaVista, H-17
applets, B-5
ASP (Active Server Pages), B-5
Assigned to list box, A-14
Associated With column, A-14
asterisk (*), B-6, B-7
attributes, of themes, C-14
authoring settings, B-4–5, H-5
Authoring tab, B-4–5, H-5
Auto Thumbnail button, D-12–13
AutoFormat feature, E-16–17
AutoShapes, D-11
AutoShapes toolbar, D-11

►B

background images, C-14, D-3, E-13. *See also* graphics
backslash (\), B-2
banner frames, F-4–13, F-16
banners, C-2–3, C-8, C-16–17
Bevel button, E-12
Bold button, A-12, B-8, E-14
boldface font, A-12, A-13, B-8, E-14
border(s)
    color, E-5
    deleting, E-14–15
    displaying, F-16
    frame pages and, F-12, F-16–17
    hidden, F-16–17
    removing, E-7

tables and, E-5, E-7, E-14–15
    thickness of, F-17
Borders button, B-9
brightness adjustments, D-4
Broken Hyperlinks report, H-7
browser(s). *See also* previewing
    described, A-2
    frame pages and, F-3, F-11, F-15
    graphics and, E-13
    lists, B-4
    page options and, B-4
    photo galleries and, D-16–17
    publishing Web sites and, H-2–3
    reports, H-16–17
    selecting, B-16
    tables and, E-13
    viewing graphics with, D-12–13
    viewing HTML documents with, B-17
Bullets button, B-9

►C

cable modems, B-16
captions, E-4–5
case sensitivity, B-3, H-12
cell(s)
    aligning, E-14–15
    borders, E-4–5
    deleting, E-8–9
    described, E-2
    formatting, E-14–15
    inserting, E-8–9
    inserting graphics in, E-12
    merging, E-10–11
    padding, E-4–5
    properties, E-5
    resizing, E-6–7
    spacing, E-4–5
    splitting, E-10–11
Cell Properties dialog box, E-5
Center button, B-6, B-7, B-8, D-12, E-14
Change Folder dialog box, D-2
check boxes
    adding, G-12–13
    described, G-12
client(s)
    described, A-2
    /server networks, A-2
Clip Art task pane, D-11
Close button, A-16
Close command, A-14, A-18

Close Site command, A-18, B-2
closing FrontPage, A-18–19
Clues to Use box, C-16
Code view, A-12
color
    border, E-5
    font, B-8, B-9, D-7
    frame pages and, F-9, F-16
    graphics and, D-6, D-7, C-14
    link, H-10
Color button, D-6
columns
    deleting, E-8
    resizing, E-6–7
comma-delimited text, G-14, G-15
components, G-2–3, G-16–17, H-7–9, H-11
Component Errors report, H-7
Component Services console (Control Panel), H-11
computer names, H-2
Confirm Save dialog box, C-14
Confirmation Form, G-2
Confirmation Page tab, G-14
confirmation pages, G-2–3, G-14
connection speeds, B-16
content, preparing, A-4
Contents frame, F-4–7, F-10, F-16
Contents pane, A-10, E-2, F-14, G-10, H-4
contrast adjustments, D-4
Control Panel, H-11
Convert Text To Table dialog box, E-9
Corporate Presence Wizard template, B-3
CSS (Cascading Style Sheets), B-5, E-5
Customer Support Web Site template, B-3
Customize Theme dialog box, C-16–17

►D

Database Interface Wizard template, B-3
databases, B-3, G-13–15
Date and Time dialog box, C-12–13
Decrease Font Size button, B-9
Decrease Indent button, B-9
Delete Cells button, E-8, E-9
Delete Frame command, F-14
Delete Task option, A-15
Description text box, A-14
Design view
    described, A-12
    image maps and, D-8–9
    opening pages in, C-2

page options and, B-4–5
shared borders and, C-12
switching to/from, A-6, A-12
WordArt and, D-10
dial-up modems, D-5, B-16
Discussion Web Site Wizard template, B-3
disk-based Web sites, A-3
Distribute Columns Evenly button, E-6–7, E-8
doc filename extension, B-6
domain names, described, A-2
domain reports, H-16
downloading
files, B-13
graphics, D-5
time estimates for, B-16, D-5
Web pages, B-16
Drawing Canvas toolbar, D-11
Drawing toolbar, D-11
drawings, inserting, D-11. *See also* graphics
Drop-Down Box Properties dialog box, G-8
drop-down boxes
adding, G-8–9
described, G-8
DSL (Digital Subscriber Line), B-16
Dynamic Web Templates report, H-7

►**E**

Edit WordArt Text dialog box, D-10–11
ellipsis (...), A-14
e-mail results, from forms, G-14
E-mail Results tab, G-14
Empty Web Site template, B-3
errors
component, H-7
page forbidden, H-16
Web site maintenance and, H-16
Estimated Time to Download menu, B-16
Excel (Microsoft), B-12–13
Excite, H-17
Existing File or Web Page button, D-8
Exit command, A-18
External Hyperlinks report, H-7

►**F**

Feedback Form, G-2
file(s). *See also* filenames
importing, B-12–13
opening recently used, A-19
types, identifying, B-6
File menu
Close command, A-14, A-18
Close Site command, A-18, B-2
Exit command, A-18
Open Site command, H-4
Print command, F-15
Recent Files command, A-19
Recent Sites command, A-19
filename(s)
conventions for, B-3

extensions, B-6, H-9
frame pages and, F-8
floppy disks, B-2
Folder List
adding pages from, C-4–5
described, A-8
frame pages and, F-6
importing files and, B-12
turning on/off, A-10, B-2
folder(s)
hidden, A-10
opening, A-8
paths, B-2
specifying Web site locations in, B-2
Folders view
changing, A-8
described, A-10
shared borders and, C-8
themes and, C-15
Folders View button, A-8, A-10, A-14, C-6, H-8
font(s)
color, B-8, B-9, D-7
size, D-7, D-10, E-14
tables and, E-14–15
Font Color button, B-8, B-9
Font list box button, B-8
Font Size list box, B-8
form(s)
check boxes in, G-12–13
components, G-2–3, G-16–17, H-7–9, H-11
creating, G-1–24
described, G-2–3
drop-down boxes in, G-8–9
fields, G-2–3
handlers, G-2–3, G-14–15
opening Web pages that contain, G-4–5
properties, G-14–15
publishing Web sites and, H-8–9
results (results file), G-2, G-13–15, H-9
saving, G-10
search, G-16–17, H-10–11
text areas in, G-6–7
text boxes in, G-6–7
understanding, G-2–3
Form command, G-6
Form Confirmation page, H-8–9
Form Page Wizard, G-2
Form Properties dialog box, H-9
Format Painter, B-10–11
Format Painter button, B-10
Formatting toolbar, B-8–9, E-14, F-8
frame(s). *See also* frame pages
creating new, F-12–13
default settings for, F-16
deleting, F-14–15
enabling/disabling, B-5
margins, F-16–17
properties, F-16–17
resizing, F-12
scroll bars and, F-16
spacing, F-16

splitting, F-12–13
target, F-10–11
Frame menu
Delete Frame command, F-14
Frame Properties command, F-14
Open Page in New Window command, F-14
Save Page command, F-14
Split Frame command, F-14
frame page(s). *See also* frames
advantages of, F-2
creating, F-1–24
disadvantages of, F-2
"no frames" pages and, F-3
printing, F-15
properties, F-16–17
saving, F-4, F-8–9
setting pages to open in, F-6–7, F-10–11
templates, F-2–5
Frame Properties command, F-14
Frame Properties dialog box, F-16–17
framesets, described, F-2. *See also* frames
FTP (File Transfer Protocol)
importing Web pages and, B-13
Remote Web Site view and, A-11

►**G**

Getting Started task pane, A-8, B-2
GIF (Graphics Interchange Format) images.
See also graphics
conversion of images to, D-6
described, D-2
thumbnail, D-12
goals, defining, A-4
graphic(s). *See also* images; thumbnail graphics
downloading, D-5
embedding, D-2
formats, D-2
frame pages and, F-6, F-12–13
inserting, D-2–3, D-6, E-12
properties of, D-4–5
resampling, D-4, F-12
saving, D-2, D-4, D-6, D-12–13
sizing, D-3, D-5, F-12–13
tables and, E-12
text over, D-6–7, D-13
themes and, C-14, C-16–17
washout effects, D-6
working with, overview of, D-1–24
wrapping text around, D-4
grayscale graphics, D-6
group names, G-10
Guest Book, G-2

►**H**

help
described, A-16–17
window, maximizing, A-16
Help task pane, A-16–17
Highlight button, B-9

Highlight Hotspots button, D-9
Hit Counter Properties dialog box, H-14–15
hit counters, H-14–15
home pages
    described, A-2
    page options and, B-4–5
HotBot, H-17
hotspots, D-8–9
htm filename extension, B-6
HTML (HyperText Markup Language)
    described, A-2
    documents, viewing, B-17
    optimizing, A-12, A-13
    tags, viewing, A-12
HTTP (HyperText Transfer Protocol)
    described, A-2
    importing Web pages and, B-13
    publishing Web pages and, H-16
    Remote Web Site view and, A-11
    Web servers and, A-3
hyperlinks. *See* links
Hyperlinks report, H-7
Hyperlinks view, A-10
Hyperlinks View button, A-10

►I

Ignore button, B-14
IIS (Microsoft Internet Information Services)
    described, H-2
    Indexing Service, H-11
    publishing Web sites and, H-2–3, H-11
image(s). *See also* graphics
    folder, D-2
    maps, D-8–9
    themes and, C-14–15
Import dialog box, B-12
Import Web Site Wizard, B-13
Import Web Site Wizard template, B-3
importing Web pages, B-12–13
Increase Font Size button, B-9
Increase Indent button, B-9
Indexing Service, H-11
Indexing Service Properties dialog box, H-11
Insert Hyperlink button, E-12
Insert Hyperlink dialog box, D-8, D-9, F-6, F-10
Insert Picture From File button, D-2, D-12, E-12
Insert Rows or Columns dialog box, E-10
Insert Table dialog box, E-2–3
Internal Hyperlinks report, H-7
Internet
    described, A-2
    importing pages from, B-13
    interacting with, A-2
Internet Explorer browser (Microsoft).
    See also browsers
    frame pages and, F-15
    page options and, B-4
    Print dialog box, F-15
    viewing HTML documents with, B-17

ISPs (Internet Service Providers), B-3, H-3, H-5, H-16
Italic button, B-8

►J

Java, B-5
JavaScript, B-5
JPEG (Joint Photographic Experts Group)
    images, D-2
JScript, B-5
Justify button, B-8

►K

keywords
    help system, A-16
    search engines and, H-17

►L

Layout tab, D-16–17
lines
    blank, D-10
    deleting, D-10
link(s). *See also* URLs (Uniform Resource Locators)
    bars, C-8, C-10–11
    broken, H-6
    color, H-10
    described, A-1
    external, C-1
    frame pages and, F-6–7, F-10, F-16
    image maps and, D-8–9
    internal, C-1
    navigation structures and, C-2–3
    properties, F-10
    recalculating, H-6–7
    verifying, H-6–7
Link Bar Properties dialog box, C-10–11
Linked Files report, H-7
localhost, H-2, H-4
logon names, A-14
logos. *See* graphics
logs, usage, H-16

►M

Macintosh, H-16
Main frame, F-7, F-9
maintenance, described, H-16–17
margins, frame, F-16–17
Mark Complete option, A-14–15
Maximize button, A-6, E-12
Merge Cells button, E-10–11
merging
    cells, E-10–11
    described, E-10
modems
    cable, B-16
    dial-up, B-16, D-5
monitor(s)
    page size settings and, B-4

resolution, C-9
    shared borders and, C-9
More Brightness button, D-4
More Colors dialog box, B-8
More Contrast button, D-4
MSN Components, G-17
My Webs folder, B-2

►N

navigation structure
    adding pages to, C-4–7
    link bars and, C-8, C-10–11
    planning, A-4
    positioning pages and, C-2–3
    resizing, C-6
Navigation view
    adding pages in, C-4–5
    described, A-10, C-2–3
    page relationships in, C-2–3
    photo galleries and, D-14
Navigation View button, A-10, C-4
Netscape Navigator browser. *See also*
    browsers
    graphics and, E-13
    page options and, B-4
    previewing Web pages with, B-16
    tables and, E-13
    viewing HTML documents with, B-17
networks, described, A-2
New Drawing command, D-11
New Page button, C-6, C-7, G-16
New Task dialog box, A-14
No Frames pages, F-3
nonprinting characters, B-10–11
Notepad, B-17, H-9
Numbering button, B-9

►O

Office Assistant, described, A-16
Older Files report, H-7
One Page Web Site icon, B-2
One Page Web Site template, B-2–3, B-6
Open button, A-8, A-9
Open last Web site option, A-19
Open Page in New Window command, F-14
Open Site command, H-4
Open Site dialog box, A-8–9, H-4
Optimize HTML command, A-12
Optimize HTML dialog box, A-12–13
option button(s)
    formatting, G-4
    groups, G-10–11
    labels, G-4

►P

page(s). *See also* Web pages
    banners, C-2–3, C-8, C-16–17
    child, C-2–3
    options, B-4–5

parent, C-2–3
positioning, C-2–3
size, B-4
Page Options command, B-4
Page Options dialog box, B-4–5, H-5
Page Properties dialog box, F-16–17
Page Size menu, B-4
Page Size pane, B-4
Page Source command, B-17
Page Templates dialog box, F-4
Page view
changing, A-12–13
default, A-12
described, A-10
paragraph(s). *See also* text
styles, B-10–11
WordArt and, D-10
passwords, case-sensitivity of, H-12
permissions
administering, H-12–13
authoring, H-12–13
browsing, H-12–13
setting, H-12–13
Personal Web Site template, B-3
photo galleries
creating, D-14–15
described, D-14
layout options, D-16–17
properties of, D-16–17
Photo Gallery Properties dialog box, D-14–15
Picture Actions button, D-4, D-5, F-12–13
Picture tab, C-16
Pictures report, H-7
Pictures toolbar, D-2, D-4, E-12, E-14
planning Web sites, A-4–A-5
PNG graphics. *See also* graphics
described, D-2
enabling/disabling, B-5
Preview view
described, A-12
displaying image maps in, D-8
switching to/from, A-12
previewing. *See also* browsers; Preview view
described, B-16–17
frame pages, F-12
hit counters, H-14–15
tables, E-12, E-16
Print button, B-16
Print command, F-15
Print dialog box, F-15
printing Web pages, B-16–17, F-15
Project Web Site template, B-3
publishing Web sites
described, A-2, H-2–3
IIS and, H-2–3, H-11
maintaining Web sites after, H-16–17
testing pages after, H-8–9

▶ R

radio buttons. *See* option buttons
Recalculate Hyperlinks command, H-6
Recalculate Hyperlinks dialog box, H-6
recalculation process, H-6–7
Recent Files command, A-19
Recent Sites command, A-19
Recently Added Files report, H-7
Rectangular Hotspot button, D-8
Refresh button, H-14
relative positioning, D-4
Remote Web Site Properties button, H-2
Remote Web Site view, A-11, H-2–4
Remote Web Site View button, H-2
Reports view, A-10, H-6
Reports View button, A-10, H-6
Resample button, D-5
Resample Picture To Match Size button, D-4, F-12
Reset button, G-4–5
Restore Down button, E-12
results file, G-2, G-13–15, H-9
root Web
described, A-5
subsites and, A-5
rows, deleting, E-8

▶ S

Save As dialog box, B-7, F-4–5, F-8
Save button, A-12, B-6, B-7, B-8
Save Embedded Files dialog box, D-2, D-4, D-12
Save Page command, F-14
Saved Fields tab, G-14–15
Saving Results dialog box, G-14
scripting languages, enabling/disabling, B-5
scroll bars
hiding/displaying, F-16
horizontal, A-10
scrolling text boxes. *See* text areas
search
engines, H-17
forms, G-16–17, H-10–11
Search Form Properties dialog box, G-16
Search Results task pane, A-16
"Search the Web" component, G-17
Select File dialog box, B-6
server(s). *See also* publishing Web sites; Server Extensions (FrontPage)
(FrontPage)
-based Web sites, A-3
described, A-2
filename conventions and, B-3
forms and, G-14
names, H-4–5
opening Web sites from, H-4–5
permissions and, H-12–13

Server Extensions (FrontPage), B-13, H-5.
See also servers
forms and, G-2
publishing Web sites and, H-3–4
Set Page Title dialog box, B-7
shapes, inserting, D-11
shared borders
changing the content of, C-12–13
described, C-1–3
design issues related to, C-9
turning on/off, C-8–9, C-13
Shared Borders command, C-8
Shared Borders dialog box, C-13
SharePoint Services
forms and, G-2
importing Web pages and, B-13
page options and, B-4
permissions and, H-13
publishing Web sites and, H-2–5, H-13
SharePoint Services button, H-2
SharePoint Team Site template, B-3
Show All button, B-10
Show All feature, B-10
Show Code View button, A-12
Show Design View button, A-6–7, D-8, D-10
Show Preview View button, A-12, D-8
Show Split View button, A-12
Site Summary Report, A-10, H-6–7
slide shows, D-16–17. *See also* photo galleries
Source command, B-17
special characters, in filenames, B-3
Specify Value check box, G-8
spell checking, B-14–15
Spelling dialog box, B-14–15
Split Cells button, E-11
Split Cells dialog box, E-10
Split Frame command, F-14
Split view
described, A-12
switching to/from, A-12
splitting
cells, E-10–11
described, E-10
frames, F-12–13
square brackets ([ ]), B-2
Standard toolbar
location of, A-7
opening files with, A-8
saving files with, A-13, B-6
Start button, A-6
starting FrontPage, A-6–7
status bar, B-16
Style list box button, B-8
Style Sheet Links report, H-7
style sheets, B-5, E-5, H-7
Style tab, C-10–11
Submit button, G-4–5
subsites (subwebs)
creating, A-5
described, A-5

▶T

table(s). *See also* cells
adding, E-2–3
aligning, E-2–3, E-6
AutoFormat feature and, E-16–17
borders, E-5, E-7, E-14–15
converting text to, E-9
creating, E-1–24
deleting cells in, E-8–9
described, E-2
entering data in, E-6–7
formatting cells in, E-14–15
inserting cells in, E-8–9
nested, E-2
previewing, E-12, E-16
properties, E-4–5
saving, E-8
search results in, H-10–11
Table of Contents pane, A-16–17
Table Properties dialog box, E-4–5
Table to Text command, E-9
target frames, F-10–11
task(s)
completing/managing, A-15
deleting, A-15
status indicators for, A-15
Task Details dialog box, A-14
Task Pane command, B-2
taskbar, A-7
Tasks view, A-10, A-14–15
Tasks View button, A-10, A-14
Tasks pane, A-15, B-2
templates
creating Web pages from, B-7
described, B-1–3
frame page, F-2–5
types of, B-2–3
viewing, B-2
testing Web sites, A-4, H-8–11
text. *See also* fonts; paragraphs
aligning, B-6, B-8, E-6
areas, G-6–7
boxes, G-6–7
color, B-8–9
comma-delimited, G-14, G-15
deleting, B-6
entering/inserting, B-6–7
formatting, B-6–9
over graphics, creating, D-6–7, D-13
tables and, E-9, E-14–15
WordArt and, D-10–11
wrapping, around graphics, D-4
Text Area Properties dialog box, G-6–7

Text Box Properties dialog box, G-6–7
Text button, D-6
Theme task pane, C-16, C-14, D-3
themes
applying, C-14–15
changing, C-15
customizing, C-16–17
deleting, C-17
described, C-1
thumbnail graphics. *See also* graphics
creating, D-12–13
described, D-12
in photo galleries, D-14–17
titles
setting, B-7
Web page, B-7
Toggle Pane button, A-8, A-10, B-12, C-5, C-6
toolbars. *See also* specific toolbars
displaying, D-2
positioning, D-2
Toolbars command, D-2
Tools menu
Optimize HTML command, A-12
Page Options command, B-4, H-5
Recalculate Hyperlinks command, H-6
traffic reports, H-16
transfer rates, B-16
Transferring RTF file to HTML message box, B-6
Tripod, H-5

▶U

Uncompleted Tasks report, H-7
Underline button, B-8
Unlinked Files report, H-7
Unused Themes report, H-7
Unverified Hyperlinks report, H-7
updates, Web site, described, A-2
URLs (Uniform Resource Locators).
See also links
described, A-2
submitting, to search engines, H-17
subsites and, A-5
usage logs, H-16
User Registration, G-2

▶V

VBScript (Microsoft), B-5
Verify Hyperlinks dialog box, H-6–7
View menu
Page Source command, B-17
Source command, B-17

Task Pane command, B-2
Toolbars command, D-2
views, changing, A-10–11. *See also* View menu; *specific views*

▶W

Web browsers. *See* browsers
Web Components button, G-16–17
Web Components dialog box, G-16
Web page(s). *See also* pages; Web sites
creating, B-7
deleting, C-4
described, A-2
filename conventions for, B-3
importing, B-12–13
organizing, A-2
planning, A-4–5
previewing, B-16–17
printing, B-16–17
saving, B-7
titles, B-7
Web site(s). *See also* Web pages
closing, A-18–19
creating, B-1–24
described, A-2
disk-based, A-3
managing, A-2
opening, A-8–9, A-19
server-based, A-3
Web Site tab, A-10, A-14
Web Site Templates dialog box, B-2–3, B-13
WebDAV (Web Distributed Authoring and Versioning), A-11, B-13
windows, maximizing, A-16
Windows 2000 (Microsoft), H-2
Windows XP (Microsoft), H-2, H-16
Word (Microsoft), B-12–13
WordArt
creating, D-10–11
described, D-10
WordPad, H-9

▶Y

Yahoo!, H-5, H-17

▶Z

Zoom list arrow, C-6, D-14